PRICING LIVES

T0317725

Pricing Lives

Guideposts for a Safer Society

W. Kip Viscusi

PRINCETON UNIVERSITY PRESS

PRINCETON AND OXFORD

Published by Princeton University Press,
41 William Street, Princeton, New Jersey 08540

In the United Kingdom: Princeton University Press,
6 Oxford Street, Woodstock, Oxfordshire OX20 1TR

press.princeton.edu

Cover graphics and design by Amanda Weiss

Library of Congress Control Number: 2018932156

First paperback printing, 2020
Paperback ISBN 978-0-691-20859-6
Cloth ISBN 978-0-691-17921-6

British Library Cataloging-in-Publication Data is available

This book has been composed in Adobe Text Pro and Gotham

Printed in the United States of America

For Robert J. Viscusi

CONTENTS

I receive frequent calls from journalists wondering if I was aware that the government is placing a dollar value on human life. The alarmed journalists believe that they have uncovered a scandal akin to the death panels that some people envisioned would accompany national health insurance. The particular practice in question is the value that risk regulation agencies use to determine the economic benefit of reducing small risks of death, or what has come to be known as the value of a statistical life.

Setting a price on life is not the province of government risk regulation policies alone. The courts have been engaged in pricing lives for centuries, as compensation in wrongful death cases sets a price on life in terms of the amounts that are paid for economic loss incurred by the survivors. In their product safety decisions, companies place a finite value on life at least implicitly every time they make a product that is not risk-free. Similarly, each of us also places a value on risks to our lives whenever we undertake potentially risky behaviors.

The principal theme of this book is that the value of a statistical life is not only an economically sound and ethically responsible approach; it has a much broader role to play in serving as the societal guidepost for valuing fatality risks. In the case of government agencies, adoption of the value of a statistical life has led to much more protective policies than when the government equated the value of expected lives saved with the economic losses in terms of medical expenses and forgone wages. While these values now serve as a much higher reference point for assessing the value of the mortality risk reductions from major new government regulations, the government still undervalues lives in other ways, as in the very low level of regulatory sanctions for job-related and product-related deaths. Companies also either tend to undervalue lives or ignore systematic valuation of risks to life altogether. Incorporation of the value of a statistical life in product safety decisions would transform the character of the corporate decision process and boost the valuations assigned to product-related risks. Finally, the courts could profit by using the value of a statistical life in assessing liability and in establishing appropriate levels of deterrence. In each of these instances, the use of the value of a statistical life will foster a safer society. And what is remarkable is that this single procedure for valuing risks to life establishes a consistent framework that can serve as the guidepost for pricing lives and promoting safety in all these institutional contexts. These principles have international ramifications as well. The shortfall from the proper valuation of life is even greater outside the United States.

My objective in writing this book is twofold. First, I hope to advance the main policy prescription in this book, which is to make responsible valuation of life the norm throughout society. While the book clearly has a strong advocacy point of view, it is grounded in economic analysis that recognizes that society does face limits in terms of the affordable level of safety. However, in most instances both in the United States and internationally, these limits have been set too low, leading to an underpricing of human life. Second, I have written this book to communicate my results and policy proposals to a broad audience. The chapters impose no technical demands on the reader.

Many of the overall policy themes in this book are new, but the fundamental underlying economic frameworks are well established. This book draws on my four decades of research and involvement in government efforts to implement policy applications of the use of the value of a statistical life. The book is an entirely new manuscript, with the exception being portions of my discussion of automobile safety risk analyses that draw on my article in *Vanderbilt Law Review*, "Pricing Lives for Corporate Risk Decisions" (68, no. 4 [2015]: 1117–1162).

Throughout the writing of this book, my publications coordinator, Sarah Dalton, undertook substantial initiative in tracking down research materials as well as formatting, editing, and producing the draft manuscript. At Princeton University Press, the senior economics editor Joe Jackson, production editor Nathaniel L. Carr, and copy editor Molan Goldstein provided valuable guidance and editorial suggestions. I am grateful to Cass Sunstein, Thomas Kniesner, and several anonymous reviewers of my draft manuscript for many insightful suggestions. Finally, I would like to thank my roster of co-authors on empirical estimates of different aspects of the value of a statistical life, including Joseph Aldy, Jason Bell, Chris Doucouliagos, Mark Dreyfus, Ted Gayer, Elissa Philip Gentry, Jahn Hakes, James Hamilton, Joni Hersch, Joel Huber, Thomas Kniesner, Wesley Magat, Clayton Masterman, Michael Moore, Thomas Stanley, Christopher Woock, and James Ziliak.

PRICING LIVES

1

How Pricing Lives Saves Lives

The Challenge of Valuing Mortality Risks

"We can't do that. That's immoral." This was the reaction I got in 1980 when I suggested to a prominent Occupational Safety and Health Administration (OSHA) official that the agency monetize the reduced risks of death from job safety regulations using labor market estimates of workers' valuation of fatality risks. The values I advocated were based on the extra amounts workers are paid for each expected workplace death. Early studies often referred to these figures as the value of life, but the terminology used to describe this approach has evolved to be the "value of a statistical life," which is both more accurate and somewhat less inflammatory.

The idea of monetizing the benefit of reduced worker fatality risks was not controversial. OSHA and other agencies had routinely attached dollar values to the expected lives that would be saved by regulations. In doing so, they followed the general approach patterned after that used by the courts in wrongful death cases, in which they equated the benefit of reduced risks of death to the value of lost earnings and medical expenses. This formulation enabled agencies to generate a mortality risk reduction benefit number and to be able to point to the use of a similar approach by the courts, thus providing some evidence of its reasonableness. However, there is a fundamental disconnect between these values and the core principle underlying benefit assessment, which is that benefit values for government policies should reflect society's willingness to pay for the benefit. An instructive way to ascertain these values is to examine the revealed preferences based on risk-taking behavior. The estimates of the value of a statistical life make such a connection by using the value that the workers themselves place on risks of death.

The benefit valuation amounts per expected fatality prevented that I suggested to OSHA were quite substantial, far in excess of the figures OSHA was using to value reductions in mortality risks. So the net effect of adopting my numbers would be to make lives considerably more valuable than the agency's practice at that time, a consequence that hardly seemed "immoral." I was also personally disappointed in their negative reaction, having just published the book edition of my doctoral dissertation on job safety,[1] as well as related articles advocating the value of a statistical life approach. But in addition to my personal stake in the methodology, I viewed valuing risks of death based on how workers themselves valued these risks as the only correct economic procedure for producing sensible policy valuations.

The idea of conceptualizing the valuation task in terms of statistical lives had a firm economic basis and was due to Nobel laureate Thomas Schelling.[2] However, given the state of empirical methods at the time of his original analysis, he was not optimistic about the prospects of assessing this value based on either surveys or empirical work: "The main problem is that people have difficulty knowing what it is worth to themselves, cannot easily answer questions about it, and may object to being asked. Market evidence is unlikely to reveal much." Fortunately, advances over the past half-century in available data, statistical methods, and survey procedures have enabled us to develop meaningful estimates of the value of a statistical life.

At the time of my original suggestion that OSHA adopt this methodology, I was on leave from my position at the Northwestern University economics department to the government, where I served as the Deputy Director of the President's Council on Wage and Price

Stability. This agency managed the pay-price guidelines and was responsible for oversight of all proposed federal regulations for the Carter administration. Under the Carter administration's Executive Order No. 12044, agencies were required to assess the benefits and costs of all major rules and to show that the chosen regulatory approach was the most cost-effective alternative. Although agencies were required to analyze the benefits and costs of policies and ideally should monetize these benefits and costs, the executive order did not require agencies to demonstrate formally that the benefits of the proposed regulations exceeded the costs. That requirement arrived in 1981 with the Reagan administration, which moved the regulatory oversight staff to the US Office of Management and Budget (OMB), Office of Information and Regulatory Affairs. Nevertheless, even without a formal benefit-cost test, there were political pressures within the Carter administration to strike a sensible balance between calculated benefits and costs, in part because of the perceived potential inflationary impact of costly but ineffective regulations.

The shift of the regulatory oversight group to OMB by President Reagan in 1981 was accompanied by other policy changes. As part of its economic reform agenda, the Reagan administration had ramped up the emphasis on bringing regulatory costs under control. The Carter administration had initiated a variety of deregulation initiatives with respect to airlines, trucking, and banking. Although the economic rationales for risk and environmental regulation are quite different than for economic regulations, as is the potential justification for deregulation as well, the Reagan administration sought to extend the deregulation concept to these newer social regulations. As part of this effort, the Reagan administration's Executive Order No. 12291 imposed a benefit-cost test for proposed major regulations. Agencies must show that the benefits exceeded the costs before being permitted to issue the regulation. This benefit-cost analysis requirement has remained in place through all subsequent administrations. The Reagan administration also strengthened the regulatory oversight process. The requirement that agencies obtain OMB approval before launching major regulatory initiatives replaced the advisory White House reviews under Carter. The Reagan administration also targeted many regulations for elimination, such as a host of recent safety regulations pertaining to the auto industry.

The Triumph of the Value of a Statistical Life Approach: The Hazard Communication Policy Debate

In this era of deregulation, agencies nevertheless continued to develop new regulatory proposals.[3] The most expensive major new initiative proposed in the early years of President Reagan's first term was the OSHA hazard communication regulation, which OSHA proposed in 1982. If this regulation was enacted, for the first time there would be regulatory requirements that firms label dangerous chemicals used in the workplace. Since these chemicals are often considerably more potent than household chemicals, the absence of any such labeling regulation more than a decade after OSHA's establishment was surprising. After having read these proposed chemical labels, workers would be aware of their chemical risk exposures and be able to take appropriate precautions, possibly including the decision to quit and seek safer employment. In addition, the regulation would require that firms maintain material safety data sheets so that if workers were exposed to a dangerous chemical, the medical personnel would be aware of the consequences of the exposure and know how to treat the worker.

OSHA's regulatory impact analysis for the hazard communication standards tallied the prospective costs and expected improvements in worker health and attached a dollar benefit to these health effects. The dominant benefit component for this regulation, as it is for most other health, safety, and environmental regulations, was the value of the mortality risk reduction. However, instead of using the value of a statistical life to monetize these effects, at that time OSHA and other agencies used the value of medical costs and lost earnings, or what they termed the "cost of death." After completing the analysis based on the costs of the deaths prevented by the regulation, OSHA submitted the proposed regulation to the OMB regulatory oversight group for the approval that was required before the regulation could be issued. Although OSHA's evaluation concluded that the regulation was desirable on balance, its economic assessment was flawed in several respects. Based on the critique of the regulatory impact analysis by the OMB economists, if OSHA had done a proper analysis, the result would have been that costs exceeded the benefits so that the regulation failed a benefit-cost test. As a result, OMB rejected OSHA's regulatory proposal.

OSHA nevertheless wished to pursue the possibility of issuing the regulation. The procedure that the Reagan administration had established for agency appeals was that in the event of a dispute, the regulatory agency could appeal the decision to then Vice President George H. W. Bush. The vice president characterized the disagreement as a technical economics dispute and suggested that an outside expert assess the merits of the competing arguments. I was asked to resolve the dispute after being approved by the Secretary of Labor and OMB. By that time, I had left the government and was then at Duke University, where my research continued to focus on risk regulation issues. The OMB regulatory oversight staff, most of whom were my former colleagues at the Council on Wage and Price Stability, raised a host of criticisms of OSHA's benefit estimates. All of these critiques were well founded. The result of adopting the OMB corrections to the analysis was that the calculated costs of the regulation exceeded the estimated benefits in terms of improved worker safety. In my assessment of the competing agency arguments, I accepted all of OMB's critiques as being sound.

Where my approach differed from that taken by both OSHA and OMB was with respect to how the expected lives saved would be valued. Both OSHA and OMB valued the lives saved based on what OSHA termed the "cost of death," or the present value of the medical costs and lost earnings that would be saved by preventing workers from being killed by chemical exposures. Under this approach, lives would have a value of several hundred thousand dollars, which was not a trivial amount, but was an arbitrary accounting measure that bore little relationship to how workers themselves valued risks of death. The approach I suggested utilized my labor market estimates of how much compensation workers required to face small risks of death. My estimate of the value of a statistical life at that time was

$3 million per expected fatality prevented, or about $7.4 million adjusted for inflation. More recent estimates of the value of a statistical life generally place its value at between $9 million and $11 million. Using this estimate in the regulatory benefits analysis instead of the cost-of-death approach boosted benefits by an order of magnitude. Following a similar approach, I also attached values to the prevention of nonfatal worker injuries, but the driving force in the benefit assessment was the value of the fatalities prevented by the proposed regulation. The result of abandoning the cost-of-death approach was that benefits now exceeded the costs so that the hazard communication regulation would now pass OMB's economic test. President Reagan approved the regulation almost immediately after my report in support of the regulation reached the White House.

The Genesis of Estimates of the Value of a Statistical Life

Where did this $3 million figure come from? The average annual worker fatality risk at that time was 1/10,000, which is more than double the current level of dangerousness. In return for bearing this risk, workers received an annual wage premium of $300, where this amount was estimated statistically controlling for other aspects of the job and worker characteristics. The result is that for a group of 10,000 workers, on average one of them would be killed on the job in the coming year. The amount of compensation that this group of 10,000 workers would receive for the one expected death is 10,000 × $300, or $3 million. Thus, the value of a statistical life is simply the total amount of compensation required per expected workplace death. The value of a statistical life reflects the values that the workers themselves believe that bearing these risks is worth rather than an accounting measure or an arbitrary number assigned by a government analyst.

But why should any finite value be applied to the expected lives saved? One could treat each expected life saved as having an infinite value. In that case, it would be desirable to expend the entire federal budget on safety measures that would eliminate a small chance of even one expected death. Given the multiple risks that we face and the limits on our financial resources, this uncompromising approach is infeasible. Consider data for 2014, the most recent year for which comprehensive accident data are available. There were 136,053 accidental deaths in the United States in 2014.[4] If the entire gross domestic product of $17.4 trillion in 2014 were allocated to preventing accidents, it would only be possible to spend an average of $128 million per death to prevent these accidents, leaving nothing left to prevent illnesses or to provide for daily living expenses.

To motivate the reasonableness of using workers' wage-risk trade-offs as the guide, it is useful to ask people to conceptualize scenarios in which the reader makes similar decisions that do not reflect an unbounded commitment to safety, whether it involves living in a riskier but less expensive neighborhood or driving a car that doesn't have all possible safety enhancements. Most transportation choices and dietary decisions entail at least some risk. We do not plan our lives to minimize all possible risks. Through daily risk-taking decisions, people reveal that they place a finite value on reduced risks to their life. People's unwillingness to display an unbounded commitment to safety is consistent with a myriad of other risk-taking decisions that we make. The labor market estimates undertake a similar comparison in which the tradeoff is based on the extra wages that workers are paid for the additional risks posed by their jobs.

Critiques of My Initial Estimates of the Value of a Statistical Life

My estimates of the value of a statistical life on the order of $3 million came under attack from both extremes. Some critiques suggested that the numbers were too big, while others thought they were too small. The critiques suggesting that they were too small involved appeals to value lives at an infinite amount and were not grounded on any actual empirical estimates. Those suggesting that my estimates were too large were more empirically based. My figure exceeded the present value of lifetime earnings, so how could it be feasible for people to value their lives so highly? Surely people could not afford to pay more for their lives than their resources permitted. The raw numbers presumably suggested that the valuations were excessive. However, what workers are valuing is not the certainty of death but rather a very small risk of death of 1/10,000 annually. It should also be noted that workers are being compensated for these small risks. They are not paying for greater safety so the budgetary constraint issues are less salient. Moreover, for small risks of death, budgetary issues are not influential whether we are talking about the amount that workers are paid to incur a risk or the amount that they would be willing to pay to reduce their level of risk. The amounts that workers require to face slightly greater risks will equal the amount that they are willing to pay to make their jobs safer to that same degree. Even if workers were paying for the risk reduction, it is not unrealistic to assume that workers would be willing to pay $300 to reduce their annual fatality risk by 1/10,000. This is a quite different matter than assuming that workers have $3 million to buy out of the risk of certain death.

A more sophisticated critique was based on the economics literature at that time. Some other competing estimates of the value of a statistical life pegged the value at well below $1 million. Didn't that lower value imply that my numbers were too high? The disparity in the estimates also gave the false impression that estimates of the value of a statistical life differed widely and were too unreliable to be used for policy analysis. However, the observed differences were quite plausible. Whereas workers in my studies faced risks that were comparable to the US average of 1/10,000 annually, the estimates of under $1 million were based on workers in very high-risk jobs with annual fatality rates of 1/1,000 per year.[5] These divergent estimates are not incompatible. The value of a statistical life is not a universal constant. Rather, it reflects the average rate of tradeoff between wages and risk for particular samples of workers. Those who place a comparatively low value on risk to their lives will tend to gravitate to higher-risk jobs and reveal through their choices a lower wage requirement per unit of risk, which will imply a lower value of a statistical life.

Notwithstanding such critiques and the political sensitivity of the task of valuing risks to life, other agencies also adopted the value of a statistical life, or the VSL. While it may be the case that agencies were swayed by the compelling economic logic of the VSL approach, it is also likely that the fact that the VSL enabled agencies to boost the calculated economic benefit estimates by a factor of ten contributes to its attractiveness. The mortality risk reduction benefit valuation approach using the VSL is now the standard practice throughout the US government as well as in many other countries. The largest benefit component of all US federal regulations is the monetized value of the statistical lives that will be saved by the regulation.[6] The VSL has become the most important parameter driving the attractiveness of government regulations generally as it plays the central role in the evaluation of health, safety, and environmental regulations.[7]

Why Monetizing the Effects Matters

The monetization of the reduced mortality risks through application of the value of a statistical life is instrumental in the assessment of the benefits by the government, as it enables these effects to be put in the same terms as other economic impacts. The benefit-cost analysis procedure that lies at the heart of regulatory analyses involves a comparison of the benefits and the costs and a judgment that the benefits exceed the costs. To make such a comparison, at some point all effects must be put in comparable units, at least implicitly. Cost figures are dollar amounts that appear to be real economic consequences. Indeed, the regulatory oversight efforts in the Ford and Carter administrations were motivated primarily by a concern with the economic burdens arising from the inflationary effects of regulatory costs, not a concern with benefits or benefit-cost balance. Monetization of risk reduction benefits puts these effects on the same footing as the cost numbers, making clear that they are just as real economic effects as are regulatory costs.

Instead of assigning an explicit finite value to the expected fatality risks, another possible benefits approach is not to monetize the fatality reduction benefits at all. Rather, one can simply note that a policy will lead to a reduction in the risk of death for some population and that these expected risk reductions are valuable but are not monetized effects. One might advocate this nonmonetized approach based on the rationale that monetizing the expected lives saved in effect denigrates them by treating lives as a commodity.[8] The danger of this attempt to skirt around the use of monetary values is that effects that are not monetized may be treated as being less consequential than the purportedly real economic costs and benefits that have a monetized market value.

In an earlier study of the use of benefit-cost analysis to value water-resource projects, I found that government agencies placed almost exclusive emphasis on the monetized effects.[9] In that era, environmental consequences received qualitative discussion but were largely set aside in favor of emphasis on the series of tangible economic benefits that were monetized. As a result, somewhat oddly the traditional evaluation of water-resource projects placed negligible emphasis on nonmonetized ecological consequences, and instead focused on monetized impacts such as the value of the irrigation water that would be sold to farmers and the value of increased municipal and industrial water supplies. Monetized benefits such as the irrigation water counted, but qualitative environmental consequences did not. If the risk reduction effects are not monetized, the greater likelihood is that they will be treated as having zero or negligible value, not that they will be viewed as being more consequential than if the value of a statistical life numbers were not used.

Failing to monetize the effects also limits the ability of benefit-cost analysis to provide a comprehensive index of the policy's attractiveness. By converting benefits into monetary terms, it is possible to compare the benefits and costs to assess the net attractiveness of the policy. Ultimately, any policy decision will implicitly make such a comparison even if the benefits are not monetized, so the failure to monetize risks disguises the hard choices being made but does not avoid the task of setting an implicit value on expected lives saved. Approval of a policy that costs $100 million and expects to save fifty lives implies that the government values lives at least at $2 million. Similarly, failure to move forward with a policy that costs $100 million but expects to save only ten lives indicates that the government values expected lives saved at less than $10 million. In instances in which there are multiple attributes that are not monetized, such as lives, cancer cases, and disabling injuries, it becomes more difficult to impute the specific implicit value of a statistical life that is incorporated in the policy decision. But whether the valuation is undertaken implicitly or explicitly, there is still some valuation judgment being made.

Exploiting the Potential of the Value of a Statistical Life

While the idea of pricing lives may seem to be morally reprehensible, the practice of valuing lives and risks to life arises either explicitly or implicitly in a variety of contexts in government policies, corporate decisions, and compensation awarded by the courts. The principal recurring theme of this book is that US institutions and practices throughout the world have consistently undervalued lives. Properly confronting issues regarding pricing lives may offend moral sensitivities but will ultimately lead to more protective policies than those that emerge when the monetization of risks to life is suppressed as being too grisly an enterprise to contemplate, much less implement in actual risk decisions.

Over the past three decades, the VSL has emerged as the most influential economic parameter in the evaluation of federal regulatory policies. All federal agencies have adopted the methodology to ascertain the benefits of different regulatory efforts and the appropriate levels of stringency of these regulations. My examination of the role of the VSL explores a variety of issues that arise in policy contexts in which the use of the VSL approach has become well established. Should, for example, reduced risks of life be valued at the same level for everyone? Should income levels matter? Are reduced risks to the lives of older people less valuable than the lives of children, who have much greater life expectancy? How should we conceptualize such issues pertaining to the heterogeneity of the VSL and tailor the appropriate policy approach? Are there any groups in the workforce, such as Mexican immigrants, who appear to be left out of this ideally functioning economic market, and what are the ramifications of this shortcoming in market performance? These are not always easy questions to answer, but available research addresses many of these issues.

The task of setting a price on life arises in many other contexts as well. My focus is on pricing lives more generally, not simply on valuing statistical lives for government policies that are directed at reducing mortality risks. Assigning either an explicit or implicit price for lives is an integral aspect of safety decisions by firms and is a routine component of court awards in wrongful death cases. Does the VSL provide more meaningful guidance in these situations? At one extreme, might it serve as an all-purpose number for valuing lives? Or should the application of the VSL in the courtroom be more focused on particular situations?

The most direct extension of the use of the VSL is to corporate decisions regarding safety. Private companies must decide on the safety features of their products, and in doing so, they are valuing risks to life just as are government agencies. While companies have not generally adopted the VSL approach, should they use the VSL estimates in their safety decisions? The failure of firms to utilize the VSL may seem to be puzzling. After all, the VSL numbers are generated by decisions made in markets. The VSL estimates from the labor market reflect the joint influence of decisions by firms to offer wages for jobs at different levels of risk and the decisions by workers to accept such jobs. The economic mechanism works analogously for products, as the VSL reflected in product choices simultaneously reflects the cost to the firm of increasing product safety as well as how much consumers themselves are willing to spend for safer products. Why have companies failed to adopt the VSL, which serves as a measure of how much their consumers will value additional safety features? Application of the VSL creates tremendous potential for providing a sounder basis for corporate risk decisions that will also lead to greater levels of safety.

But there are pitfalls companies face that might account for their failure to adopt the VSL. Using the VSL may expose corporations to greater liability threats than if they didn't undertake a thorough risk analysis. Just as government agencies periodically come under fire for valuing lives, corporations may be subject to similar and even more costly critiques. However, unlike government agencies, corporations are not shielded from potential liability costs. Much like government agencies before the adoption of the VSL, corporations have a history of shortchanging safety. Establishing a legal structure that enables companies to undertake responsible risk analyses is essential. Applying the VSL to corporate behavior as well as to government policies establishes a consistent and more protective safety framework across societal institutions.

In addition to the prospective safety decisions by government agencies and corporations, there are also situations in which mortality risks must be valued retrospectively. Government regulators levy fines on firms when workers are killed on the job as well as penalties on firms that generate product and environmental hazards that lead to fatalities. Courts make damages awards to companies in wrongful death cases ranging from routine automobile accident cases to mass tort actions, such as for pharmaceutical products. Both the regulatory sanctions and the court awards entail the pricing of identified lives after the fact. In neither instance is the VSL the standard approach now used to value these deaths. As I will indicate, the VSL does have a pivotal role to play for government regulatory sanctions but a more nuanced role in the courts, for which the principal concern is addressing the economic losses incurred by the accident victims. In these instances as well as in valuing prospective risks, the VSL establishes safety guideposts that will lead to more protective outcomes than current approaches.

Risk Awareness and Beliefs

The application of the VSL estimates appears to offer enormous potential dividends in a variety of contents, but is there any reason to believe the numbers are credible? Do workers even understand the risks posed by their jobs? This is an important question, since the VSL estimates are based on economic frameworks that assume that workers are aware of the risks they face. An assumption of fully informed workers seems unreasonable for hazardous exposures that cannot be readily monitored and that lead to illnesses not captured in accident statistics. However, the VSL estimates are based on acute fatality risks generally caused by accidents rather than deferred risks associated with occupational illnesses. Basing the VSL approach on a framework that presupposes awareness of the risk is reasonable for the types of hazards captured in labor market studies, which are the more visible risks, such as motor vehicle hazards and risks of fires and falls, rather than less apparent risks, such as the cancer risks of asbestos.

The evidence that workers' risk beliefs are plausible is quite strong.[10] While the economic theory does not require that every worker can identify the job risks with pinpoint accuracy, workers' subjective risk perceptions do follow the expected patterns. Workers are more likely to believe their jobs expose them to dangerous or unhealthy conditions if they work in industries with higher reported accident rates. Whereas only 24 percent of workers in low-risk industries view their jobs as dangerous, all workers in the highest-risk industries believe that their jobs are dangerous. The most prominent hazards cited by workers are inherently dangerous materials, inherently hazardous equipment, inherently hazardous procedures, dangerous exposure to dust, and transportation hazards. A particularly striking result is that for my survey of hundreds of chemical workers described below, workers' perceptions of the accident rate in their jobs were equal to the objective measure of the average injury risk in the chemical industry.

The sources of information about risks are quite diverse. Many hazards, such as the dangers of high-rise construction work, are readily apparent. Moreover, over two-fifths of all workplace fatalities are related to motor vehicles, which pose quite familiar risks. Workers also learn through their on-the-job experiences. Workers who have experienced an on-the-job injury on their current job are more likely to regard their jobs as being dangerous, as 71 percent of those who have experienced such an injury view their jobs as dangerous. These patterns of risk beliefs are consistent with the notion that people learn about risks in a sensible way. If the wages paid for these perceived risks are inadequate, they may quit. My estimates have found that one-third of all manufacturing quit rates are attributable to this learning response to job risks. Moreover, after quitting these jobs, workers switch to positions for which they receive appropriate risk compensation in line with the VSL estimates.

How do estimates of the wage premiums workers receive for subjectively assessed risks compare with economists' estimates derived using objective risk measures in the statistical analysis of compensation for risk? There are in fact strong parallels in terms of the wage-premium effects implied by objective measures of the risk and subjective worker assessments. The wage-premium estimates for risk that I obtained using fatality risk measures conditional on workers perceiving that their jobs exposed them to dangerous or unhealthy conditions were the same as the values obtained with empirical estimates based on objective industry risk measures. Also, if workers are completely ignorant of the hazards, there will be no market mechanism that generates wage premiums for risks, so the existence of observed wage differentials provides additional evidence of some underlying risk awareness. Situations in which there are gaps in the provision of such risk compensation, such as for immigrant workers in dangerous jobs, serve as a red flag that there is something amiss and more vigilant government regulation might be beneficial.

Linkage to Hazard Communication

It is particularly noteworthy that the OSHA hazard communication regulation that led to the adoption of VSL is closely linked to a linchpin of the economic theory used to derive the VSL estimates, which is that workers will demand compensation for the risks they face. If workers are unaware of the risks, as is possible when facing dimly understood chemical hazards, they will not require extra wages to face these hazards. Communicating information about the risks through a labeling effort is consequently a pivotal mechanism for fostering the kind of market response that underlies the VSL approach.

But what effect would such labeling regulations actually have? The regulatory impact analyses of the proposed hazard communication standard by OSHA and OMB were based largely on hypothesized possible impacts and plausible conjectures. The 1980s was a period in which there was substantial interest in the comparatively novel informational regulations, but little was known about their efficacy. Other than cigarette warnings (in place in the United States since 1966), warnings for prescription drugs, and warnings for a short list of highly dangerous chemicals such as hydrochloric acid, there was much less reliance on informational approaches than is the norm today. OSHA's hazard communication regulation was an innovative policy, but it was not the only informational effort in that era. Other informational initiatives followed. Congress passed legislation requiring new rotating cigarette warnings in the mid-1980s, and in that decade the US Environmental Protection Agency (EPA) also embarked on various right-to-know efforts for chemical exposures and toxic environmental releases. However, despite the flurry of policy activity, agencies did not have a firm grasp of the efficacy of the warnings policies. In many instances, policymakers regarded informational efforts as a holding action until the pertinent policy response became evident or political obstacles to more stringent regulation could be overcome.

At the time of my evaluation of the OSHA hazard communication regulatory proposal, there was no firm empirical basis that could be used to ascertain the likely efficacy of the regulation. In collaboration with a chemical industry official, I designed a survey with an experimental structure to explore how workers would respond to the warnings.[11] This survey also illuminated how workers perceive and respond to risks, providing a detailed exploration of the formation of workers' risk beliefs and how these beliefs translate into the wages they require for the job. The survey involved showing different warnings to hundreds of workers at several major chemical plants. The products ranged from very dangerous chemicals, such as asbestos, to fairly innocuous materials, such as sodium bicarbonate (household baking soda). If the worker had to work with the warning on the chemical label instead of the chemicals at the worker's current job, would that affect the assessment of the risks of the job? The results were remarkably strong. Before being shown any warnings, workers were asked to assess the injury risks of their jobs. The average response was exactly equal to the reported injury rate in the chemical industry, which is a number that they were not told. These remarkably accurate risk beliefs were consistent with workers being cognizant of acute accident risks, as the theory underlying the VSL assumes. The study told the workers that the new chemicals that had the warning label would replace those chemicals currently used in their jobs. Giving workers information about potentially dangerous chemicals boosted their risk beliefs for chemicals that were more dangerous than the chemicals that the workers were currently exposed to on their jobs.

This change in risk beliefs also had the expected effects on workers' attitudes toward their jobs. If workers were not offered higher wages for greatly increased risks, they indicated that they would be unwilling to take the job again or they would be willing to quit their position. In addition, the wage rate that they required to face greater risks from the hypothetical chemical exposures were in line with existing labor market estimates of wage premiums for objective measures of injury risks. This study consequently documented the reasonableness of worker risk beliefs and the broad tradeoff that workers must make in terms of the discrete decision to work on a particular job based on whether the wage and job-risk package made the job as attractive as alternative positions.

The chemical worker study addressed many key aspects of individuals' responses to hazard warnings, particularly those related to risk beliefs and wage responses, but did not focus on the pivotal regulatory issue, which was whether there would be an increase in precautionary behaviors that the worker would take when using the chemicals. Whether warnings would also foster safety-related behaviors also was a particular concern for the EPA, which had in place a series of regulations regarding chemicals and pesticides used by consumers and workers. The agency wanted to ascertain whether it was sufficient to utilize warning labels for dangerous chemicals and pesticides to promote safe handling of risky chemicals rather than banning these chemicals or greatly restricting their use, such as requiring that users be certified pesticide applicators. The trade-offs in this instance involved risk-averting choices the individual makes, conditional on use of the product, rather than the discrete decision to use a product to take a job. Would the consumer take appropriate precautions such as wearing rubber gloves and mixing herbicides with water at the recommended levels? For that agency I directed a series of studies of how best to design chemical and pesticide warnings.[12] In this household-chemical situation, the tradeoff was not in terms of wages and risk. Risk and precautionary efforts were often the focus, as consumers had to choose the precautions they would take with the product. In other studies that we undertook, consumers could pay a higher price for a safer product that required fewer precautions during use or that was safer generally, which is more analogous to the wage-job risk situation. Thus, there are two dimensions by which warnings could exert their influence. They could affect a consumer's discrete decision to use a product at all, in much the same way as hazard warnings could affect whether the worker would take a job, or they could influence how consumers choose to use the product. We found that properly designed warning labels could be effective in influencing each of these dimensions.[13]

The underlying principle for understanding such informational efforts is that their function is intrinsically related to the economic principles pertaining to the VSL. The tradeoffs embodied in decentralized decisions by consumers and workers involve decisions to engage in potentially risky activities, the precautions they take in such activities, and the other aspects of the activity that govern its overall attractiveness, such as the job's wage rate and the product's price. Informational efforts seek to make these decisions function in a sound way. Similarly, the use of the VSL serves as a mechanism for replicating the guidance for how policies would be structured if they were designed based on the patterns of behavior reflected in informed consumer and worker decisions.

The Organization of This Book

My exploration of the issues pertaining to pricing lives begins with the fundamentals. Chapter 2 considers the key components of government practices. What is the most reliable evidence for the VSL, and how have agencies incorporated these values in their policy assessments? The dominant approach in the United States has been to rely on labor market evidence, but survey approaches also have a role to play to address risks such as cancer and in countries such as the United Kingdom where labor market studies are less reliable. US estimates of the VSL based on labor market evidence are greater than those using other techniques, such as asking people in surveys how much they value risks.

The basic elements of the VSL involving setting a monetary value on the worth of risks to life should extend beyond government policies to corporate risk decisions, such as whether more costly safety devices should be added to the product design. Corporations' failure to adopt the VSL and the causes of their reluctance to undertake meaningful risk analyses are the subject of chapter 3. Historically, companies have been vilified for undertaking risk analyses that strive to balance costs and safety, but this impediment to responsible risk analyses could be addressed by providing appropriate legal protections for corporations undertaking responsible risk analysis. The attendant liability costs in the absence of such protections have led to the suppression of meaningful risk analyses, as exemplified in the policy practices at General Motors (GM) with respect to defective ignition switches. This case study of corporate neglect dramatizes the dangers of shunting explicit risk-cost tradeoff issues to the side. Banishing explicit discussion of the underlying risk-cost concerns led to over one hundred deaths. Chapter 4 takes an in-depth look at the GM ignition switch defect experience and the potential transformation of corporate practices that would be achieved through the use of the VSL estimates. This case study also illuminates the shortfall in government policies that fail to incorporate the VSL in setting regulatory sanctions for corporations' safety infractions.

While the basic components of the VSL approach suffice for providing guidance in most instances, many modifications of the approach may be desirable. Chief among the potential refinements in the use of the VSL estimates is recognition of possible heterogeneity in these values. Chapter 5 examines differences by age, as there is substantial variation across society in remaining life expectancy.

Should risks to the lives of people with very short life expectancy receive the same value as lives of the very young? Should any such quantity adjustments guide our thinking with respect to setting the price on reducing risk, setting levels of compensation, or levying penalties after fatalities have occurred, and are the appropriate age adjustments the same in each context? If we are striving for a more equitable approach, does that mean that all lives are valued equally or that each year of life should have the same value? While posing such questions raises potentially troubling moral issues, framing the answer to such queries to inquire how much the person values risks to his or her own life mollifies many of these concerns. Moreover, the fact that the VSL does not plummet with age and people place a considerable value on risks to each year of life makes the VSL a more protective way to address these issues than some current practices.

Basing the VSL on people's valuation of the risk might serve to disadvantage those who have lower income levels, both within countries and across the world. Chapter 6 considers differences by income, and chapter 7 examines related risk equity issues generally. Whose lives should be saved, and what is the most insightful way to conceptualize what we mean by equity when dealing with risks? There are potential differences in the VSL estimates along these and other dimensions. In some cases, the differences are not as great as one might think. In many other cases, the differences are not critical because government policies, environmental pollution, and consumer products generate risks that often cut across a broad swath of the population so that reliance on average valuations is reasonable. Nevertheless, there are some circumstances in which heterogeneity in valuations matters and should be taken into account. The pertinent VSL that should be used in very low-income nations is less than what is used in the United States. Nevertheless, use of the US VSL after appropriate adjustments for income differences across countries will lead to greater valuation of mortality risks than the practices in those countries or in the practices advocated by international bodies such as the Organisation for Economic Co-operation and Development (OECD), an international organization of 35 countries, most of which are advanced nations.

That this is the case indicates the systematic undervaluation of life throughout the world.

Although the basic components in the VSL literature are clear, there are several ongoing areas of refinements and professional debates, which are considered in chapter 8. An ongoing issue is how illnesses with substantial morbidity components should be addressed. Labor market studies provide insight into the valuation of acute accident risks, but how can we derive valuations for mortality risks such as cancer and other dread diseases? Should cancer risks be accorded a premium, and if so, how much? That chapter also considers issues such as whether the VSL estimates are distorted by publication selection biases in terms of what values are selected to be submitted to journals and published in the literature.

Our understanding of the role of morbidity effects and related complications also has ramifications for how the VSL can best be incorporated in reform of judicial practices with respect to determinations of liability and setting of damages amounts, which is the focus of chapter 9. The VSL does have a legitimate role to play in each instance but in a manner not currently used by the courts. The variations with respect to considerations such as age and income arise in judicial contexts as well, but these are not new issues for the courts. Indeed, the courts treat matters such as income levels and age in a starker fashion than current VSL practices.

Despite the potential controversies and misconceptions that the VSL generates, basing risk determinations on the risk valuations of those exposed to the risk serves as the most meaningful and responsible guide. Refinements in the VSL levels used for policy will remain a worthwhile endeavor. However, the most pressing tasks are to extend the use of the VSL to additional domains and to strike an efficient balance between risk and cost for a wide range of societal decisions. The VSL can serve as the guidepost for establishing appropriate safety levels as well as setting the level of financial sanctions needed to promote safety. Tremendous opportunities remain for incorporating the VSL as an integral part of society's efforts to address health, safety, and environmental risks. Corporations, government agencies, and the courts all should give the VSL a more prominent role. Previously, government agencies sought to disguise their valuation of lives saved by relabeling it the "cost of death." Corporations have sought to suppress such decisions altogether as being off-limits. The main consequence of these failures to value fatality risks properly is that safety levels fall short and lives are being lost.

2

How the Government Values Risks to Life

The Valuation of Statistical Lives

Government agencies no longer hesitate to value risks to life as part of the benefit assessment for policies that reduce mortality risks. The misguided efforts to sidestep such intrinsically sensitive valuation issues by equating the value of expected lives saved to the financial cost of death have been abandoned. The VSL approach has become the norm throughout the US government and many other countries.

Because the VSL is based on preferences with respect to small risks of death, it is well suited to serving as a benefits measure for government programs that generate benefits in terms of saving statistical lives involving risk changes that are comparable to or smaller than levels of occupational fatality risks. Policy efforts do not transform situations of certain death into situations of guaranteed survival. Rather, they have small, probabilistic impacts on well-being. Lifetime risks of cancer from chemical exposures of 1/10,000 or more—or just above annual risks of death of one in a million—are sufficient to trigger US Environmental Protection Agency criteria that hazardous waste sites should be cleaned up. Often the changes in the risk levels due to government policies are much less. Guard-rails have a small effect on safety for any particular passenger, and environmental air quality standards likewise have very modest effects on any particular individual's health. Government policies almost invariably have incremental effects on statistical lives rather than impacts on identified lives in which certain deaths are being prevented.

This chapter examines the types of VSL estimates used for government policies and the VSL levels used by various agencies and different countries. There are two principal sources of evidence that are used to establish VSL levels. It is possible to infer VSL levels based on revealed preferences regarding risky decisions or based on stated-preference values elicited in surveys. Each of these approaches has a similar conceptual basis, as the focus is on valuing mortality risk reductions based on attitudes toward small changes in risk rather than the monetary cost of death. US government agencies place the greatest emphasis on revealed-preference estimates, but other countries often place greater reliance on survey evidence because their labor market data are less reliable. While my focus here is on the economic literature generating the VSL estimates, agencies' selection of the VSL is not a dispassionate academic exercise, but it involves a political component as well. Higher levels of the VSL will lead to more stringent and more costly governmental regulations. Not surprisingly, industries subject to these regulations have opposed my efforts to increase the VSL, as this chapter's discussion of previous practices at the US Department of Transportation will indicate.

The Revealed-Preference Approach: Estimating the VSL Based on Actual Decisions

Decisions in market contexts are generally instructive about how people value different commodities, since they are expending their own funds to obtain the particular combination of product benefits. The payment of wages in return for accepting jobs with its mix of job attributes involves analogous tradeoffs, as does the higher price level that people are willing to pay for safer products. Because the tradeoff is not between money and risk alone but between money and a combination of different attributes of the product and the job, it is necessary to impute statistically the money-risk tradeoff, controlling for other aspects of the product, job, and personal characteristics. This approach has provided the basis for several lines of research.

The explorations seeking to identify the wage premium for worker fatality risks necessarily entail the use of a multivariate statistical analysis to isolate the wage-risk tradeoff. Casual examination of the pay that workers get for different jobs suggests that the most dangerous jobs are not the highest paid. Indeed, most of the jobs at the top of the pay spectrum entail very low levels of risk. A principal driver of this relationship is that safety is a normal economic good. Richer people will pay to live in safer neighborhoods, buy safer cars, and be more reluctant to boost their income by work on a hazardous job.

Because of the widespread availability of employment data, the most prevalent approach to analyzing the VSL implied by actual market behavior involves the use of labor market data to estimate the VSL. The observed wage premium is the result of the joint decisions of firms and workers. From the standpoint of the firm, providing increased safety is costly so that paying higher wages to induce workers to accept dangerous jobs may be less expensive than investing in a technology that reduces the risk. Because health and safety risks make the job less attractive to workers, economists beginning with Adam Smith observed that workers will demand extra pay to incur extra risk.[1] The statistical estimates directed at obtaining a labor market estimate of the VSL focus on a quality-adjusted or hedonic wage equation, which simultaneously reflects the extra pay workers need to incur extra risk as well as the extra cost to the firm of reducing the risk. The empirical challenge is to properly control for characteristics of workers and their jobs to isolate the amount of extra pay that workers in dangerous jobs receive compared to what they would have received had they been employed in safer positions.

Over the past four decades, there has emerged a substantial VSL literature based on labor market data. This literature will provide the basis for my discussion of not only the level of VSL but also its variation with age and other personal characteristics. The risk levels analyzed in these studies are relatively small. In the 1970s the average annual US worker fatality rate was 1/10,000, but due to improved levels of safety and the changing job mix in the economy, this figure has now diminished to 1/25,000. Thus, if the VSL was $10 million in each instance, then the annual compensation needed to generate that VSL number for the average risk level is $1,000 for the 1/10,000 risk, and $400 for a risk of 1/25,000.

New Occupational Fatality Data and Why Estimates Have Changed over Time

Estimates of the VSL differ across studies and datasets even if we restrict the focus to labor market estimates, which are the dominant source of revealed-preference estimates of the VSL. There is no single VSL. The VSL is not a natural constant but is a reflection of the money-risk preferences of the particular population and the trade-offs exhibited during that economic era. The observed differences across studies are not reflective of underlying instability of the values but instead embody the heterogeneity of VSL, the use of different samples with a different occupational mix, different econometric approaches, and different fatality risk measures. Over the course of this line of research, there have been many changes, including the increased affluence of society, the expanding role of workers' compensation benefits, technological improvements that promote greater workplace safety, and more refined employment data. Meta-analyses that pool the results of these different studies, controlling for different study characteristics, serve as an attractive means for exploiting the increased statistical power of a larger sample size as well as taking into account factors that could lead to differences in the VSL across studies.

Perhaps the greatest strides from the standpoint of research seeking to pin down the VSL have been with respect to the measures of fatality rates used in the studies. In the early era of the literature, such as my estimates of the VSL used in the hazard communication regulation debate, the best fatality rate data that could be matched to workers in various worker datasets was the Bureau of Labor Statistics (BLS) fatality rate data based on voluntary reports to the BLS from a sample of firms. The BLS then used this information to construct average fatality rates by industry, not distinguishing risks across different occupations within an industry. A subsequent era in US fatality rate data was the data series compiled by the National Institute of Occupational Safety and Health, which involved less measurement error but still did not permit detailed matching of fatality rates to the employee's particular job situation. Consistent with what one would expect if measurement error is random, use of this improved data series would lead to a larger VSL estimate. The impact of the better data was considerable, as it led to about a doubling of the estimated VSL using the same econometric specification as with the earlier BLS data.[2]

Although the data were much improved, they nevertheless were not ideal and did not permit matching of fatality rates to workers in a refined manner but instead were restricted to broad aggregates, such as industry-wide average risks. Beginning in 1992, the BLS developed the gold standard in fatality rate data through its Census of Fatal Occupational Injuries (CFOI).[3] Instead of relying on a sample of firms and individual reports of fatalities, these data are based on a comprehensive census of all occupational fatalities, each of which must be verified using multiple sources, such as reports by the firm, death certificates, and workers' compensation records. These statistics are also available on an individual fatality basis including information about the characteristics of the worker and the fatality event. As a result, instead of assuming that all workers in the industry face the same risk, it is possible to construct risk measures based on both the industry and occupation of a worker, thus providing a much more accurate reflection of the risk faced by the worker. In addition, researchers have also used the CFOI data to construct risk measures that are also contingent on gender, race, age, immigrant status, nature of risky event, type of death, and length of time receiving treatment before death, permitting a fuller exploration of the heterogeneity of the VSL in different contexts and for different worker groups. The principal data improvement was with respect to being able to fine-tune the objective measures of the risk to make them more directly applicable to the risks posed by the particular job for workers in an employment dataset used to estimate the VSL. Subsequent chapters explore some of these differences in VSL estimates based on these different risk measures.

The CFOI occupational fatality data are superior in many respects. These data involve less measurement error, thus reducing potential bias in the VSL estimates. The data can be refined based on a broad array of characteristics, providing precise matching to particular workers' situations and characteristics. The studies using the CFOI are also subject to less publication selection bias, which is an issue that we will examine in chapter 8. The distribution of the VSL estimates based on a sample of all 621 VSL estimates drawn from twenty published studies using the CFOI data is shown in table 2.1.

The VSL estimates using the CFOI fatality rate data vary depending on the sample that is used and the control variables included in the study. Based on the full set of VSL estimates using the CFOI data, as shown in table 2.1, the mean value is $13.1 million, and the median value is $11.1 million. If one focuses instead on the values from these studies that the authors regard as the "best estimates" in the studies because of the inclusion of pertinent statistical controls, the mean value is $12.2 million, and the median value is $10.1 million.[4] The stability of the VSL estimates is reflected in the similarity of these estimates to the $9.6 million median VSL estimate in my earlier meta-analysis with Joseph Aldy, which several government agencies have used in setting their VSL level.[5] In these as in many recent studies, the estimated VSL is often in the $9 million to $11 million range. For concreteness, I will use a VSL estimate of $10 million as the reference figure in much of my discussion.

In recognition of the superiority of the CFOI data in its selection of the pertinent VSL, the US Department of Transportation now relies only on labor market estimates based on the CFOI data. In particular, it utilizes VSL estimates based on a series of fifteen labor market studies, ten of which I authored or coauthored and five of which I did not.[6] Based on the department's assessment of which of the estimates in the literature were most reasonable, it concluded

TABLE 2.1: Distribution of the VSL Estimates in CFOI Studies

Percentile	VSL Estimate ($ millions)
10th	4.3
25th	7.3
50th	11.1
75th	16.8
90th	27.7
Average	13.1

Note: All estimates are in 2015 dollars.

that a VSL of $9.4 million is appropriate, which is a value in the estimated range above.

Perhaps the main continuing deficiency of all available occupational fatality data is that while these statistics do an excellent job of capturing traumatic injuries, they are not well suited to monitoring many occupational illnesses. Traumatic events that generate acute injuries and for which the job-related linkage can be ascertained are reflected in the CFOI data. However, the data underestimate deaths from longer-term exposures that have a latency period, such as the mesothelioma risks of asbestos and cancer risks from excessive radiation. An inherent difficulty is that for illnesses that are not signature diseases and that occur long after the worker's period of exposure to the hazard, the job-related linkage may be difficult to ascertain. The VSL statistics consequently are most directly related to accidental deaths. How these numbers can nevertheless be used to value illnesses such as cancer is examined in chapter 8.

Estimating the VSL Based on Product Market and Self-Protection Decisions

The VSL estimates from outside the labor market have also yielded VSL figures in the millions. As with the labor market estimates, the values from other revealed-preference studies will differ. In some cases, the VSL estimate from a product choice can indicate a floor or ceiling on the VSL. Suppose that a ski helmet reduces a skier's risk of death by 1/50,000, costs $200, and has no other positive or negative attributes. Setting aside other product attributes such as comfort, consumers who purchase the helmet have revealed a VSL of at least $10 million (i.e., $200 divided by 1/50,000), and those who don't purchase it reveal a VSL of less than $10 million. In each instance, their decision establishes a bound on their VSL. Unlike the labor market studies that address a continuum of risks, product risk decisions often are only instructive in indicating whether the VSL is above or below a critical value. Product market data generally tend to be less refined than employment data, usually with less information about individual characteristics and the risk levels associated with particular products. Nevertheless, these explorations provide valuable corroboration of the general magnitude of the labor market VSL estimates.

Economists first established the implicit VSL embodied in private choices involving transportation risks based on analyses of consumers' use of safety equipment. Studies of the use of seatbelts, beginning with Blomquist, imputed the VSL based on the monetary value of the time-and-effort cost of buckling that consumers incur in return for the reduced risk levels.[7] The time-and-effort costs are not generally observable, but using estimates of these costs and their monetary value, one can generate a VSL associated with safety gains from seatbelts. Similarly, in my joint work with Jahn Hakes, we found that respondents who indicate a higher VSL in stated-preference surveys are more likely to use seatbelts so that decisions to engage in safety-related behaviors are consistent with their levels of the VSL, which is a useful check on the rationality of risk-taking decisions.[8] An extension of the general approach in the seatbelt analyses provides VSL estimates associated with motorcycle helmets as well as for the use of child safety seats for children, who have comparatively higher VSL levels, based on their parents' purchase decisions.[9] The purchase of smoke detectors and bicycle helmets also have led researchers to impute an implicit VSL based on these products.[10]

Consumers similarly are willing to pay more for safer cars. Several studies have examined how the product price varies with safety. In my study with Mark Dreyfus, we found that used cars with a better safety record command a higher price, yielding a substantial implicit value of associated fatality risks, controlling for other automobile characteristics.[11] Similarly, houses that are exposed to the cancer risks of nearby hazardous waste sites have lower values, after taking into account other aspects of the house and the neighborhood. These housing price estimates imply an implicit value per expected case of cancer of \$5.9–\$7.0 million (in 2015 dollars).[12] More recently, Rohlfs, Sullivan, and Kniesner have shown that the price premium for cars equipped with airbags yields a VSL estimate very similar to the VSL range from labor market studies.[13] The study was particularly well designed in that it isolated the price effect associated with the introduction of airbags and then linked this effect to the risk reduction to estimate the VSL. They find that the airbag premium yields a VSL of \$10.5 million (in 2015 dollars). One ramification of these results is that basing corporate decisions on a benefit-cost analysis using a VSL will replicate the decisions that would emerge if consumers were fully informed of the vehicle safety levels and had the opportunity to pay a higher price for safer cars.

Given the expected safety benefits of protective equipment and safety devices, are people irrational if they fail to take advantage of these protective options? Whether that is the case depends on whether the safety measure passes a private benefit-cost test. Just as the benefits of safer vehicle design features for motor vehicles may not pass a benefit-cost test, consumers who forgo some precautionary opportunities may do so for quite rational reasons, such as a higher value of time.[14]

The Stated-Preference Approach: Estimating the VSL Based on Hypothetical Choices

Instead of relying on market data, many researchers have also utilized various survey techniques in which respondents are asked how much they would be willing to pay for a particular risk reduction. The advantage of this approach is its flexibility. One need not be constrained by the specific aspects of market data. Thus, it is feasible to obtain stated valuation amounts for population groups not in the labor market. In addition, survey questions provide the leeway of being able to alter the particular type of death. Fatalities involving possibly severe morbidity effects, such as cancer, may have different valuations than traumatic injuries. The context of the death may be influential as well. Particularly fearful deaths, such as burn deaths or being killed in an airplane crash, may lead to higher individual valuations of the risk than less dramatic hazards. Chapter 8 explores some of the refinements in VSL estimates that are made possible using stated-preference results, the most important of which is as-certaining whether VSL estimates should incorporate a cancer risk premium and, if so, to what extent.

The disadvantage of the stated-preference approach is that the hypothetical valuations derived from these surveys may not be re-flective of the decisions people would make if actually confronted with a particular risk. Concerns about the problems of hypothetical-question bias emerged when stated-preference methods were intro-duced to assess natural resource damages from the *Exxon Valdez* oil spill.[15] The subsequent literature has led to substantial refine-ment in the stated-preference approach, which now must meet exacting criteria. It is essential that such studies convey a credible scenario incorporating a realistic payment mechanism, a plausible mechanism for altering the risk level, and a well-specified linkage to a particular risk reduction. Particularly when dealing with small probabilities, these studies should educate respondents with respect to thinking about risks so that they can understand this probabilistic information. Conveying the risk level in terms of a concrete popula-tion denominator is often a well-understood method of conveying probabilistic information. For example, people are much more likely to be able to comprehend the magnitude of a risk of 13 deaths in a population of 1,000 rather than being told the risk is 0.013. Underly-ing this difference in perceptions is that the brain processes these values differently, as my colleagues and I found doing an fMRI study in which we analyzed the difference in brain images depending on the manner in which health risk information is presented.[16]

To be credible, the survey responses also must pass a series of rationality tests to indicate that respondents understood the sur-vey. Rational responses should pass several kinds of scope tests.

Respondents should be willing to pay more for a safety policy as the magnitude of the risk reduction generated by the policy increases. Similarly, they should be willing to pay more for a mortality risk reduction accompanied by reductions in nonfatal risks than if there was only a mortality risk effect. There are also behavioral scope tests in which responses should be consistent with fundamental economic predictions. For example, more affluent respondents should be willing to pay more for a specified risk reduction than those with less adequate financial resources.

Despite the challenges of undertaking credible stated-preference studies, it may nevertheless be the case that this approach yields more reliable estimates of VSL in situations in which either the fatality rate data or the employment data are deficient, making it infeasible to obtain stable VSL estimates using market data. Although one might expect such problems to be confined to less-developed economies without a well-developed governmental data series, the stated-preference approach has received its greatest prominence in the United Kingdom with respect to a series of studies focusing primarily on traumatic transportation-related risks.[17] Labor market estimates of the VSL in the United Kingdom are highly unstable, sometimes leading to small values and other times generating extremely large values several times greater than those observed in the United States.[18] As a result, while the underlying VSL methodology in the United Kingdom is the same as in the United States, the evaluation approach in the United Kingdom uses stated-preference values for governmental benefit assessments rather than the findings of revealed-preference studies from the labor market.

Agency Performance and Convergence

Historically, agencies that first valued mortality risks for policy purposes used variants of the cost-of-death approach patterned after the components of court awards. Since these values are roughly an order of magnitude lower than those implied by VSL estimates, the starting point for agency valuations was a substantial underestimation of the VSL. After the Occupational Safety and Health Administration hazard communication policy debate, agencies began to adopt the VSL approach, but there was a tendency to remain anchored on the earlier cost-of-death numbers, making the upward adjustment to the VSL only partial. This anchoring phenomenon is evident in the estimates formerly used by the US Department of Transportation (DOT) as well as in the practices at many other agencies.

Consider the following trend in the VSL used in government agencies' risk analyses, where all figures have been converted to comparable 2015 dollars.[19] The DOT's Federal Aviation Administration (FAA) evaluation of protective breathing equipment in 1985 used a VSL of $1.3 million. That amount reflected a major policy shift, as it was several times greater than the cost-of-death benefit values that it used previously, but it still fell short. The FAA was not ignorant of the pertinent estimates of VSL, as I had prepared a major review of the literature for the FAA in which I had suggested a substantial increase in VSL estimates, which is a change that FAA officials supported.[20] Raising the VSL to be in line with my VSL estimates had potential ramifications throughout the agency and would have led to more stringent transportation regulations, including additional automobile safety regulations. At a meeting at the office of the Secretary of Transportation in which I presented my report, I advocated substantial boosting of the VSL for the entire department and particularly for the FAA. Because a higher VSL would lead to justification of more government regulations, representatives of the auto industry attending the meeting favored a lower figure of $1 million per life. There was substantial upward movement in the VSL after this meeting, but the DOT's VSL still fell short. The auto industry's opposition to responsible estimates of the value of human life is reflected in the companies' own analyses, which I examine in the next two chapters. Despite industry opposition, after my report for the FAA, the DOT raised the VSL beyond the industry's preferred $1 million figure. For example, in 1996 the VSL amount used by the DOT had risen to $4.1 million in the agency's evaluation of aircraft simulator use in pilot training, testing, and checking and at training centers. This value reflected continued upward movement in the FAA's VSL, but remained below the more recent labor market estimates of VSL.

What accounts for the succession of partial but upward movements in the VSL at the DOT? The combination of anchoring biases and the regulatory ramifications of a higher VSL led to a more gradual VSL approach that would lead to less protective but less expensive government policies. Subsequent levels of VSL used by the DOT reached $6.4 million in the 2008 analysis of new entrant safety assurance processes by the Federal Motor Carrier Administration, railroad tank car transportation regulations for hazardous materials in 2008, roof crush-resistance standards for motor vehicles in 2009, and air cargo screening standards in 2009, with comparable valuations for roof resistance standards in 2010. After convening a group of economists, including me, the DOT boosted its VSL for all agency analyses. Beginning in 2013, the DOT adopted an agency-wide VSL figure of $9.0 million based on the series of labor market estimates incorporating the CFOI data, thus increasing the VSL by almost 50 percent. Periodic updates have now led to a departmental VSL of $9.4 million.

Particularly in the case of the DOT, for which transportation safety regulations are subject to meaningful benefit-cost tests, this increase in the VSL estimates will lead to the justification of more stringent and more protective safety standards. At other agencies, such as the EPA, the enabling legislation in different policy areas often imposes requirements that prevent benefit-cost guidance from being a binding test. Indeed, the Clean Air Act specifically excludes the consideration of costs in the setting of national ambient air quality standards. Nevertheless, EPA must submit a benefit assessment to the US Office of Management and Budget as part of the regulatory approval process, and being able to tout a substantial level of benefits for the policies enhances their political salability.

There was similar but more rapid escalation in the VSL figures used by the EPA. In conjunction with its Science Advisory Board and its National Center for Environmental Economics, the EPA has always made an effort to remain attuned to academic research developments and to incorporate these values in policy assessments. While in 1985 it used a VSL of $2.3 million to value the regulation of fuels and fuel additives, including lead content, by 1996 the agency had moved to a VSL of $8.5 million for national ambient air quality standards for particulate matter and for ozone, applying similar values to a broad variety of other regulations ranging from arsenic in drinking water in 2000 to emissions control from non-road diesel engines in 2004. By 2005, EPA's VSL would round off to figures in the $10 million range, with the preponderance of the estimates by different agency branches being between $9.9 million and $10.4 million.

It is noteworthy that EPA and DOT are the agencies responsible for the most costly government regulations, and these agencies have made notable efforts to incorporate appropriate VSL levels in the policy assessments. Other agencies have likewise raised their valuations of mortality risks to be more in line with the economic estimates of VSL. The Food and Drug Administration used a VSL of $8.3 million in its 2011 evaluation of labeling for bronchodilators to treat asthma, which pertained to "cold, cough, allergy, bronchodilator, and antiasthmatic drug products for over-the-counter human use."[21] Similarly, in 2012, the Mining Safety and Health Administration used a VSL of $9.0 million in its proposed regulation for examinations of work areas in underground mines for violations of mandatory health and safety standards. In 2015, OSHA used a VSL of $9.3 million to value fatality risks from confined spaces in construction. Agencies have converged in terms of the general range of the VSL, as they have adopted values more in line with a sound economics approach than the cost of death.

The adoption of the VSL conceptual approach to valuing mortality risks has been encouraged by formal agency guidance from OMB.[22] Agencies must submit to OMB a benefit-cost analysis for all major government regulations with annual costs of $100 million or more. In undertaking these and other analyses, OMB has specified that the VSL is the correct conceptual approach but has not indicated a specific government-wide number. Three agencies have issued detailed recommended internal guidelines. The US Department of Transportation now has an official guidance document indicating that the VSL is $9.4 million across the department.[23] The EPA formerly had agency guidance of $9.7 million (in 2013 dollars), and in 2016 it was considering increasing the VSL to $10.3

million (in 2013 dollars).[24] Similarly, the US Department of Health and Human Services issued a guidance VSL figure of $9.6 million (in 2014 dollars).[25]

Should agencies all use the same VSL or should there be differences such as distinguishing the demographic profile of the particular lives being saved, the change in the risk levels generated by the policy, or the causes of death? In each instance, there may be strong economic evidence that uniformity does not reflect the underlying willingness to pay for the risk reduction. Whether and how such differences should be taken into account will be discussed in chapters 5, 6, and 7. However, it is noteworthy that most government policies have a broad impact across a spectrum of risk-taking preferences, not targeted at specific groups, so that an average VSL for the economy may be quite reflective of the pertinent valuation amount.

Valuing Risks of the Military

An apparent omission from the roster of government policies utilizing the VSL is consideration of the evaluation practices in the particularly hazardous area of security and national defense. However, even in this policy area, agencies have adopted the VSL approach. For example, recent joint regulations issued by the US Coast Guard and the US Department of Homeland Security have used a VSL of $9.1 million.

The VSL also has a constructive role to play in valuing risks in combat situations. Shouldn't risks to the lives of soldiers be treated as having value beyond any death benefits that might be paid out and the recruitment costs of finding replacements? Despite the inherent risks of military operations, prospective enlistees place a value on risks to their lives that is similar to that of workers in risky civilian occupations.[26] The VSL could serve as a guidepost for the appropriate risk-cost tradeoffs involving military risks. Kniesner, Leeth, and Sullivan illustrate this applicability using a case study of force-protection investments involving the replacement of wheeled ground vehicles used for day-to-day operations.[27] Vehicles can have light armor, medium armor, or heavy armor, but the procurement and operational costs increase with the degree of armor. Lightly armored vehicles are the least expensive, so the decision pertains to whether to purchase the vehicles with more protective medium or heavy armor instead. The vehicles with medium armor cost about three times as much as those with light armor but reduce fatalities for infantry units at a cost of $1–$2 million per expected life saved, thus easily passing a benefit-cost test. However, medium armor is not cost-effective for lower-risk uses such as administrative support units. The heavy armor costs three times as much as medium armor but does not reduce fatalities appreciably and consequently does not pass a benefit-cost test.

The application of the VSL to such military decisions regarding force-protection investments such as armaments illustrates the parallels with product safety decisions generally. As in the case of product safety decisions in the private market, application of the VSL can highlight the desirable allocations across the many available opportunities to promote safety. However, just as it is not cost-effective to make the cars we drive as safe as tanks, there likewise may be only negligible benefits but substantial costs in making all military vehicles as safe as tanks.

International Differences in the VSL

The recent international performance with respect to the selection of the VSL has been less reassuring.[28] Recent policy estimates of the VSL are $5.6 million in Canada, which is well below the current US level but in the range of some recent US values. It is the other countries that are the truly stark outliers. The VSL estimates used for policy purposes in the United Kingdom include $2.4 million for transport accidents and $2.1 million for flooding risks. The current Australia guideline value of $3.5 million is in a similar range.[29] Countries that have adopted even lower VSL values in recent policy analyses are $0.9 million in Mexico, $0.9–$1.0 million in Columbia, $1.6 million in Peru, and $1.0 million in Malaysia. The VSL estimates for more affluent countries are greater. The values recommended by the OECD lie in the $1.8–$5.5 million range in 2015 dollars, where countries can adjust their values from a base value of $3.6 million depending on the international differences in income levels.[30] These figures are also too low, as I will demonstrate in chapter 6.

It is unsurprising that the VSL estimates differ across countries. One would of course expect lower estimates in these countries based on the differences in income levels. But, as chapter 6's discussion of the income elasticity of the VSL will indicate, these differences with the VSL levels in the United States are far too great to be explained by income differences alone. Anchoring the choice of the VSL based on past practices is a contributing factor to the continued low VSL levels, as was also the case in the United States for many years. International estimates of the VSL also tend to be based on stated-preference studies rather than revealed-preference evidence. These survey values have tended to be lower than those derived from labor market studies, perhaps because hypothetical risks presented in survey contexts are less fearsome than actual threats to one's life.

Table 2.2 provides a representative selection of international labor market estimates of the VSL for thirteen countries. The labor market data and fatality rate data in these countries are not as reliable as in the United States, making some of these estimates less credible. There is also a tendency for authors of international studies to report VSL estimates that are anchored on the US VSL levels, creating a form of publication bias, which is explored in chapter 8. For example, the VSL estimates of $4.9 million for India and $12.3 million for Pakistan are implausibly high. As a result, transferring the US estimates to other countries after accounting for income differences is a sounder approach, as will be detailed in chapter 6. Increasing the VSL in countries outside of the United States is a remaining policy challenge. Adopting more pertinent VSL estimates will lead to more protective policies throughout the world.

How the VSL estimates are used to value fatality risks also may differ. In the United States, the VSL properly serves as the overall value to the individual of reducing the risk of death. This value reflects how much the individual values the risk to the entire trajectory of well-being that will be lost, including any lost earnings. The US benefit calculation procedure is to multiply the expected number

TABLE 2.2: A Selection of International Labor Market VSL Estimates

Country	VSL ($ millions)
Australia	7.1
Austria	11.6
Canada	6.7
Chile	10.8
Germany	2.6
India	4.9
Japan	6.6
Pakistan	12.3
Poland	2.5
South Korea	1.5
Switzerland	10.9
Taiwan	0.8
United Kingdom	10.8
Average	13.1

Source: These estimates are from W. Kip Viscusi and Clayton J. Masterman, "Anchoring Biases in International Estimates of the Value of a Statistical Life," *Journal of Risk and Uncertainty* 54, no. 2 (2017): 103–128.

of lives saved by the VSL to obtain the benefit amount for reduced fatality risks. In the United Kingdom, the governmental procedure has instead included adding the VSL to the cost-of-death value, which is a form of double counting. In particular, the UK Department for Transport's fatalities benefit measure of £1,428,180 was the sum of the lost output value of £490,960, the medical and ambulance costs of £840, and the human costs of £936,380 reflected in the VSL amount derived from survey evidence.[31] While the Department for Transport viewed the VSL numbers as excluding forgone consumption of goods and services, the labor market estimates are all-inclusive. Similarly, any survey measure is unlikely to be able to exclude them as well.[32] Including external financial costs such as medical and ambulance expenses is appropriate, as these would not be privately valued in the VSL calculation.

The Economy-wide Price for Job Safety

By almost any standard, the market incentives for risk reduction created in the United States through the VSL are considerable. In 2014, there were 4,821 fatal job injuries.[33] Using $10 million per expected fatality for purposes of this example, the total annual wage compensation for the economy-wide risk of fatalities is $48 billion. But there is similar market compensation for nonfatal injuries as well. The rate of wage compensation for injuries severe enough to cause the loss of a day of work or more is in the range of $50,000 or more.[34] With 1.15 million such injuries in 2015,[35] the total wage premiums for these nonfatal risks was $58 billion. Together these wage effects establish powerful incentives for safety of at least $106 billion.

There are other forces at work that generate safety incentives as well. Workers' compensation premiums establish safety incentives to the extent that they are experience-rated based on the firm's accident performance or an insurance adjuster's assessment of the riskiness of the firm. These premium levels were $40.9 billion in 2013.[36] Workers' compensation premium levels in turn establish strong safety incentives, as empirical estimates suggest that the overall worker fatality rate would be one-third higher than it currently is if there were no workers' compensation system and no tort liability system to replace it.[37] These financial incentives for safety dwarf the financial incentives created through job safety regulations by several orders of magnitude.

Regulatory Costs per Life Saved and the VSL: Why Might There Be an Imbalance?

The VSL levels used in benefit assessments also can serve as a reference point for assessing policy attractiveness. Thus, if the agency's VSL is $10 million, then regulations with a cost per expected life saved less than that amount have benefits in excess of costs, and policies for which the cost per life saved exceeds that figure do not. Although reduced mortality risks are not the only regulatory benefit, they are typically the driving force of benefits. In calculating the cost per expected life saved, one can account for other benefit components as part of the analysis.[38]

With few notable exceptions, such as the legislative mandates governing DOT regulatory policies, the laws that provide the basis for regulatory policies do not establish benefit-cost balancing as a policy objective but instead have a narrower agency mission, such as to make the workplace safe. The executive orders governing the regulatory oversight process for new regulations do not require that agencies demonstrate that benefits exceed costs when doing so conflicts with the agency's legislative mandates. As a result, almost all government regulations other than those within the DOT formerly imposed inordinately high costs per expected life saved, with some of the extreme examples being the OSHA formaldehyde exposure limit with a cost per expected life saved of $103 billion and the EPA sewage sludge disposal standards with a cost of $700 million per expected life saved.[39] These high costs per expected fatality prevented are the result of a very small number of expected lives saved in the denominator rather than a high level of costs in the numerator. Notwithstanding the restrictive legislative mandates, such ineffective regulatory policies are no longer common, as agencies increasingly tout the substantial benefits of the regulation that now exceed the overall regulatory costs.[40]

Although the regulatory oversight process appears to have led to some internalization of the application of VSL estimates to policy assessments, government policies that are not new regulatory initiatives are not subject to that process and are more likely to retain the tunnel vision approach focusing on the agency's specific mission rather than on overall net benefits to society. The EPA Superfund program for cleaning up hazardous waste sites exemplifies this emphasis. The cleanup criteria are governed by the actual and hypothetical future risks of cancer and other health effects from the chemical wastes at the sites. Based on EPA's upper-bound risk assumptions, the median site in terms of cost effectiveness has a cost per expected case of cancer averted of $10.5 million.[41] If one assumes that an expected case of cancer has the same value as an expected death, this value is in the same neighborhood as the VSL estimates. However, these estimates, which are based on risk levels under the agency's worst-case scenarios, overstate the policy's actual efficacy.[42] Using EPA's mean risk estimates rather than upper-bound values generates staggering cost estimates. Actual costs per expected case of cancer averted exceed $1 billion per case of cancer for two-thirds of the Superfund sites.[43] Chapter 7 will propose targeting cleanups based on equitable risk tradeoffs, which perhaps surprisingly is both a less costly and a more protective approach than current profligate policies.

Toward Sound Government Policies

The availability of the VSL estimates does not ensure that all government policies will strike a sensible balance between program costs and benefits. Agencies can and do have other institutional objectives. What the VSL estimates accomplish is providing government agencies with a procedure and an empirical framework for monetizing the mortality risk reduction benefits of these policies, should the agencies wish to do so. This approach has already become the norm for benefit assessment for major new government regulations. The current US emphasis in selecting the VSL levels is on labor market evidence regarding the wage-risk tradeoffs for dangerous jobs. Based on the most reliable fatality risk data, the Census of Fatal Occupational Injuries, the estimated VSL is in the $10 million range. US government agencies are converging in their choice of the VSL estimates in that range. The use of the cost-of-death approach to valuing fatality risks has been abandoned, though it took decades for agencies to increase the mortality risk valuation amounts to accurately reflect the level of the VSLs. Extending the use of this approach for all other government policies is a remaining challenge and would enable government agencies to better target the policies so that they will be most beneficial to the citizenry.

There are also additional opportunities to use the VSL estimates to foster responsible risk policies. Subsequent chapters will identify such extensions, including setting regulatory sanctions based on the VSL, incorporating the VSL in corporate risk decisions, and integrating the VSL into liability and damages determinations by the courts. The VSL should not be limited to its current well-established function of providing guidance for new regulatory initiatives.

In addition to expanding the scope of domestic application of the VSL, there are also international opportunities to foster more protective and cost-effective policies. The values that countries outside the United States assign to fatality risks are seriously inadequate and greatly undervalue lives. As I will indicate in chapter 6, transferring the US VSL estimates internationally is feasible and will generate more accurate estimates than the current international approach. Estimates of the VSL should serve as the guidepost for establishing risk tradeoffs.

3

The Hazards of Corporate Valuations of Product Risks

Extending the Domain of the VSL Methodology

Application of the VSL estimates to value fatality risk reductions need not be restricted to government policies. Companies should also use this methodology when assessing the value of safety improvements for products and jobs. Taken at face value, the VSL estimates provide the average tradeoff between costs and product risks that consumers would make if they were cognizant of the product risks. Incorporation of the VSL estimates in product design decisions consequently enables producers to design products with the safety features that consumers would find desirable if they understood the product risks. Corporations devote substantial effort to getting a handle on consumers' preferences so that they can market products with valued attributes. Much of this marketing research is based on hypothetical responses in focus groups or conjoint studies of product attributes. Even though the VSL estimates are more concrete and pertinent in that they reflect actual market-based tradeoffs, companies have not incorporated these values in their product design decisions.

The corporate failures with respect to such risk analyses can be traced to challenges that are more fundamental than those faced by government agencies. In the 1980s, when government agencies adopted the use of the VSL estimates, agencies had already been undertaking extensive efforts to monetize the safety-related benefits of these policies, which they were required to do as part of the regulatory oversight efforts. The VSL estimates simply gave government agencies a higher price tag that they could use in valuing mortality effects in analyses that they were already doing. Private corporations don't have a similar history of regulatory analyses or requirements that they undertake such analyses.

The shortcoming in how corporations incorporate safety concerns in their decision making is consequently more fundamental. It is not simply a matter of failing to use the VSL estimates in an otherwise sound analysis balancing risk and cost. Systematic risk analysis involving a meaningful comparison of safety benefits and costs is not the norm. As I will examine in this chapter, private companies, particularly in the automobile industry, often undertook risk analyses but based these analyses on the cost-of-death approach rather than the VSL. These analyses fared particularly badly in the courts, leading companies to abandon the risk analysis approach in ways that will be further illuminated by considering the GM ignition switch experience in chapter 4.

Simply replacing the cost-of-death numbers with the VSL will rectify companies' undervaluation of life, but may not be in the company's self-interest. Just as the government's adoption of the VSL has generated controversy, companies may be even more vulnerable. To examine the potential ramifications of companies adopting the VSL, I undertook a series of legal case experiments using hundreds of jury-eligible citizens. The disturbing findings suggest that jurors may use a high VSL as an anchor in setting the damages award, possibly boosting liability costs even though the VSL leads to safer products by placing a greater value weight on the harm consumers suffer from product risks. What is needed is fundamental legal reform to facilitate company efforts to utilize the VSL estimates in the context of systematic risk analyses.

Risk Analyses at Ford, Chrysler, and GM:
The Ford Pinto Debacle and Other Controversies

Automobile companies historically were leaders in assessing the benefits and costs of safety aspects of vehicles and using these findings in the product design decisions. Their experience with these analyses highlights the pitfalls that companies face when venturing into this sensitive valuation terrain. A useful starting point is to review some examples of the corporate risk analysis experiences based on the results of successful litigation against the companies. After this review, I will explore possible ways in which these barriers to corporate risk analyses can be overcome.

The potential hazards of undertaking a corporate risk analysis are exemplified by the experiences of Ford, Chrysler, and GM. The first such analysis to receive scrutiny was Ford's assessment of gas-tank location risks for the Ford Pinto. The Ford Pinto experience is not unique, as gas-tank location issues often played a prominent safety role because of the fire-related hazards. There were similar analyses of various safety measures for design aspects by Ford, Chrysler, and GM. In each case, the company undertook an analysis seeking to ascertain the appropriate balance between cost and safety improvements and ultimately decided not to adopt the additional safety measures. The companies' analyses were flawed in serious ways, with the most important being that the lives at risk were valued based on the level of tort liability damages in wrongful death cases. In addition to this specific shortcoming in the economic methodology, there appears to be an overriding problem in that explicitly considering risk-cost tradeoffs in such analyses generates controversy and, in some cases, very large punitive damages awards.

THE ADVERSE REPERCUSSIONS
OF THE FORD PINTO RISK ANALYSIS

The first product risk analysis to garner national attention involved the Ford Pinto, which, much like the GM cars implicated in the ignition recall problems, was an entry-level vehicle. The Ford Pinto case,

Grimshaw v. Ford Motor Co.,[1] also involved the first documented blockbuster punitive damages award of at least $100 million. The injury occurred in 1972 when a Ford Pinto was rear-ended after it stopped on the freeway. The thirteen-year-old passenger, Richard Grimshaw, suffered a serious injury, and the driver was killed. The impact caused a fire that the plaintiffs attributed to a defective product design for the fuel filler pipe and the placement of the gas tank behind the rear axle. In addition to a compensatory damages award of $2.5 million to Grimshaw and $600,000 to the driver, the jury awarded $125 million in punitive damages. The punitive damages award was later reduced to $3.5 million.[2]

What was most noteworthy about the case and the ensuing debate about Ford's safety practices is that Ford had performed a risk analysis and concluded that the less-safe design was preferable.[3] Trial lawyer Stuart Speiser termed the analysis "the most remarkable document ever produced in an American lawsuit." Although the *Grimshaw* case pertained to the risk of fire due to rear impacts, Ford's risk analysis pertained to gas-tank design changes that might reduce risks of fires associated with rollovers. Ford undertook the study in anticipation of a prospective safety regulation by the National Highway Traffic Safety Administration (NHTSA). Even though Ford's study was not related to fire risks arising from rear impacts, the analysis was used in court to characterize Ford's alleged callous disregard for life.

Table 3.1 summarizes the benefit and cost calculations in Ford's analysis. The calculated $137.5 million cost associated with the design change is almost triple the $49.6 million safety benefit, making the change apparently undesirable from a benefit-cost perspective. However, the components of the benefits analysis are seriously flawed. Consider the $200,000 value that Ford placed on each burn death. Ford based this figure on a variant of the cost-of-death approach, which is the principal methodology used in litigation and was also the methodology used at that time by the Department of Transportation to value mortality risk reduction benefits. The Ford analysts selected the amount that the estate for a fatally injured person is typically compensated in court cases, which is principally the

TABLE 3.1: Benefit-Cost Calculations for the Ford Pinto

PANEL A: BENEFIT CALCULATIONS FOR INCREASED SAFETY IN PINTO GAS TANK DESIGN

Outcome of Faulty Design	Ford's Unit Value	Ford's Total Value
180 burn deaths	$200,000	$36.0 million
180 serious burn injuries	$67,000	$12.1 million
2,100 burned vehicles	$700	$1.5 million
Total		$49.6 million

PANEL B: COST CALCULATIONS FOR INCREASED SAFETY IN PINTO GAS TANK DESIGN

Number of Units	Unit Cost	Total Cost[a]
11 million cars	$11	$121.0 million
1.5 million light trucks	$11	$16.5 million
Total		$137.5 million

[a] Excluded is the minor cost component of the lost consumer's surplus of customers who do not buy Pintos because of the $11 price increase.

Source: W. Kip Viscusi, *Reforming Products Liability* (Cambridge, MA: Harvard University Press, 1991), 112, which in turn cites the internal 1973 Ford Motor Company document by E. F. Grush and C. S. Saunby, "Fatalities Associated with Crash Induced Fuel Leakage and Fires," archived at https://perma.cc/7XFH -3KDG, discussed in Brent Fisse and John Braithwaite, *The Impact of Publicity on Corporate Offenders* (Albany: SUNY Press, 1983).

present value of the net income of the deceased. However, these amounts are focused on meeting the income losses suffered by the survivors, not on preventing the loss of life to the accident victim. The correct economic valuation of preventing a small risk of death is governed by the VSL, which is at least an order of magnitude greater than this figure. Even if jurors were not aware of the VSL approach, they would certainly be on sound ground in their belief that focusing only on the earnings that are lost when a person dies greatly under-states the value of preventing any expected death. Similarly, burn injuries suffered in a crash often inflict severe pain and sometimes permanent disfigurement so that the value of preventing these risks will surely be greater than the average compensatory damages value.

Ford was pilloried for undertaking an analysis that tried to take a hard look at the costs and benefits of a design change.[4] Ideally, we want to encourage companies to think systematically about safety. However, companies should do so in a responsible way. Dramati-cally underestimating the value of reducing the risk of death was a serious deficiency of Ford's approach. Use of a compensatory damages payment to value lives should have evoked legitimate concerns about whether Ford was placing adequate weight on the lives at risk.

THE INHERENT CHALLENGE TO RISK
ANALYSIS POSED BY HINDSIGHT BIAS

The Ford Pinto analysis also highlights a challenge that Ford would have faced even if it had done a proper analysis. The cost of the design change to prevent the fuel-related fire injuries and deaths was only $11 per vehicle. When jurors confront an identifiable fatality that could have been prevented for $11, they will not be considering a comparison of the total costs and total expected benefits across the entire product line. Rather, the comparison is between the life that has been lost and a relatively inexpensive change to the car. This ex post frame of reference that is an inherent feature of tort litigation is certainly not the appropriate frame to use in judging any risk decision that must be made before the risk outcomes are known. Because it is so difficult for people to overcome hindsight bias and place themselves in the pre-accident situation, it is vital that firms avoid undervaluing the lives at risk.

The prominent role that hindsight bias plays in jury deliberations with respect to product safety has been a major concern of Seventh Circuit Judge Frank Easterbrook. In an escalator injury case in which a person was injured after someone pushed the stop button on an escalator, Judge Easterbrook made the following observations:

> The ex post perspective of litigation exerts a hydraulic force that distorts judgment. Engineers design escalators to minimize the sum of construction, operation, and injury costs. Department stores, which have nothing to gain from maiming their customers and employees, willingly pay for cost-effective precautions. . . . Come the lawsuit, however, the passenger injured by a stop presents himself as a person, not a probability. Jurors see today's injury; persons who would be injured if buttons were harder to find and use are invisible. Although witnesses may talk about them,

they are spectral figures, insubstantial compared to the injured plaintiff, who appears in the flesh.[5]

In this case, the company's tradeoff involved the identified person who was injured by someone pushing the escalator button, as compared with all the unidentified persons who were protected by the safety button. In the jury's mind, identified lives that have been harmed will count more than an unknown number of statistical lives that have been protected.

OTHER CONTROVERSIAL FORD RISK ANALYSES

The role of hindsight bias coupled with corporate risk analyses extended beyond the Pinto. Ford did not fare much better in a subsequent case involving a risk analysis that the court termed "safety science management."[6] In *Ford Motor Co. v. Stubblefield*, Terri Stubblefield was in the rear seat of a Ford Mustang II and was killed after being hit from behind by a car traveling about sixty miles per hour, turning the rear seat of the car into a "ball of fire." To punish Ford for making an explicit—and unacceptable—tradeoff between cost and risk reductions, the jury awarded $8 million in punitive damages:

> The evidence here was sufficient to authorize the jury to find that the sum of $8 million was an amount necessary to deter Ford from repeating its conduct; that is, its conscious decision to defer implementation of safety devices in order to protect its profits. One internal memo estimated that "the total financial effect of the Fuel System Integrity program [would] reduce Company profits over the 1973–1976 cycle by $109 million," and recommended that Ford "defer adoption of the [safety measures] on all affected cars until 1976 to realize a design cost savings of $20.9 million compared to 1974." Another Ford document referred to a $2 million cost differential as "marginal."[7]

The economic use of the term "marginal" means "incremental" with respect to the additional costs of a design change, not that the costs were very low and sufficiently trivial that being guided by marginal costs reflects a flagrant disregard for safety. However, misinterpreting this terminology reinforces the callous image of the company that the attorneys sought to create.

In a subsequent case involving a systematic risk analysis, Ford was penalized with a punitive damages award in *Miles v. Ford Motor Co.*, an award that was subsequently overturned.[8] In this instance, the controversial risk analysis concerned a "tension eliminator" for the shoulder harness on a seatbelt.[9] The failure of this part caused Willie Miles, the passenger, to slide through the seatbelt after a collision and suffer head and spinal injuries. Once again, Ford was faulted for undertaking a risk analysis and not incurring the cost for the safety improvement:

> Syson [the plaintiffs' accident reconstruction expert] testified that when Ford identified what it believed was a defective product it would first run a "cost benefit" analysis to see what the cost would be to fix or repair the defect. Next, Ford would assign arbitrary values to each death or serious injury and would predict the number of occurrences which would involve either death or serious injury. Finally, Ford would determine the cost to litigate such deaths and injuries. Syson testified that if the cost to repair the defect exceeded the other costs, Ford would not correct the defect.[10]

Ford's efforts to undertake a benefit-cost analysis were well founded from an economic standpoint. However, using court awards in personal injury cases as the yardstick for valuing risk to life and health dramatically understates the level of benefits associated with greater safety. In this instance, the court overturned both the punitive damages award and the finding that Ford was "grossly negligent" because Ford's tension eliminators were consistent with those found to be acceptable in a regulatory analysis by NHTSA.

A SIMILAR RISK ANALYSIS CONTROVERSY FOR CHRYSLER

Chrysler Corporation has also been faulted for undertaking a risk analysis. In the blockbuster awards case, *Jimenez v. Chrysler Corp.*, the jury awarded $250 million in punitive damages because of risk-cost comparisons very similar to those in the Ford Pinto case.[11] After his mother ran a red light, Sergio Jimenez, who was an unbuckled passenger in his mother's Dodge Caravan, was thrown from the vehicle and killed. A better door latch could have prevented him from being thrown from the vehicle, but Chrysler concluded that the costs of such a door latch outweighed the value of reducing the risks. According to the plaintiff's post-trial memorandum:

> Chrysler officials at the highest level cold-bloodedly calculated that acknowledging the problem and fixing it would be more expensive, in terms of bad publicity and lost sales, than concealing the defect and litigating the wrongful death suits that inevitably would result.[12]

The cost and risk reduction comparisons mirror the types of concerns in Judge Easterbrook's hindsight example. On the cost side, there would be a one-time tooling cost of $100,000 and a unit cost of $0.50 per vehicle for the new, superior part. Comparison of the $0.50 cost with the loss of an identified person's life will lead to an adverse judgment for Chrysler, but this is not the appropriate comparison. At the time of the product safety design decision, the company must deal with assessed probabilities of accidents, not identified prospective deaths. Even if the Chrysler analysis had been undertaken using sound benefit values, taking the jury back to the decision Chrysler faced before the accident occurred would require overcoming the well-established role of hindsight bias.

THE GM RISK ANALYSIS OF FUEL-TANK RISKS

GM also has not fared well in instances in which it has undertaken a risk analysis pertaining to the tradeoffs between vehicle cost and risk. In the 1998 Georgia case *GM Corp. v. Moseley*, GM had undertaken a risk analysis pertaining to the design of the side-saddle fuel tanks.[13] Although Moseley survived the initial impact when his GM pickup truck was broadsided by a drunk driver, he suffered fatal burn injuries after his truck's gas tank ruptured and caught fire. The design of the fuel tank, which led to Moseley's death, had been the subject of a previous GM analysis and a corporate decision not to increase the safety of the vehicle.[14]

After a witness presented GM's detailed risk analysis of fuel-fed fires, a "constant refrain among the jurors interviewed" was that "they knew" about the risk.[15] The inherent problem of undertaking a risk analysis for any safety-related feature is that, if the company does not adopt the most protective safety option, the perception that the company chose to ignore a known risk will always be a danger. According to GM's risk analysis, which was prepared by GE engineer Edward Ivey in 1973, fuel-fed fires would lead to a maximum of around "650–1000 fatalities per year in accidents with fuel-fed fires where the bodies were burnt." Ivey's analysis assigned a value per fatality of $200,000, which is the same cost-of-death figure used by Ford in the Pinto analysis. The memo's calculations found that the estimated fatality cost per automobile currently operating would be about $2.40. For new cars produced in the current model year, the estimated accident cost would be $2.20 per vehicle. Preventing fuel-fed fires at costs greater than this $2.20 per vehicle figure therefore would not be worthwhile based on this calculation. Ivey's bottom-line conclusion on the accident costs was the following:

> This analysis indicates that for G.M. it would be worth approximately $2.20 per new model auto to prevent a fuel fed fire in all accidents. . . . This analysis must be tempered with two thoughts. First, it is really impossible to put a value on human life. This analysis tried to do so in an objective manner but a human fatality is really beyond value, subjectively. Secondly, it is impossible to design an automobile where fuel fed fires can be prevented in all accidents unless the automobile has a non-flammable fuel.[16]

Notwithstanding his expressed misgivings about the value of a human fatality, Ivey's analysis produced an extremely low value of safety that would make safety improvements to eliminate fuel-fed fires not worthwhile if they cost more than $2.20 per new vehicle.

The jury awarded $4 million in compensatory damages, $1 in pain and suffering, and a blockbuster punitive damages amount of $101 million.[17] This blockbuster punitive damages award was based on the company's risk analysis and the specific fuel fire risks involved in the case, not the overall safety of the vehicles, as GM trucks were involved in only slightly more fatalities per 10,000 crashes than Ford trucks (1.51 deaths versus 1.45 deaths).[18] The construction of the punitive damages number was based on an irrelevant mathematical exercise—the value of $20 per vehicle multiplied by 500,000 GM trucks on the road, plus an extra $1 million "exclamation point."[19] It is noteworthy that the value of the lives that were lost due to the product design never entered the plaintiff attorney's damages request or the jury's conceptualization of the punitive damages amount. From the standpoint of proper deterrence, the number of fatalities and the VSL associated with these fatalities should play a central role in establishing the appropriate level of deterrence.

USE OF THE FUEL RISK ANALYSIS MEMO
AGAINST GM IN AUTOMOBILE LITIGATION

The Ivey memo resurfaced in a subsequent rear-end crash involving a 1979 Chevrolet Malibu. Patricia Anderson, her four children, and a family friend suffered severe burns after her car was hit in the rear by a speeding drunk driver when Anderson was approaching a red light.[20] The six burn victims received a compensatory damages award of $107.6 million and a punitive damages award of $4.8 billion, making it the largest blockbuster award in any motor vehicle case. Some observers speculated that the November 1998 landmark Master Settlement Agreement in the cigarette litigation had an anchoring effect, leading jurors to think in terms of award levels in the billions rather than the millions.[21]

Once again, the VSL and the value of preventing risks of death did not enter the procedure for setting the punitive damages award. The jury used two benchmarks—linking the $4.8 billion figure to GM's advertising expenses over a long period[22] and "two-thirds more than GM's entire profit for 1998."[23] Such reference points should be irrelevant, though from the plaintiff's perspective they help to establish very high anchors for conceptualizing the appropriate level of the punitive damages award. In any reasonable approach to setting punitive damages to promote safety, the value of preventing fatalities must be a critical component. Instead, the jury utilized a form of voodoo economics that led the *Washington Post* to observe that such punitive damages awards "send a message to the public at large that the courts are more like a casino than a hall of justice."[24]

The risk-cost tradeoff in the Ivey memo played a central role in assessing the safety of GM's designs. According to the plaintiffs, moving the tank an additional nine inches away from the bumper would have eliminated the risk at a cost of $8.59 per vehicle. Compared to a benefit of reduced risks to life that averages $2.20 per vehicle for new vehicles and $2.40 per vehicle for existing vehicles, the measure failed a benefit-cost test, since costs were about four times as great as benefits.

The plaintiffs' lawyers were able to demonize GM based on this analysis. In post-trial comments, one plaintiff's lawyer concluded: "The jurors wanted to send a message to General Motors that human life is more important than profits."[25] Jurors echoed this perspective: "Jurors told reporters that they felt the company had valued life too lightly. 'We're just like numbers, I feel, to them,' one juror, Carl Vangelisti, told Reuters. 'Statistics. That's something that is wrong.'"[26]

Economists are more comfortable with numbers than these jurors, but a critical problem with GM's numbers for determining the value of lives is that they were too small. GM grossly undervalued the reduced fatality risks from preventing fuel-fed fires. The conclusion that the costs of preventing the fires exceed the benefits hinges quite critically on the value assigned to the reduced fatalities. Based on estimates in the economics literature around at the time of the trial, the VSL was $7 million (in year 2000 dollars), or thirty-five times greater than what GM used in the analysis. Rather than failing a benefit-cost test, moving the gas tank to prevent fuel-fed fires provides safety benefits that greatly exceed costs, easily passing a properly executed benefit-cost test.[27] Using statistics need not undervalue life or lead to less-safe cars if the valuations are undertaken properly.

However, even if the analysis had been done properly, GM would have faced a considerable challenge in convincing jurors of the desirability of making risk-cost tradeoffs. One juror expressed a "zero-risk mentality" in her observation: "There was no evidence that the car they put out there was as safe as what they could have put out there."[28] If vehicle cost is irrelevant, there are no limits to additional improvements in safety. A similar zero-risk mentality, or certainty premium, distorts risk preferences more generally.

OTHER GM RISK ANALYSIS CONTROVERSIES

GM's problems with risk assessments also have included its risk analyses of allegedly faulty door latches in the Chevrolet Blazer. Based on the plaintiff's experts, GM's estimate of the cost of fixing the safety latch problem was $916 million, or $216 million for parts and $700 million for labor.[29] As characterized in the court proceedings, the presence of the risk analysis showed that GM was aware of the risk based on crash tests, had calculated the costs to fix the problem, and had concluded that the costs outweighed the risk reduction benefits. A man who was paralyzed in a crash implicating the alleged door latch problems received a total award of $150 million, including a $100 million punitive damages award. Once again, a corporate risk analysis played a central role in a blockbuster punitive damages awards case.

LESSONS LEARNED

Officials at GM and other US automobile companies have been able to observe the ramifications of risk analyses undertaken by their company and by other firms. Such analyses leave companies vulnerable to charges that they were aware of possible safety improvements but chose not to incur the costs to bolster product safety. Companies have been vilified for undertaking these assessments, often triggering substantial punitive damages awards. Because these assessments can lead jurors to the conclusion that companies have a callous or indifferent attitude toward consumer safety, companies might reasonably respond by ceasing to undertake risk analyses at all. I have not found any recent risk analyses with respect to the GM ignition switch problems to be examined in chapter 4, and the internal review of the ignition switch problem commissioned by GM did not report any such assessments.

Recall that the previous assessments undervalued lives by using the value of tort awards in wrongful death cases to calculate the benefits from additional safety measures. A risk assessment based on sound economic principles might be less vulnerable in court. We should not be so quick to dismiss a potential role for meaningful risk analyses because the corporate alternative of forgoing risk analyses, as well as failing to address safety concerns and associated tradeoffs in vehicle design, would be less effective in advancing consumer welfare. Even from the standpoint of corporate profits, it is not in society's best interest to adopt a corporate culture in which frank discussions of safety matters are discouraged and sanctioned. The costs of ignoring the safety concerns may be greater than the costs of adequately addressing product defects.

Would Sound Risk Analyses Fare Better or Pose New Hazards?

Whether analyses with different valuations of life might be more successful in addressing jurors' concerns can be examined using experimental studies. Here I summarize the results for my series of experiments in which jury-eligible citizens considered various case scenarios involving corporate risk decisions. The findings document the substantial resistance that remains to even sound economic risk analyses. This resistance suggests that legal reforms are needed to incentivize corporations to undertake sound risk assessments.

Historically, juries hit GM and other auto companies with considerable penalties when the companies attempted to systematically examine the tradeoffs between risk and cost. Is undertaking such a risk-cost analysis necessarily a red flag that leads jurors to conclude that the company has displayed a callous disregard for human health? Ideally, companies should not be found liable for punitive damages if they used an appropriate VSL and adopted all safety measures for which the expected health benefits exceeded the cost. Indeed, companies are not even negligent if the safety measures they did not adopt had costs exceeding benefits.

To examine these issues, I completed two experimental studies that explored jurors' potential sensitivity to responsible risk-cost tradeoffs using a total sample of almost seven hundred jury-eligible citizens.[30] The studies presented respondents with case scenarios that differed in terms of whether the company did a risk analysis and the nature of the analysis that it undertook. Each sample group received a different case scenario. The scenarios principally differed in terms of how expensive it was for the company to reduce fatality risks with improved designs.

Consider the first study, in which all scenarios given to respondents stated that the additional manufacturing cost of the vehicles per expected life saved was $4 million. More specifically, the company could change the electrical system design of the vehicle at a cost of $40 million to prevent ten expected deaths. Doing so would cost $400 per vehicle. Additionally, in all of the scenarios, the survey told respondents that the courts had awarded each victim's family $800,000 for pain and suffering and other compensatory damages and that after this case, the company altered future designs to eliminate the problem. After providing participants with standard jury instructions for punitive damages, they were asked whether they would favor an award of punitive damages and, if so, what the amount would be.

In the first scenario, the company did not perform any benefit-cost analysis and chose not to adopt a particular safety-enhancing feature. The respondents received the following information about the company: "The company thought there might be some risk from the current design but did not believe it would be significant. The company notes that even with these injuries, the vehicle has one of the best safety records in its class."[31] A striking 85 percent of the participants favored punitive damages, with a median punitive award of $1 million.[32] Table 3.2 summarizes the results of this and other scenarios.

In the next case scenario, the company undertook a risk analysis of the prospective safety improvement. The approach was similar to that used in the Ford and GM examples, in that the company assigned

TABLE 3.2: Summary of Jury Experiments on Corporate Risk Analyses

Scenario	Percentage Favoring Punitive Damages	Median Award ($ millions)
No risk analysis	85	1
Risk analysis valuing lives at $800,000	93	3.5
Risk analysis using DOT value of $3 million	93	10
Company performed but ignored risk analysis	89	3
Company conveyed constructive role of its risk analysis	76	1

a value to the expected lives lost based on court awards and used the compensatory damages amount of $800,000 to value each fatality. Undertaking such analysis in this scenario boosted the median award level to $3.5 million. Thus, valuing lives based on the compensatory damages amount led to a larger punitive award than undertaking no risk analysis at all. The compensatory damages value established a reference point for possible punitive damages. In this instance, respondents resisted the company's attempt to monetize fatality risks and wanted to send the company a price signal that exceeded the $800,000 amount the company used to value lives.

What if the respondents are told that the company used the VSL that NHTSA uses in its regulatory analyses of safety measures, which at the time of the study was $3 million? This scenario should have been more favorable to the company in two ways. First, the value assigned to the fatalities at risk is almost four times as great as when the company uses court awards; thus, the company is not undervaluing the lives lost. Second, the company is following established safety norms adopted by the government agency charged with setting safety standards. Nevertheless, the respondents continued to take an unfavorable view of benefit-cost analyses. There was no reduction in the frequency of punitive damages awards, and the median award escalated to $10 million.

Why did placing a higher value on the lives at risk and consequently making safety a more prominent concern adversely affect the damages levied against the company? A reasonable hypothesis is that the $3 million VSL figure used by the company established an anchor that the jurors had to top in order to establish greater financial incentives for safety than the company already displayed in its risk analysis. Thus, instead of high VSL numbers reducing the sanctions against the company, valuing lives more highly and adhering to the benefit-cost practices of a government agency had counterproductive effects. If these experimental results are borne out in practice, doing the analysis correctly with higher valuations of fatalities may boost court verdicts rather than reduce them.

To explore ways in which this discouraging outcome could be avoided, a sequel to the study, involving over one hundred jury-eligible adults for each scenario, altered the company risk analysis description.[33] In one scenario the company performed a benefit-cost analysis but ignored it, while in another scenario the company attempted to persuade jurors that benefit-cost tradeoffs are reasonable. Perhaps if jurors understood the constructive role that risk analyses could play in fostering appropriate vehicle designs with safety features that consumers truly valued, there would be less of a tendency to want to punish corporations for risk analyses.

Consider first the scenario in which an employee at the company undertook a benefit-cost analysis but the company didn't utilize the employee's analysis in the safety design decision: "The company said it never used the study in the design of the vehicle. It was an analysis by a staff engineer that did not play any role in the design decision."[34] Apparently doing an analysis and ignoring it is slightly less reprehensible than doing an analysis and applying it, but more reprehensible than doing no analysis at all. Compared with the situation in which the risk analysis guides the company's safety decision, doing an analysis that is ignored led to a frequency of punitive award verdicts of 89 percent and reduced the median award to $3 million.

Conceivably a more favorable scenario is one in which, instead of ignoring the analysis or not undertaking a risk analysis at all, there is information provided in an attempt to persuade jurors that benefit-cost analyses have a useful, constructive role to play. Such a scenario that attempted to overcome jurors' aversion to risk-cost tradeoffs provided the following additional information:

The company had undertaken a series of similar risk analyses for other safety measures. These studies led to improved structural reinforcements in the doors, stability controls, and other improvements. But in this instance the company concluded that the extra costs to consumers were too great in comparison to the safety benefits. The company chose instead to make other design changes that might save more lives at less cost.[35]

This effort to convey the constructive role of benefit-cost analysis reduced the frequency of jurors favoring punitive awards to 76 percent, which is the lowest punitive award percentage in the scenarios tested in the two studies, and reduced the median award to $1 million. Note that this median award level of punitive damages is the same as was found when the company did no benefit-cost analysis at all.[36] In effect, providing a rational basis for the benefit-cost analysis can neutralize and have some modest reduction in resistance to risk analyses as compared with the no-analysis situation.

How a risk analysis would fare based on current fatality benefit assessment practices is unclear. A more vigorous and concrete articulation of the benefits of risk analysis and use of the current, higher VSL of $9.4 million adopted by DOT may persuade jurors of the legitimacy of risk-cost tradeoffs. However, the higher VSL also may have a counterproductive anchoring effect in instances where punitive damages are awarded, pushing jurors to award higher levels of punitive damages in order to provide greater financial incentives for safety than the company's own valuations of risk would provide.

Even with a well-motivated benefit-cost analysis, the public will generally be uncomfortable with a risk decision that leads to a higher fatality rate when other, more expensive choices are available. Government safety agencies generally claim that their mission is to make cars, planes, drugs, and food "safe."[37] They could make more accurate claims, such as that the agency hopes that the food safety regulations can limit the annual number of fatalities related to food illnesses to under two thousand. Confronting safety decisions in a responsible and open manner will continue to pose challenges, but failing to think systematically about these issues will lead to policies that are less effective in saving lives.

A Proposal for Overcoming the Aversion to Risk Analyses

To address the inherent challenges proposed by risk analyses and to simultaneously encourage companies to think systematically about safety, it is desirable to give companies legal protections so that the content of the risk assessments cannot be used against them in trials. It would be beneficial to establish a safe harbor for risk analyses that follow the procedures used for federal regulatory impact analyses and that adopt the VSL used by the US Department of Transportation in the case of motor vehicle risks. If such an analysis indicates that a particular design feature implicated in an accident did not pass a benefit-cost test, the company should be able to introduce this evidence in its defense, but the plaintiff should not be permitted to introduce it separately. A company that does not adopt a safety measure that fails a benefit-cost test is not negligent. Economic models of the meaning of negligence standards imply that a company is not negligent if the costs of the safety feature outweigh the benefits. However, plaintiffs may misconstrue such studies as indicating that the company knowingly chose to market an unsafe product. If the analysis indicated that the design feature did pass a benefit-cost test and the company nevertheless chose to not adopt the design, there should be no legal protection for the analysis.

If a safety feature fails a benefit-cost test, not adopting it is economically efficient, so that company should not be found to be negligent. In such situations, I would prohibit introduction of the analysis by the plaintiff. The plaintiffs would not be able to introduce as evidence information indicating that the company had done a benefit-cost analysis or the results of this analysis. If, however, the safety measure passes a benefit-cost test and the company decides to not implement the safety measure anyway, then there would be no legal protection for the analysis.

One could easily envision that over time there might be a rationale for stronger versions of such a proposal. There could, for example, be a regulatory compliance defense against lawsuits alleging negligence for the particular design choice if the company's analysis met government standards and the company adopted designs that passed a benefit-cost test. To formalize this process, companies could file the risk analyses with the US Department of Transportation, which could assume a formal role of reviewing and approving the risk assessments.

Either of these safe harbor proposals could yield several dividends. By stimulating risk analyses, there would be a dramatic shift in the current corporate culture in which there has been a pronounced retreat from confronting safety issues explicitly. Incentivizing companies to utilize the same methodology and the VSL levels that the government uses would put the analysis on sound footing. The VSL is the value of mortality risk that a benefit-cost analysis should use in evaluating the desirability of a safety feature. This approach, in turn, would lead to design changes that are in consumers' best interest. Dampening the liability risks posed by undertaking benefit-cost analyses would also shift the focus of these cases to the substantive merits of the accident and away from a conception that anything less than an unbounded commitment to safety is an irresponsible corporate act.

The emphasis of this safe harbor proposal is on the determination of liability, not on the damages remedy. An alternative approach would be to cap punitive damages or eliminate them altogether when companies undertook responsible risk analyses. However, companies would still be liable for some damages in this instance that would be triggered by behavior that ideally society should encourage. Thus, the safe harbor approach eliminates the disincentives that otherwise might discourage companies from undertaking risk analyses.

The rationale for this safe harbor approach is similar to that for proposals for safe harbor provisions for treatment decisions that have been made with respect to medical malpractice reform by Blumstein.[38] In much the same way that there is inequality of information between doctors and patients, there is similar asymmetry of information between companies manufacturing potentially dangerous products and consumers. Analogous types of legal protections are provided in the medical malpractice context through apology laws.[39] Thirty-two states have enacted such laws, which reform state evidence rules so that statements of apology from physicians to patients are excluded from being admitted into evidence.[40] A complete parallel with apology laws would always prevent the introduction by plaintiffs of evidence regarding risk analyses.

Legal structures that will incentivize companies to undertake systematic risk analyses and balance benefits and costs in a responsible manner should be encouraged. In the case of corporate risk analyses, there are generally accepted professional, scientific standards of practice of undertaking such benefit-cost tests so that ascertaining whether a company conforms to that standard is feasible. Courts have long been engaged in such assessments for government regulatory analyses.[41]

The safe harbor mechanism also takes matters that jurors are not well suited to address out of their hands. The selection of the VSL and benefit-cost criteria are well-developed economic methodologies that may not conform to jurors' conceptions of what the customary practices should be. Moreover, companies are undertaking the analyses from a different vantage point than jurors. The product risk analyses that companies do before a product is marketed necessarily deals with statistical lives that are not yet identified, whereas jurors are dealing with identified lives that have already been harmed. The influence of hindsight bias that affects juror judgments of liability generally is also likely to impede jurors' efforts to conceptualize what a proper risk analysis should be.

This safe harbor approach has the characteristics of an effective solution to the current impediments to corporate risk analyses. It is a precise ex ante standard that is narrow in terms of its design and scope. The main challenge is to institute a standard that will truly serve as a safe harbor. Legislation has the force of law and is the most desirable approach. A more modest alternative is for government agencies to establish specific norms for such analyses, such as DOT issuing guidance for procedures that companies should adopt. In the absence of specific guidance, companies could turn to existing regulatory analysis guidelines issued by the US Office of Management and Budget in conjunction with agency practices with respect to the VSL. A defense such as this may not be fully persuasive but at best may serve to reduce the company's financial exposure, as the jury scenario using the NHTSA VSL indicated. There is also the danger that such criteria may have an asymmetric effect in that falling short of professional norms indicates that the company was negligent, but adhering to the norms does not persuade the jury that the company was not negligent.

Toward More Responsible Corporate Risk Decisions

Use of the VSL amounts in corporate risk analysis has a strong theoretical foundation for establishing safety incentives and, as I indicate in chapter 9, would bring greater discipline to the setting of punitive damages. However, the potential hazards of meaningful risk analysis have had a chilling effect on corporate risk analyses. I have identified over one hundred punitive damages awards of at least $100 million in the United States. Table 3.3 lists the eleven "blockbuster" punitive damages amounts (i.e., in excess of $100 million) that have been awarded to date in motor vehicle cases involving personal injury. Ten of these awards are against major US auto companies, and one is against the Bridgestone and Firestone tire companies. The final column in table 3.3 describes the nature of the case and the alleged defect. Although there are some exceptions involving several victims, most of these cases involve an alleged product defect causing a single fatality. Based on economic theories of punitive damages that are designed to create efficient incentives for safety, an award in the $100 million range could be warranted in such instances, provided that the jury believed the probability of detecting the wrongful conduct is low. Thus, a large award is needed because the company believes that the odds of having the wrongful conduct detected are very small. However, there is no evidence that this deterrence-based logic has played any role in these awards. Plaintiff attorneys' requests for punitive damages typically are based on irrelevant anchors that are divorced from the task of establishing appropriate levels of deterrence.[42]

TABLE 3.3: Blockbuster Punitive Damages Awards against Automobile Companies

Case	Year	State	Punitive Damages Amount ($ millions)	Punitive Damages Amount ($2015 millions)	Nature of Plaintiff's Claim
Grimshaw v. Ford Motor Co.	1981	CA	125	318.6	Ford was aware of design flaws with the Pinto's fuel system and fuel tank placement. The rear-end collision punctured the Pinto's tank, burning the vehicle and its occupants.
Moseley v. General Motors	1993	GA	101	161.9	GM placement of the fuel tank outside the vehicle frame of its GMC Sierra truck. GM analysis showed that the design was dangerous, leading to a fire and the death of a vehicle occupant following a side-impact collision.
Hardy v. General Motors	1996	AL	100	147.7	Some GM door latches were substandard and problematic (according to engineers' reports), resulting in the ejection of vehicle occupants in a crash.
Jimenez v. Chrysler	1997	SC	250	360.9	A defective rear liftgate latch in a 1985 Chrysler minivan resulted in the opening of the liftgate during a rollover accident, leading to the death of a boy who was ejected from the van.
Robinson v. Ford Motor Co.	1998	MS	120	170.6	A defective design in a 1976 Ford Ranger increased the risk of a rollover during turns, injuring two people and killing one.
Romo v. Ford Motor Co.	1998	CA	290	403.3	During a rollover, different components of a Ford Bronco's roof collapsed or broke, killing three people and injuring two people.
Anderson v. General Motors	1999	CA	4,775	6,640.6	The fuel tank in a Chevrolet Malibu exploded during a collision, resulting in severe burns to six passengers.
White v. Ford Motor Co.	1999	NV	153.18	213.0	A parking brake failed to stop a Ford F-350 truck from rolling down a hill, killing a boy when the truck was inadvertently shifted from first gear to neutral.
Dorman v. Bridgestone/Firestone Inc.	2000	MO	100	134.5	A multi-piece tire exploded while a man was filling it with air, seriously injuring him.
Jernigan v. General Motors	2002	AL	100	128.8	A design defect in an Oldsmobile 88 resulted in inadequate protection for the passenger compartment.
Buell-Wilson v. Ford Motor Co.	2004	CA	246	301.7	A Ford Explorer was defectively unstable and not crashworthy because of a design defect in the roof.

Note: All amounts are converted to 2015 dollars.

Five of the cases listed in table 3.3 played a prominent role in the discussion of the corporate risk analyses above. Thus, half of the blockbuster award cases in which auto companies were defendants were those in which a purported transgression of the company was that it undertook a systematic risk analysis. The powerful message conveyed by these blockbuster awards is to discourage sensible balancing of product design costs and benefits. Consequently, there has been a diminished prominence of such risk analyses in more recent auto liability cases, perhaps in part because companies have been severely sanctioned for attempting to think systematically about the risk and cost of vehicle design. As the review of the GM experience in the next chapter will indicate, the corporate response has been to almost completely stymie explicit consideration of any hazards posed by vehicle design features.

This policy of committed corporate neglect of product risk issues is unfortunate because risk analyses in which there is a systematic assessment of costs and benefits can play a pivotal role in fostering efficient levels of safety. Benefit-cost analyses using appropriate levels of the VSL have played an increasingly prominent role in regulatory policy and now guide the development of regulatory standards by government agencies. In contrast, corporate risk analyses have not adopted the VSL, and the role of any corporate risk analysis for products has diminished over time. Early efforts by companies to assess the risks and costs associated with design choices appear to have been well intentioned but were hindered by the use of a cost-of-death approach, which systematically undervalues risks to life and health. Valuations more in line with government agencies would certainly have bolstered the credibility of the analyses and would have led to different safety decisions in some instances. But as my jury experiments indicated, undertaking any analysis poses inherent problems of a company becoming aware of the risks and costs and, in some instances, choosing to not incur the costs to reduce the risks, both of which makes the company vulnerable to punitive damages awards. Although a concerted effort to educate jurors on the overall merits of systematic analysis of the competing concerns may diminish the repercussions from undertaking a benefit-cost analysis, the role of hindsight bias will continue to discourage prospective risk and cost assessments.

A potential solution to this problem would be the analog of a regulatory compliance defense for regulatory analyses. If a company undertakes an analysis consistent with the procedures used by the pertinent regulatory agency (e.g., NHTSA for auto safety), and if the analysis indicates that the safety design feature is not warranted, then these analyses should not be used against the company in tort litigation. This risk analysis regime would also make the VSL the financial guidepost for safety decisions rather than compensatory damages awards, which undervalue lives at risk. The critical importance of changing the corporate culture to use the VSL to guide product safety decisions will be evident when we consider the GM ignition switch recall experience.

4

Corporate Risk Analyses and Regulatory Sanctions

LESSONS FROM THE GM IGNITION SWITCH RECALL

The GM Ignition Switch Defect

The GM ignition switch experience illustrates the consequences of corporate suspension of meaningful risk assessments. The defective GM ignition switch led to 124 deaths. What was particularly notable about this defect incident is the insight it provides into the workings of corporate decision making involving product risks. As this chapter will document, there has been almost complete suppression of meaningful risk analysis, as the legal penalties inflicted for past risk analyses no doubt have been influential. Unfortunately, the regulatory remedies have also been inadequate due to the government's failure to utilize the VSL in setting corporate penalties because of the statutory caps imposed on regulatory penalties.

The GM ignition switch controversy attained prominence in 2014, when General Motors Company (GM) incurred government fines of $35 million for failing to report the safety problems stemming from defective ignition switches in several lines of vehicles.[1] The nature of the defect is that the ignition switch was designed with too-low torque that was below the company's own specifications.[2] As a result, the switch could move too easily from the "run" position into the "accessory" or "off" position, resulting in a loss of power, loss of power steering and power brakes, and disabling of the frontal airbags. This problem was well known to GM, as an engineer involved in the testing of the switch emailed that he was "tired of the switch from hell."[3] The US Department of Transportation's National Highway Traffic Safety Administration levied the maximum penalty for failing to report the defect, which at that point had been blamed for causing thirteen documented fatalities.[4] The death toll attributable to the ignition switch failure subsequently increased by an order of magnitude to 124 deaths.[5] After the NHTSA penalty, GM launched a series of automobile recalls for defective ignition switches and other vehicle defects, with total recalls of twenty-nine million vehicles.[6] This incident highlights a wide range of fundamental problems plaguing corporate risk decisions generally, as well as the failures of tort liability and government regulation to rectify these problems.

GM'S FAILURE TO SET ADEQUATE LEVELS OF PRODUCT SAFETY

From an economic efficiency standpoint, a company's product risk objective should provide a level of product safety that is consistent with the level of safety consumers would choose if they were fully cognizant of the product's risk characteristics. Ascertaining which safety attributes are desirable and which features are not worthwhile should not be an entirely haphazard process. What procedure should companies adopt in making this product safety decision? A principal theme of this book is that companies should confront the pertinent tradeoffs directly and think systematically about product safety; striking a responsible balance between safety and other competing concerns such as cost should be a fundamental component of corporate operations.

Surprisingly, the detailed NHTSA assessment of GM's practices and the investigative report GM commissioned to examine the ignition switch recall fail to indicate any systematic economic assessment by GM of safety-related issues.[7] Similar to how a dog's failure to bark became the critical clue in the Sherlock Holmes mystery, "Silver Blaze," the glaring missing element in the 315-page GM investigative report on the ignition switch failure is that there is no mention of any safety-related studies pertaining to the ignition switch or any other aspect of vehicle safety. Instead, there is overwhelming evidence that GM's corporate culture officially discouraged any frank discussion of safety. Even suggesting that there might be a product defect that posed liability concerns was off-limits.[8]

The emergence of GM's lax safety culture was not a historical accident. The company's systematic neglect of safety is not an institutional quirk but rather was likely a response to past treatment of corporate risk analyses in tort cases. In the 1970s, 1980s, and 1990s, as discussed in chapter 3, all the major US automobile companies undertook detailed economic analyses of the cost and risk implications of safety-related product characteristics. However, frank assessments of the risks and costs of different design possibilities led these companies to be vilified in the press and penalized by juries for undertaking such safety studies, not simply for specific alleged deficiencies in the analyses. A particularly controversial component of the analysis was the use of tort damages amounts to value the lives lost by failing to adopt additional safety measures. This cost-of-death approach led to an economic value of risks to life that appeared to be offensively low to jurors and also was inconsistent with a sound economics approach. These adverse experiences no doubt have contributed to the corporate abandonment of systematic assessments of safety decisions.

THE ROLE OF THE VSL

The linchpin of all these interrelated issues—from the standpoint of both the regulatory agency and corporations—is the price that is attached to risks to life. In particular, what level of higher costs is worthwhile to incur for each expected fatality that will be prevented?

The VSL serves as the guidepost used by NHTSA in setting regulatory standards for motor vehicles and could serve a similar function for establishing the appropriate risk-cost tradeoff for automobile companies.

Additionally, as I will indicate, the VSL should play a role, but currently does not, with respect to setting penalty levels for violations of safety regulations, such as GM's failure to report the ignition switch defect. Should companies' risk assessment efforts fall short, government regulations and sanctions can come into play. However, regulatory sanctions are often limited and do not contain sufficiently severe financial penalties to deter corporations from failing to provide adequate levels of safety. As a result, regulatory agencies provide insufficient impetus to lead companies to engage with safety-related issues in a thorough and responsible manner. Applying the VSL to regulatory sanctions would consequently dramatically increase the level of these penalties. Furthermore, the VSL could exert a restraining function in the context of punitive damages awards, providing a methodology for establishing appropriate levels of deterrence.

In all of these domains, the VSL should play a pivotal role. Surprisingly, there is no evidence that the VSL played any role either in setting government sanctions for vehicle-related regulatory violations—even though its function in setting regulatory standards is well established—or in driving corporate risk decisions. Overhauling the institutional approaches to corporate safety will require a commitment to deterrence-based analyses and sanctions. Reform will also require additional legal protections such as those outlined in chapter 3, so that when corporations do undertake systematic analyses of safety measures, they will not be vulnerable to punitive damages awards simply because they have undertaken a thorough examination of the safety-related issues.

Guidelines for Product Risk Analyses

The nature of GM's ignition switch decision was far removed from a systematic economic assessment that balanced the costs and risks of a defective switch. Systematic assessment of the costs and safety decisions had formerly been an integral part of company safety policies, as indicated by the experiences at Ford, Chrysler, and GM that are described in chapter 3. However, these evaluations fell short in terms of their economic approach and also led companies to be punished with very high punitive damages awards. The result was that GM apparently abandoned making thorough risk analyses.

PRICING RISKS TO LIFE

Automobile safety decisions fit the standard paradigm for how one should use VSL estimates in setting the appropriate level of safety: there are well-defined categories of product costs as well as anticipated benefits from additional safety-related product characteristics. Auto safety decisions inquire which safety enhancements should be adopted and whether there should be a limit to the safety features incorporated in the design of the vehicle, or whether cars should be made as safe as possible. If all cars were designed to be as safe as tanks, there would be fewer auto-related injuries and deaths. But doing so imposes a cost in terms of higher vehicle prices, lower fuel efficiency, and adverse environmental consequences. The safety design task is to strike an appropriate balance between risk and cost, recognizing that at some point the value of the added safety to the consumer will not be worth the additional expense or loss of vehicle performance.

The intuitive appeal of thinking about vehicle cost and safety tradeoffs plays such a fundamental role in our general understanding of risk-cost tradeoffs that US Supreme Court Justice Stephen Breyer uses auto safety as an example to illustrate the unacceptability of unbounded commitments to reducing risk. Justice Breyer asks whether it is worthwhile to promulgate a regulation that will save ten lives annually over forty years at a cost of $100 billion, which is not an entirely hypothetical regulatory problem. He repositions this question as being equivalent in risk-cost terms to asking how much a person would be willing to pay for a slightly safer car that would reduce the death risk by 5 percent:

Would we pay an extra $1,000 for such a car? An extra $5,000 for that added contribution to safety? To spend $100 billion as a nation to save ten lives annually assumes we value safety so much that each of us would pay $48,077 extra for any such new, slightly safer car.[9]

It is likely that few consumers would find it worthwhile to pay such a price premium.

MEASURING THE VALUE OF A STATISTICAL LIFE

In practice, we need not repeat Justice Breyer's thought experiment for every auto safety device considered. The tradeoff that people are willing to make between risk and cost is embodied in the VSL estimates. The DOT uses VSL estimates to decide whether it is worthwhile to impose motor vehicle safety regulations, such as tire pressure monitoring systems, roof crush-resistance standards, and limits on hours of service of truck drivers. The agency sets regulations after undertaking detailed regulatory impact analyses of the costs and benefits of standards with varying levels of stringency using a VSL of $9.4 million.

The DOT's adoption of the VSL approach is consistent with recognition of the prominent role of risk-cost tradeoffs in the motor vehicle market. Because the costs of motor vehicle safety and airplane safety are shifted to consumers in terms of higher prices for cars and airplane tickets in a competitive market, the costs are more salient than costs spread throughout the economy. Most of the costs of transportation regulations are directly borne by the people who benefit from the safety improvements generated by the regulations, and using consumers' valuation of risk as reflected in the VSL formalizes a link to the market.

In much the same way that government agencies assess the desirability of prospective safety regulations in terms of their benefits and costs, ideally private firms should undertake similar assessments for potential vehicle design changes. Use of the VSL to value these benefits would establish the appropriate price for safety that consumers would be willing to pay if they understood the benefits that the safer car offered. Thus, there is a direct market linkage between safety improvements and consumers, as making cars safer will raise the cost of vehicle production and consequently vehicle price. But making these safety improvements also boosts how much consumers are willing to pay for the safer vehicles. For that reason, the costs of government auto safety regulations that pass a benefit-cost test, as the NHTSA safety standards generally do, should not be viewed as a deadweight societal loss but as providing consumers with a better, highly valued product that average consumers would choose if they understood the risk reduction benefits.

The GM Faulty Ignition Switch

While systematic thinking about costs and risks is the desired product safety framework, how GM set about dealing with the ignition switch design issues was quite different. As the discussion here will demonstrate, GM became aware of the ignition switch defect, but the organizational procedures for dealing with such safety issues fell short due to an ingrained lax corporate safety culture. Application of a responsible economic balancing of risks and costs indicates the desirability of the ignition switch recall that the company had failed to undertake.

THE IGNITION SWITCH DEFECT AND RECALL COSTS

What role, if any, did a balancing of benefits and costs of safety play in one of the most prominent product safety problems in this century—GM's faulty ignition switch?[10] There is no publicly available, comprehensive description of whatever analysis GM did of the defective ignition switch recall. The two main components of an analysis of a product defect are the nature of the risk and the cost to eliminate it. While there is substantial information about GM's assessment of the nature of the defect, there is little information about GM's assessment of the risk consequences and the costs of eliminating the defect.

At the time of the NHTSA sanctions in 2014, GM attributed thirteen deaths to the ignition switch problems first linked to the Chevrolet Cobalt.[11] However, the acting administrator of NHTSA, David Friedman, correctly hypothesized that the death toll could be greater than the number of deaths GM has blamed on the defect. Given that the overall death rate for drivers of the Chevrolet Cobalt is the highest of all vehicles in its class,[12] Friedman's fear that the risk might exceed the thirteen fatalities initially estimated by GM proved to be well founded. The possibility of additional human costs from the defect was also bolstered by the fact that at that point GM had identified at least fifty-four frontal-impact crashes involving ignition switch problems that led the airbag to not deploy.[13] Based on the results of the compensation fund GM established, the final death toll of 124 fatalities was far out of line with the estimates in 2014.

From the standpoint of corporate risk analysis, what were the cost and risk estimates at the time when GM could have undertaken a design change to eliminate the defect, and what were the implications of such an assessment? GM has not made public any information regarding its risk and cost assessment other than the statement by its current CEO, Mary Barra, who testified that as of 2007, GM estimated that the cost of a recall for vehicles with the faulty ignition switch would be $100 million.[14] Since the recall did not begin until regulatory pressures were exerted in 2014, GM concluded—at least implicitly—that the recall was not merited given this cost level.

The 2007 recall analysis date and the $100 million cost given by Barra provide my principal reference points for assessing GM's recall analysis decision. One could also examine other cost assessments at different points in time, but the analysis identified by Barra appears to be the most comprehensive. Subsequent news reports indicated other dates and different cost assessments for problems related to the ignition switch. For example, in 2005, a GM engineering manager emailed other engineers and design team members that it would cost ninety cents per vehicle, plus $400,000 for production machinery, to change the switch.[15] Another cost estimate in a similar range is that modifying the head of the key for less than a dollar per car would have significantly reduced the risk of an unexpected shutoff.[16]

Retrospective cost estimates for ignition switch recalls reached as high as $700 million in 2014, but this figure includes model years not included in the 2007 analysis.[17] Even incurring this high cost estimate would be warranted based on the ultimate fatality record of 124 deaths. All of these cost assessments mention the cost associated with the recall but do not estimate the risk in terms of the expected number of lives that would be lost or the monetary value that should be placed on these lives.

Based on Mary Barra's testimony regarding the 2007 analysis and the information in the NHTSA Consent Order's summary of the ignition switch problem,[18] for at least the seven-year period between 2007 and 2014, the company was aware of the risk, undertook a cost analysis, concluded that a recall was not worth the cost, and failed to notify either consumers or the government of the problem.[19] By law, the company was required to notify NHTSA of any safety-related defects within five days after a defect has been determined to be safety related.[20] However, it was only on February 7, 2014, or seven years after the 2007 GM cost analysis of a recall, that GM notified NHTSA that there was a safety defect in 619,122 Chevrolet Cobalt vehicles and model year 2007 Pontiac G5 vehicles. Later that month, GM added 748,024 more vehicles with that defect, including model year 2006–2007 Chevrolet HHR and Pontiac Solstice, model year 2003–2007 Saturn Ion, and model year 2007 Saturn Sky vehicles. The following month, GM added another 823,788 vehicles that may have received faulty service parts during repairs to the list. These vehicles included model year 2008–2011 Chevrolet HHR and model year 2008–2010 Chevrolet Cobalt, Pontiac Solstice, Pontiac G5, and Saturn Sky vehicles. The GM recalls in 2014 for this defect and recalls for other vehicle defects that were apparently stimulated by the ignition switch recall total an astounding twenty-nine million vehicles.

THE FAILED GM CORPORATE SAFETY CULTURE

Although it is not known whether GM did a full-blown benefit-cost analysis or just a cost analysis in 2007, GM nevertheless developed corporate practices that reflect the company's desire to suppress any critical comments by the staff relating to product safety. A confidential

Judgment Words

Documents used for reports and presentations should contain only engineering results, facts and judgements. These documents should not contain speculations, opinions, vague non descriptive words, or words with emotional connotations. Some examples of words or phrases that are to be avoided are:

always	deathtrap	gruesome	rolling sarcophagus (tomb or
annihilate	debilitating	Hindenburg	coffin)
apocalyptic	decapitating	Hobbling	safety
asphyxiating	**defect**	Horrific	safety related
bad	defective	impaling	serious
Band-Aid	detonate	inferno	spontaneous combustion
big time	disemboweling	Kevorkianesque	startling
brakes like an "X" car	enfeebling	lacerating	suffocating
cataclysmic	evil	life-threatening	suicidal
catastrophic	eviscerated	maiming	terrifying
Challenger	explode	malicious	Titanic
chaotic	failed	mangling	tomblike
Cobain	failure	maniacal	unstable
condemns	flawed	mutilating	widow-maker
Corvair-like	genocide	**never**	words or phrases with a biblical
crippling	ghastly	potentially-disfiguring	connotation
critical	grenadelike	powder keg	you're toast
dangerous	grisly	problem	

GM

GM Confidential

FIGURE 4.1. GM's List of Controversial Words. Source: U.S. Department of Transportation, National Highway Traffic Safety Administration, "TQ14-001 Consent Order," May 16, 2014, www.nhtsa.gov/staticfiles/communications/pdf/May-16-2014-TQ14-001-Consent-Order.pdf [https://perma.cc/A95H-LALY], p. 41.

GM memo included as an exhibit to the NHTSA Consent Order admonished the staff to avoid controversial "judgment words." The memo explained that "documents used for reports and presentations should contain only engineering results, facts, and judgments. These documents should not contain speculations, opinions, vague nondescriptive words, or words with emotional connotations."[21] Among the examples of forbidden words provided in the memo in figure 4.1 were seemingly accurate characterizations of potentially recallable cars, including the following words: asphyxiating, bad, critical, dangerous, defect, defective, failure, maiming, potentially disfiguring, problem, safety, safety-related, serious, and unstable.[22] In addition, the memo admonished against using more colorful and possibly inflammatory language, including language such as the following: apocalyptic, big time, cataclysmic, catastrophic, Corvair-like, deathtrap, decapitating, detonate, evil, ghastly, inferno, powder keg, suicidal, terrifying, Titanic, tomblike, and you're toast.[23] With even seemingly innocuous words such as "safety" and "defect" being ruled out of bounds, GM in effect discouraged frank discussion of product risks.

Another GM memo also apparently sought to head off litigation threats by providing guidance for how company drivers of GM vehicles should discuss problems that they encountered while driving the vehicle. The confidential GM memo "What every company vehicle driver must know . . ." apparently sought to rein in potentially damaging characterizations of safety problems.[24] The memo listed the following "examples of comments that do not help identify and solve problems:

> 'This is a lawsuit waiting to happen . . .'
> 'Unbelievable Engineering screw up . . .'
> 'This is a safety and security issue . . .'
> 'This a very dangerous thing to happen. My family refuses to ride in the vehicle now . . .'
> 'I believe the wheels are too soft and weak and could cause a serious problem . . .'
> 'Dangerous . . . almost caused accident.'"[25]

Instead, the company encouraged comments that downplayed the potential safety implications and opted for blander descriptions of the problems. Perhaps because of such suppression of safety-related concerns, GM officials categorized the ignition switch problem as a matter of "convenience" rather than safety.[26]

Other remarkable aspects of the GM corporate culture embody a similar inattention to safety. CEO Mary Barra described what she referred to as the "GM nod" in which, through their nod, participants in a meeting signal that there should be action taken. However, there is an understanding that this was an empty gesture as they did not intend to actually implement the plan.[27] The investigation commissioned by GM to examine the ignition switch failure identified the GM nod as a common commitment to inaction at safety committee meetings.[28] Another noteworthy GM behavior became known as the

"GM salute." Participants in the meeting fold their arms and point in each direction, away from themselves, to indicate that they have no responsibility for taking action, as all responsibility lies with others.[29] The investigation of the GM ignition switch recall indicated that the shift of responsibility epitomized by this salute was an ingrained aspect of the GM safety culture "that permeated the Cobalt investigation for years."[30] The Chevrolet Cobalt had been a prominent model in the ignition switch recall discussions.

As evidenced by the suppression of frank safety discussions and the behaviors designed to deflect personal responsibility for safety matters, GM had apparently developed a bunker mentality in which honest efforts to confront safety issues and take action were discouraged. As the discussion in chapter 3 demonstrated, GM had a previous history of undertaking systematic risk and cost analyses of safety-related matters, but these analyses were used against it in litigation. My hypothesis is that the fear of substantial legal sanctions played a key role in fostering the lax corporate safety culture at GM. While the causal link between litigation fears and the current GM safety culture is unknown, there is clearly a litigation-related overtone to the avoidance of controversial safety-related language. Moreover, as one would expect, GM recognized the potential for legal liability. Beginning in 2010, GM officials were aware of the potential for punitive damages in their discussion of the ignition switch defect.[31] GM was vulnerable to litigation with respect to the ignition switch defect and sought to impose structure on these efforts by establishing a victim compensation fund from which the injured recouped scheduled compensation amounts for ignition-related injuries, which will be discussed in chapter 9.[32] GM's anticipated exposure to legal liability might have been even greater if it were not for some of the legal protections that the company claimed were afforded by its Chapter 11 bankruptcy reorganization in 2009.[33] However, a 2016 decision by the US Court of Appeals for the Second Circuit ruled that GM's bankruptcy did not preclude the ignition switch claims, so that there may be additional costs resulting from this litigation.[34]

GM's suppression of meaningful risk analyses is a corporate failure that has implications across the entire menu of vehicle safety decisions. In much the same way that GM ignored the safety implications of the defective ignition switch, it also chose to utilize the defective but less expensive Takata airbags.[35] GM chose to trim vehicle costs with these slightly less expensive airbags even though corporate officials had been apprised of the potential hazards of this brand of airbags due to the volatility of the ammonium nitrate compound used in the inflaters. GM's suppression of a responsible risk management culture led to systematic neglect of product safety.

A SOUNDER APPROACH TO THE IGNITION SWITCH DEFECT

GM has apparently shunted safety issues to the side, but what would have been the implications of a sound benefit-cost analysis of the ignition switch defect? Did GM take the economically justified action by failing to address the defect? Making this assessment by relying on our current knowledge of the extent of the risk takes advantage of hindsight because the internal assessments by the company are not available. However, a benefit-cost analysis drawing on the information that has become public indicates that a recall would have been worthwhile. Even using GM's early estimate of thirteen defect-related deaths and the US Department of Transportation's VSL figure of $9.4 million, the value of the expected lives that would be saved by preventing the ignition-related deaths would be $122 million (i.e., 13 lives × $9.4 million per life).[36] This amount alone exceeds the $100 million estimated cost of the recall. Based on the final death toll of 124 fatalities, the total value of the fatality risks was $1.17 billion. The appropriate benefit amount surely would have been higher had the value of the additional 275 injuries and the costs of the property damage to crashed vehicles linked to the defect been included. This calculation treats the VSL for a product defect in which customers are experiencing an increase in risk as being the same as the VSL for a risk reduction. If there is a discrepancy between the valuation of defects and safety improvements, the benefits of addressing the defect would be even greater.

Given that GM sold new and used cars with a known product defect and did not report the product defect to NHTSA as required by law, what regulatory sanction is warranted? For simplicity, assume that an expected increase in the fatality rate from a defect has the same value as an expected decrease in the fatality rate by a safety improvement. To determine the level of regulatory penalties needed to provide adequate incentives for safety, the VSL provides the appropriate guidance. To convey the value of the lives that are lost by failing to report a defect, NHTSA should impose a penalty based on the DOT VSL of $9.4 million per expected death.[37] However, the regulatory sanction needed to provide an appropriate incentive for efficient control of risks—$9.4 million per expected death—greatly exceeds the penalty caps NHTSA is permitted to levy, which was only $7,000 per violation with a limit of $35 million for a related series of violations.[38] In 2016, the Obama administration updated the penalty schedule for inflation, leading to a new penalty limit per violation of $21,000 and a total limit of $105 million for a related series of violations.[39] Note, however, that any single violation could have resulted in a fatality, and a related series of violations could have led to a much greater number of fatalities than in the defective ignition switch situation. Thus, the failure of the National Motor Vehicle Safety Act to establish any meaningful linkage between the violations, the extent of the harm, and the expected economic value of the prevented risks impedes the role of these sanctions to function as a safety incentive mechanism.

An appropriately set sanction would have dwarfed the current penalty amount. Suppose that there are only thirteen deaths related to the defect, as GM indicated initially, and that the VSL for product defects is the same as for safety improvements. Then, consistent with the benefit-cost analysis summarized above, the appropriate sanction for a readily identifiable risk would have been $122 million rather than $35 million. Based on the ultimate death toll of 124 deaths, the sanction would be $1.17 billion. Note that these penalty values are the same as the benefit estimates that GM would have calculated had it done a proper analysis. What regulatory sanctions based on the VSL accomplish is to force the company to incorporate the same kind of risk-cost tradeoffs that they would use had they undertaken a proper risk analysis.

AN INVENTORY OF FINANCIAL SANCTIONS AGAINST GM

There have been three principal types of financial costs that GM incurred as a result of the ignition switch failure. In addition to the $35 million penalty levied by NHTSA, GM also incurred payments for the injuries and deaths caused by the defective switch as well as a payment to settle criminal charges. GM's settlement fund, which will be discussed in chapter 9, provided $595 million in compensation for the deaths, injuries, and property damages caused by the defect.[40] The levels of compensation were set below the amounts that would be implied by reliance on the VSL. There may be additional costs arising from the claims that have not yet been litigated. The final payment component is that GM paid $900 million to settle criminal charges associated with the defect.[41] These payments were not for producing a product that caused injury. Rather they were for "engaging in a scheme to conceal a deadly safety defect from its US regulator, in violation of Title 18, United States Criminal Code, Section 1001, and committing wire fraud, in violation of Title 18, United States Code, Section 1343."[42]

Using Punitive Damages and Regulatory Penalties to Generate Adequate Incentives for Safety

The VSL statistics that should play a fundamental role in corporate risk decisions also should be the pivotal values in other institutions' response to safety matters. That is, the VSL can serve as the guidepost for regulatory agencies in setting sanctions and for the courts in their quest for the appropriate punitive damages amounts. This section outlines the general pertinence of the VSL measure to establishing safety incentives and compares the likely award levels using the VSL to the blockbuster punitive damages awards that have been levied in motor vehicle cases.

REGULATORY SANCTIONS AND PUNITIVE DAMAGES TO PROMOTE SAFETY

In a situation of product risk design, companies should use the VSL to value the expected fatalities that are reduced. But what if the company uses an inappropriately low value for prevented fatalities, ignores the implications of a risk-cost tradeoff analysis, or doesn't do any systematic analysis at all, leading to vehicles that lack highly justified safety improvements? If the company is found liable for the wrongful death of a person injured by the company's product, the usual form of compensation is equal to the present value of lost earnings that the household has suffered and the value of the services provided by the deceased—not the VSL. That compensatory damages amount will not provide adequate incentives for deterrence.

Similarly, government-imposed penalties are often quite limited by statute. Even with the recent increase in penalty levels, NHTSA can only levy modest penalties.[43] Regulatory damages are capped, whereas court awards usually are not.

If the company's behavior meets the criteria for awarding punitive damages, which are intended to punish and deter such conduct in the future, the court award or regulatory penalty can achieve levels of deterrence that sufficiently incentivize the company to choose the efficient level of safety. In situations where there is a 100 percent chance that the company will be caught for its behavior, the appropriate financial incentive for deterrence purposes is provided by a cost penalty equal to the VSL. Thus, either the regulatory penalty or, in the case of the courts, the total award of compensatory and punitive damages should equal the VSL. This amount will price safety at the correct levels.

It may be, however, that the company's behavior is not always detectable. The company may, for example, have not disclosed key information about defects or may have settled cases and sealed the information relating to the case to prevent others from ascertaining that there was a systematic defect in the product. If the chance of detecting the company's behavior is 50 percent, then the appropriate total award amount is $2 \times VSL$. If instead the chance of detection is only 10 percent, then the efficient level of setting the award is $10 \times VSL$.

This straightforward mathematical approach to damages has a long history in the literature but has not yet been adopted by the courts.[44] One practical difficulty is that once a company has been brought to trial for marketing a defective product, the company's behavior has been detected with certainty. The appropriate question to ask is what was the probability of detection at the time the company undertook the wrongful conduct? That probability and the VSL serve as the two main components to setting the damages amount.

Basing the sanction for failing to report the ignition switch defects on a readily identifiable risk is not appropriate in this situation. The ignition switch defect does not fit the well-known risk paradigm. GM was able to keep the defect secret from NHTSA, the government agency to which it is required by law to report safety-related defects, for at least seven years.[45] GM officials knew of the defect no later than 2005, were aware no later than spring 2012 that the defect had consequences that were deadly, took the defect "offline" so that it would not be part of a normal recall process, concealed the defect from the public, falsely reassured purchasers of certified used cars of the safety of the ignition switches and keys for the vehicles, and failed to report the defect to NHTSA.[46] In addition, GM settled some claims related to the ignition defect but did so with confidential settlements in which the nature of the risk was not disclosed.[47] Thus, in both the regulatory arena and judicial contexts, GM made a concerted effort to keep the risks hidden. This established policy of keeping the risks hidden lowers the probability of detection. If, for example, the chance of identifying the defect and linking it to all the harms was 1/10, the appropriate regulatory sanction for thirteen deaths valued at $9.4 million each would be $122 million/0.1, or $1.22 billion. Had NHTSA identified 124 deaths, the sanction would be $11.7 billion. Even if the agreement in which GM paid $900 million to settle criminal charges for failing to report the defect to regulatory authorities and for continuing to mislead the public is viewed as a partial substitute for the appropriate penalty related to the low probability of detecting the company's behavior, the penalty is still too low.

GM's corporate strategy of fostering secrecy with respect to product-related risks is not unique to auto safety situations. Hersch identified a similar phenomenon with respect to medical devices.[48] In particular, companies settled cases involving leaking breast implants, keeping the terms of the settlement confidential as well as the nature of the risks. The companies did not notify the Food and

Drug Administration (FDA) of the defects and kept the information out of the public domain by making the settlements confidential.

Government safety agencies such as NHTSA and the FDA lack the resources to undertake the kind of detailed monitoring needed to track the performance of products. Even if companies do not disclose the financial terms of the settlements, they are required to disclose the product defect to the respective government agency, which has the option of making the information public.[49] While companies already have such an obligation to report product defects, the sanctions for subsequent efforts to keep the defects hidden by utilizing such confidentiality agreements should be enhanced. These secretive efforts serve to lower the probability of detection and dampen the safety incentives that the courts and regulatory agencies can provide. If the regulatory sanction for failing to report defects is linked to the probability of detection, then efforts to hide the defect through confidential settlements of litigation could be used in assessing the probability of detection and boosting the appropriate regulatory sanction.

The role of the VSL in product safety situations is consequently twofold. First, it sets the price that companies and regulatory agencies should use in valuing the fatality risks associated with alternative designs. Second, if the company has been found to be remiss and either the courts or regulatory agencies wish to levy a penalty that incentivizes the company to produce and sell products that provide for an efficient level of safety, then incorporating the VSL in this procedure is essential.

Wholly apart from fostering more responsible corporate risk analyses, the VSL could play a central role in reformulating the penalty structure of current safety regulations. The limitations on the penalties that NHTSA has imposed on company failures have resulted in potential regulatory sanctions that are far below either the value of the lives at risk or the costs to the company of addressing the defect. The corporate strategy of suppressing information about safety defects and failing to fix the defects should not become a profitable option simply because government sanctions are better suited to promoting carefully completed paperwork rather than disclosing fundamental product risks. Pricing lives by integrating the VSL into corporate risk practices and government regulatory efforts would produce more protective safety policies.

Policy reform also includes a meaningful role for the VSL in terms of the regulatory sanctions. Rather than using $21,000 per violation, NHTSA should use the VSL to set the penalty level in the case of fatalities, boosting the scale of penalties by a factor of almost 500. Altering the penalty structure in this way would require a change in the agency's legislation. Creating efficient levels of deterrence becomes more complicated and requires larger sanctions if the probability of detecting the wrongful conduct is below 1.0.

Extending the Domain of the VSL

At present, the principal use of VSL estimates is by government agencies evaluating the fatality risk reduction benefits of proposed government regulations. This practice now has over three decades of experience and has been substantially refined over that period. The most direct counterpart to regulatory risk analyses is for corporations to use the VSL estimates in product safety decisions. The safe harbor reforms that I proposed in chapter 3 will go a long way in addressing the current corporate aversion to meaningful risk analyses. The GM ignition switch recall and the emerging picture of corporate product risk practices indicates that there has been substantial retrenchment in terms of addressing risk tradeoffs explicitly. Shunting safety issues to the side in this manner is not in the best interests of consumers. But until the liability environment of corporations is altered so as to foster such risk assessments, it is likely that few companies will undertake the necessary risk assessments and utilize VSL estimates when doing so.

There are also substantial opportunities for regulatory agencies to better utilize the VSL estimates in setting the level of regulatory sanctions. The VSL establishes a much more pertinent price that should be imposed on companies for behavior that violates regulations and leads to fatalities. Unfortunately, transportation safety regulatory efforts are hindered by ill-conceived damages caps that, in effect, trivialize the value of lives that are lost due to transportation violations. In the case of NHTSA, the legislative strictures on regulatory sanctions need to be either increased or removed altogether.

Many other health, safety, and environmental agencies also impose regulatory sanctions for violations that lead to risks such as workers killed due to faulty construction practices and deaths due to pharmaceutical products marketed for inappropriate off-label purposes. The use of the VSL provides an analytic framework to assist in conceptualizing the appropriate regulatory sanctions needed to establish efficient levels of deterrence.

This function can also be generalized to determinations of damages amounts in situations in which punitive damages are warranted. At present, jurors are engaged in a rudderless task in which they are given fairly meaningful guidance to ascertain whether the wrongful conduct merits a punitive award, but are given no guidance in the jury instructions regarding the setting of the punitive damages amounts. As a result, jurors are subject to the influence of irrelevant anchors that will be presented to them in the hope of giving them a quantitative handle in setting the punitive damages amounts. Incorporating the VSL statistics in setting efficient levels of punitive damages would serve to bolster the rationality of jury awards. There would be a desirable increase in very modest awards as well as greater discipline on the outlier awards.

5

The Devaluation of Life

SHOULD AGE MATTER?

The Potential Importance of Age Differences

Without question, the most strident controversies generated by the VSL have not involved the overall practice of placing a monetary value on expected lives saved, but rather have stemmed from the lowering of the VSL. The EPA's use of a smaller VSL for those over age 65 and the reduction of the VSL by the EPA Office of Air Quality Planning and Standards (or what most officials refer to as the EPA Air Office) each created a media firestorm. This chapter examines the role of age and the resistance that will likely accompany any devaluations of life based on age or other considerations.

Government policies that reduce fatality risks do not confer immortality but simply reduce the chance of premature death. Who benefits and to what extent is often a critical issue in assessing policy benefits. The incidence of the policy effects may not be uniform, as regulatory policies often have targeted impacts, affecting some segments of the population more than others. This differential impact can even occur for EPA air pollution regulations and other policies, which may have a broad geographical impact, but for which the beneficiary group includes populations who are particularly at risk, perhaps because they are asthmatics, have advanced respiratory diseases, or are otherwise more vulnerable to risk exposures. Using a uniform VSL treats all individuals symmetrically, irrespective of the magnitude of the expected additional life expectancy that is extended by the policy.

The role of life expectancy in setting the VSL for EPA policy achieved prominence in the Clear Skies regulation controversy when the agency placed a lower value on the lives of older victims of pollution. This chapter examines whether there should be such age differences in the VSL and, if so, how great the age differences should be. That such age adjustments might be consequential is reflected in the substantial differences in the life expectancies affected by different government policies. However, whether there are in fact pronounced differences in the VSL derived from such adjustments depends on how these valuations vary with age, which I examine here.

In the extreme case, a policy may have a minimal effect on life expectancy, perhaps with gains measured in terms of additional months of life to live, not years. How we should value such modest gains is particularly important in health care contexts. As in the case of risk reduction, generally, application of the insights afforded by the VSL approach will lead to higher values and more protective policies than the alternative techniques that have been used.

THE EPA SENIOR DISCOUNT CONTROVERSY

In 2003, the EPA attempted to grapple with the potential age-related heterogeneity of the VSL in its regulatory analysis of the Clear Skies Initiative. This analysis included an evaluation of the proposed air pollution regulation in which the expected mortality risk reductions for people aged 65 and older were accorded a lower VSL than mortality risk reductions for younger age groups. The EPA's devaluation of the lives of senior citizens generated a political firestorm, with senior citizen groups such as the AARP protesting against the apparent disregard of the policy importance of older citizen's well-being.[1]

The lower value associated with the reduced mortality risks for those over age 65 became known as the "senior discount" or the "senior death discount." Because the EPA policy analysis reduced the VSL for those over age 65 by 37 percent, there were outcries such as "Seniors on sale, 37% off" and "What's a granny worth?"

The EPA soon abandoned the "senior discount" approach, and no other US agencies have ventured into this sensitive terrain. Nevertheless, it is worthwhile to revisit this controversy to examine how EPA handled the VSL-age issue, how such matters should be addressed, and whether making such distinctions regarding age variations in the VSL are likely to have a policy impact. It is noteworthy that while the Clear Skies Initiative generated the most prominent controversy of any VSL-age adjustment, it was not the first such attempt to incorporate age variations. During the Clinton administration, in 2000 the EPA undertook a similar, but less publicized, sensitivity analysis of the benefits of a highway diesel rule.[2]

The principal impetus for raising the issue of whether the VSL should differ by age is that air pollution policies such as the Clear Skies Initiative may have highly differentiated impacts across the population, with young children and older population groups being particularly affected. At the very minimum, it is desirable from a policy assessment standpoint to have information regarding which population groups are affected and the extent to which their lives are influenced by the policy. Agencies often don't disclose such information so that compared to other federal agencies, the EPA was relatively forthright in this respect. After obtaining such a breakdown of the incidence of the policy impacts, the next policy assessment task is to place a value on the reduced mortality risks incorporating any legitimate differences in the benefit value for different fatality risks. The EPA undertook these steps, both providing the age distribution of the policy effects and attaching dollar values to these impacts.

The key components of the benefit assessment were the mortality benefits to the different population groups.[3] The EPA provided estimates of benefits based on long-term and short-term pollution exposures, each of which embodied age distribution effects. To

simplify the discussion, let us focus on the larger, long-term exposure benefits. The EPA estimated that the regulation would reduce
the number of annual fatalities by 1,900 for people aged 18 to 64
and by 6,000 for those aged 65 and over. Clearly the impacts on the
older segment of the population were critical to the overall benefit-
cost performance of the regulation. Using a VSL of $6.1 million (in
1999 dollars, or $8.7 million in 2015 dollars), the EPA estimated that
the total benefit value would be $11.6 billion for people aged 18 to
64. Although the EPA presented an analysis of the monetized benefits for those aged 65 and over using the same $6.1 million figure,
it also presented a sensitivity analysis applying a senior discount
of 37 percent to the benefits to the group aged 65 and over, or a
VSL of $3.8 million. Doing so reduced the total estimated benefits
for those aged 65 and over from $36.6 billion to $23.1 billion, or a
benefit reduction of over $13 billion annually.

WHY DID EPA DEVALUE OLDER LIVES?

Where did the 37 percent figure come from? Should fatality risks to
seniors really be valued at less than two-thirds of the value attached
to fatality risks to the rest of the population? While the senior discount number was not an entirely arbitrary choice, it was a provi-
sional figure based on a different approach than the usual market-
based tradeoffs that govern estimates of the VSL.[4] In particular, the
agency relied on a stated-preference survey question in which UK respondents of different ages gave their valuations of improvements in
traffic safety.[5] This study was an unusual choice and a substantial leap
from a benefit transfer perspective for several reasons. The governmental VSL levels based on UK stated-preference studies have been
much lower than the VSL estimates in the United States, compared
with what one would expect given the income differences between
the two countries. The UK Department for Transport formerly used
the cost-of-death approach, which anchored their values at a low
starting point. When they shifted to the VSL estimates derived from
a stated-preference study, they adopted the median survey values,
which were more similar to the cost-of-death numbers than the

higher mean estimates.[6] Subsequent updates in the VSL for inflation and income growth have still left the official UK VSL well below
US levels. The current governmental guidelines for policy analysis in
the United Kingdom specify that the VSL used for UK Department
for Transport regulations derived from stated-preference studies of
transportation safety is $2.29 million (in 2015 dollars), which is less
than one-fourth of the VSL used by the US EPA and the US Department of Transportation.[7] Respondents' valuations at different
ages also are likely to be sensitive to differences across countries
in income levels across the life cycle, retirement policies, social insurance structures, and attitudes toward health risks. Setting apart
these differences in the influence of age in the United Kingdom and
in the United States, the UK VSL-age relationships found in these
studies involve complicated impacts of age.[8] The structure of the
VSL-age relationship also differs across stated-preference studies,
as other more recent survey studies of willingness to pay for risk
reductions as a function of age have yielded other patterns, such as
either a continual steady level of VSL with age or a flat relationship
between VSL and age until the age of 70, after which there is some
decline.[9] In the absence of basing the senior discount on robust estimates that were clearly pertinent to the United States, the EPA was
in an untenable position of adopting a highly controversial valuation
approach utilizing initial exploratory findings.

Even if the downward adjustment in the VSL for older age groups
had been based on impeccable economic grounding, it is likely that
any downward age adjustment would have received a hostile recep-
tion. From an external vantage point, lowering the VSL for older
age groups is a form of economic loss for those whose lives are now
accorded a lower value. Something is being taken away from this
population group that they already had before, which was a VSL
that indicated that their lives were equally valuable. Psychologists'
studies of the loss aversion phenomenon by Kahneman and Tversky
suggest that the aversion to such losses will be a powerful effect.[10]
The resistance to the senior discount is not simply a matter of arcane
economic parameters, as it will have real policy impacts by making
policies that protect older age groups appear to be less worthwhile.

POSSIBLE DEFENSES OF THE DEVALUATION
OF OLDER LIVES

Appealing to other societal precedents for age adjustments may be helpful but is not directly on point with respect to the VSL-age variation. That there might be some rationale for age variations in the valuations of death risks does have other societal precedents that are even harsher than the EPA's senior discount. The compensation for fatalities that is provided in the courtroom in wrongful death cases is based largely on the present value of the decedent's lost earnings. Older people have shorter remaining future work lives, thus diminishing the value of their future earnings loss. If the decedent was retired, as many people aged 65 and over are, the compensation in wrongful death cases will not include earnings losses at all but will be limited to medical expenses and impacts such as lost services, loss of consortium, pain and suffering, and other non-income components. The substantial age-related reduction in court awards for fatalities is consistent with the stated objective of such compensation, which is to address the income losses incurred by the survivors. In contrast, the purpose of monetizing the mortality reduction benefits of government policies is not to reflect the income losses of the survivors but the value of reducing the risk of death to the people who might otherwise have died. It is more akin to the deterrence function of court awards than the compensation and insurance function.

Appealing to the precedent of a senior discount being consistent with policy practices in other countries conceivably may help dampen the public's resistance to using a different VSL based on age. For example, analyses in Canada applied a 25 percent discount when valuing reduced fatalities for those aged 65 and older.[11] Similarly, the European Commission recommended a declining VSL with age.[12] Pointing to other countries that use perhaps arbitrary senior discount numbers may be instructive to the extent that they are based on sound economic studies, but simply noting the parallels with other countries is unlikely to completely quash the potential controversy, given the strident reactions to the age adjustments.

Rather than seeking a shortcut to making a VSL-age adjustment, it is instructive to return to the basics of benefit assessment. Proper conceptualization of age variations in the VSL requires that one go back to first principles rather than attempt to analogize based on age differences in seemingly related contexts. The underlying principle for these benefits is that they should be governed by society's willingness to pay for the risk reduction. If the amounts that people are willing to pay for particular risk reductions decline substantially with age, such a decline would be a signal that the VSL does in fact decline. Casual observation does not suggest greater risk taking on the part of the older segments of society that might be an indicator of a declining VSL. They do not choose to gravitate to unsafe neighborhoods, to work in dangerous jobs, or to drive unsafe cars, as one might expect if they really do have much lower VSL amounts. Whether and how much the VSL declines with age requires a sound empirical basis for making such an assessment rather than a brute-force discounting of their VSL.

The Hazards of Being an Older Worker

Whether it is feasible to use labor market data to determine if the VSL exhibits variation with respect to age depends on whether any older workers are exposed to potential hazards on the job and potentially receive wage compensation for fatality risks. If all workers tend to sort themselves into extremely safe occupations as they age, then there would be no sound basis for imputing an age-adjusted VSL based on labor market data. Extremely dangerous occupations such as high-rise construction work tend to be the province of younger employees, and it is true generally that the average nonfatal injury risk in the industries in which people work declines steadily from the levels for the 20–24 age group to the 55–62 age group.[13] But most occupational fatalities are not the result of highly dangerous pursuits, as evidenced by the very large share of motor-vehicle-related deaths.

The advent of the BLS CFOI data, discussed in chapter 2, made it feasible to get a more precise assessment of whether older workers are exposed to more fatality risks. A contributing factor to the risk level is that there are age-related differences in vulnerability. Deaths from falls tend to increase with age, as does the fatality rate from motor vehicle accidents involving personal injury. As a result, it would not be entirely surprising that older workers might be exposed to fatality risks on the job even if they tend to shift to safer types of employment as they age. Calculations of the fatality rates by age and by industry indicate that within particular industries, the average worker fatality rates increase by a modest amount for older age groups. Comparison of the annual fatality rates for workers aged 20 to 24 with those aged 55 to 62 indicates a rise in the fatality rate per 100,000 workers for these two age groups in the construction industry (10.5 to 15.1), manufacturing industry (3.0 to 4.8), transportation (6.9 to 14.4), wholesale trade (4.6 to 7.5), retail trade (2.0 to 5.9), financial industry (0.6 to 2.2), and services (1.5 to 2.3). The consistent result is that older workers remain substantially at risk and have a higher fatality rate within particular lines of work.

What this pattern means for the age variation in the VSL is not evident without supporting empirical evidence. Are older workers more likely to be killed in any particular job, or do they work in different kinds of jobs? Older workers within particular industry groups may be exposed to greater risk due to their increased vulnerability, but workers move across industries over time, typically to safer employment. Many of these workers in the older age groups have shifted from higher-risk industries to lower-risk industries, which is consistent with them having a relatively high VSL despite their shortened life expectancy.

The Inverted U-Shaped VSL-Age Relationship

If people were endowed with their lifetime wealth at birth and could draw on these funds to purchase risk reductions throughout their lives in an idealized economic model, the VSL would be steadily declining with age, reflecting the shorter future expected lifetime that remains.[14] However, perfect borrowing, lending, and insurance opportunities are not available, so individuals' financial resources change markedly over time and are critical determinants of how greatly safety will be valued. One practical problem stems from moral hazard or incentives issues. It is not possible to draw on your lifetime earnings independent of actually putting forth work effort, as there is no assurance that you'll do the work if you are paid your lifetime earnings in advance. As a result, there is no strong theoretical basis for predicting that the lifetime trajectory of VSL follows a steadily downward path.

One can, of course, generate such results by using a restrictive empirical model. My early estimates of the VSL-age relationship assumed a constant utility level per year of life, so the empirical task was to estimate the constant value of a statistical life year, appropriately discounted. Policy applications that use a constant value of a quality-adjusted life year (QALY) make similar assumptions.[15] The assumption of a constant value per discounted life year was driven by the aggregate nature of the early fatality rate data, which did not permit refined estimation of the VSL-age relationship.

The utilization of the CFOI data makes it possible to construct worker fatality rates by age group, permitting age-specific estimation of the VSL-age relationship. The result of such labor market studies is that they all yield a similar inverted U-shaped pattern.[16] Figure 5.1

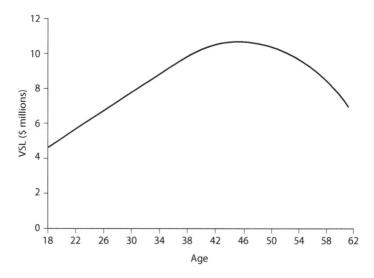

FIGURE 5.1. Age Variations in the Value of a Statistical Life. Original figure based on data in Joseph E. Aldy and W. Kip Viscusi, "Adjusting the Value of a Statistical Life for Age and Cohort Effects," *Review of Economics and Statistics* 90, no. 3 (2008): 573–581. The figure has been adjusted for inflation.

presents an illustration of the rise and subsequent decline of the VSL with age based on one set of empirical estimates.[17] The VSL starts at a fairly modest level just below $4.7 million for workers aged 18, rises through middle age to peak at $10.8 million for workers aged 46, and then tapers off to a value of $7.0 million for 62-year-old workers. The VSL does eventually decline with age but does not drop off the table. The actual VSL levels vary depending on the sample used in the different articles, the time period of the data, and other aspects of the empirical analysis, but the general inverted U-shaped pattern is consistent across several labor market studies. In many instances, the differences in the estimated VSL levels for those aged 55–62 as compared with those aged 18–24 are not statistically significant. There is no justification for singling out older workers as having especially low valuations of mortality risks.

Why the VSL Rises and Falls over the Life Cycle

The VSL is a reflection of two components—the mortality risk level of the job and the average amount of wage compensation workers receive for these risks. Each of these components changes with age. Consider the results for another labor market study of the VSL-age relationship.[18] The steeper change is with respect to the average mortality risk level, which rises continually from a level of 3.3 per 100,000 workers for those aged 18–24 to 5.46 for those aged 55–62. The total compensating differential workers receive for bearing the risk also rises with age, from $0.21 per hour (in 2015 dollars) for those aged 18–24, to $0.35 per hour for those aged 35–44. Subsequently, the hourly compensation for fatality risks diminishes to $0.23 per hour for those aged 45–54 and $0.22 per hour for those aged 55–62. The hourly compensation for fatality risks is fairly similar across age groups except for the peak years of 35–44, but the steady increase in the risk levels with age leads to a dampening of the VSL and the observed temporal trajectory of VSL levels.

The age-related pattern of VSL levels takes on a shape that is quite familiar to economists. Annual earnings rise and then fall over the life cycle, with changes that are particularly pronounced for white-collar workers. Similarly, individual consumption patterns exhibit a trajectory that mimics the overall shape of the VSL-age relationship. This similarity is not a statistical quirk, as there is a theoretical linkage of one's valuation of safety to income and consumption levels.[19] On an empirical basis, inclusion of life-cycle consumption measures as a determinant of the VSL yields the strong positive relationship on the estimates of the VSL by age group that one would expect.[20] The temporal trajectories displayed by individual income, consumption, and VSL all adhere to a similar inverted U-shaped pattern.

Implications for the Clear Skies Benefit Assessment

Based on these various results, would the estimated benefits of the Clear Skies Initiative be affected if instead of using a constant VSL for all age groups, the government analysts adopted an age-dependent VSL implied by these analyses? While the substantial concentration of benefits to this regulation among people aged 65 and over will tend to lead to a reduction in benefits, the extent of the benefit adjustment varies depending on what age variations are incorporated in the empirical results. Some VSL estimates based on industry fatality rates matched to workers by age yield a 39 percent reduction in the assessed benefits for those aged 65 and older, which is a result that is very similar to the EPA Clear Skies analysis.[21] However, for econometric models that also account for the dependence of the VSL on lifetime consumption levels, the effect is less dramatic, on the order of a 7 percent reduction.[22] Thus, it may be the case that age adjustments that are warranted are not very stark even in the case of the Clear Skies Initiative.

Consideration of possible age adjustments to benefit assessments also is not simply a matter of reducing the VSL for older age groups. Should policymakers wish to fine-tune their efforts to incorporate age variations in the VSL, such refinements should reflect the entire structure of the VSL over the life cycle. Because of the VSL's inverted U-shaped relation with age, the estimates tend to be lowest for both the youngest and the oldest age groups. The absence of statistically significant difference between the VSL for those aged 18–24 and those in the 55–62 age group in many studies reflects the lower VSL at both tails of the distribution. Singling out the older age groups for a lower VSL is certainly not warranted based on the empirical evidence and does not appear to be reflective of that age group's willingness to pay for safety. As people age, the commodity they are buying through risk reduction efforts is smaller than it is when they are younger. However, their financial resources are also greater, and it is the net effect of financial resources and changes in remaining life expectancy on the person's valuation that is most consequential. It is clear from the empirical evidence that the VSL does not plummet dramatically with age. For most policies with broad societal impacts, use of the average VSL estimate for all benefits will both be reflective of the benefit values across the population and avoid unnecessary controversies with respect to targeting specific population groups who might have lower VSL levels.

Implications of Normalized Lifespans

The EPA's Clear Skies Initiative was not distinctive in terms of the substantial component of the benefits accounted for by the affected population aged 65 and older. EPA air pollution regulations often affect people at the upper end of the age distribution. For example, the average age of the population benefitting from the mortality reductions from the decrease in particulate-matter emissions associated with the sulfur dioxide content of gasoline was over age 70.[23] Differential impacts by age group are not unique to EPA air pollution regulations, as many health care interventions raise similar issues of how one should conceptualize the different life expectancies being affected. A brute-force way to address this issue is to standardize the lives saved based on the amount of remaining life at risk. Doing so incorporates an age adjustment in the VSL by accounting for the length of life at risk. This approach highlights the potential importance of age adjustments but ignores the substantial variation across policies in the duration of life being extended.

The first part of any mortality risk-benefit calculation is to understand the effect on individual mortality, its distribution across the population, and the length of life at risk.[24] Not all affected lives have the same remaining duration. The expected number of years of life lost from a fatality declines with age. The remaining life expectancy at age 5 is 73.7 more years of life; but conditional on a person reaching age 75, an additional 11.7 years of life are expected.[25] The age at which the policy affects the mortality risk is clearly consequential in terms of the magnitude of the benefit. Deferred risks that occur with a latency period will tend to lead to the loss of fewer years of life so that policies addressing deferred risks generate shorter life-expectancy gains than those that reduce more immediate hazards. Whether such latency effects influence the applicable VSL depends on how much the VSL declines over the life cycle. Abstracting from various latency issues, the lost life expectancy is greatest for deaths affecting the young. The lost life expectancy for different ailments is 75 years for perinatal conditions, 58 years for congenital abnormalities, 37 years for auto accidents, 14 years for neoplasms (cancer), 10 years for cardiovascular disease, and 9 years for pneumonia/influenza. Acute accident risks are not subject to latency periods, so they are not much affected by concerns with respect to the timing of the fatalities. For causes of death that respond with a lag after the exposure, the value of the lost life expectancy diminishes.

One might be tempted to simply scale back the VSL based on the proportion of the remaining life at risk. Making adjustments for the length of life at risk is something that people may do implicitly when thinking about the severity of different risks. One of the most well-established biases in risk beliefs is that people greatly overestimate very small risks that they face, such as the risk of being killed by lightning strikes or botulism, and they underestimate the truly substantial risks, such as heart disease and cancer.[26] The apparent bias appears to be attributable in large part to people taking into account the amount of life lost when rating the importance of such risks.[27] Risks of death for which there is a large loss in life expectancy tend to receive much higher mortality risk assessments than those involving much shorter loss of life, which tend to receive lower assessments. People tend to confound the severity of the risks and the level of the risks in their assessment of the risks.

These types of intuitive judgments could be incorporated to measure the performance of regulatory policies to account for both the mortality risk and the loss in life expectancy. Suppose that instead of inquiring how the VSL declines with age, we approach the issue from the standpoint of the quantity of life at risk and then make quantity adjustments to the estimates of the cost per life saved by the regulation, using auto accident deaths as the reference point. Thus, if a traffic safety policy saves lives at $3 million per life and a pharmaceutical policy also costs $3 million per life saved but has half of the effect on life expectancy as the transportation policy, its cost per normalized expected life saved would be $6 million. Based on life-expectancy-weighted estimates for a wide variety of diseases, it is feasible to calculate the regulatory cost per normalized expected life saved. These calculations shift the focus to the cost incurred per normalized life, which one can then compare with the pertinent VSL estimates to assess whether the regulation is worthwhile. The normalized life reference point of a traffic accident death risk involves acute deaths that are similar to that of the average worker in studies estimating the VSL for occupational fatalities, many of which are attributable to transportation or motor-vehicle-related deaths. As one would expect, policies that target acute hazards are not much affected by such normalization considerations. The real lap/shoulder belt regulations that DOT proposed for automobiles had a cost per life saved (in 2015 dollars) of $6.9 million and a cost per normalized life saved of $6.9 million. For policies with a deferred impact, such as OSHA's arsenic occupational exposure limit, the cost per life saved is $230.4 million, but the cost per normalized life saved rises to $575.4 million. OSHA safety standards entail less of an adjustment as their effects are more immediate and with an age distribution more similar to that of auto accidents. The cost per life saved for the OSHA auto wheel-rim servicing standard is $0.9 million, with a cost per normalized life saved of $1.1 million. EPA regulations almost invariably involve effects that occur with some time lag and may affect older age groups. Typical in its performance is the arsenic emission standard for glass plants, with a cost per life saved of $29.1 million and a cost per normalized life saved of $72.8

million. The FDA diethylstilbestrol (DES) cattle-feed ban performs with a comparable disparity between the normalized and the conventional values, with a cost per life saved of $269.0 million and a cost per normalized life saved of $671.9 million.

Calculation of the cost per normalized life saved highlights the important role of both latency periods and age in influencing the cost-effectiveness of policies. Efforts directed at reducing the risk of accidents are generally more cost-effective than those addressed to illnesses based on the cost per normalized life. The policy impact on the probability of death alone is not a sufficient guide for assessing the attractiveness of policy options. It is also noteworthy that transportation regulations fare particularly well even without the normalization since they are more strongly grounded on benefit-cost tests than are regulations of many other agencies. Consideration of the factors that normalize the mortality risk reduction benefits reinforces the already strong performance of transportation safety policies.

Such adjustments for the expected quantity of life saved clearly would have a huge impact on the economic performance of regulations that are targeted to older age groups and which have effects that occur with some latency period, thus both deferring their impact and shortening the length of the future lifetime that might be affected. Valuation approaches that apply a standardized value per expected year of life across the population and adopt the brute-force approach of scaling back the value based on life expectancy at risk consequently will have a profound effect on the benefits of mortality risk reductions. However, such quantity adjustments are not based on how people's willingness to pay for the risk reduction varies across these policies. The proper solution is not to chop down the VSL to recognize age-related factors. Doing so will undervalue the lives at risk. Similarly, we will find that brute-force adjustments for very short life extensions such as a year or less also undervalues lives.

The Value of a Statistical Life Year

Using a one-size-fits-all approach for VSL sidesteps many potential controversies and may not be a bad approximation of overall benefit values based on age-specific VSL estimates. Such a uniformity in the

VSL levels is suitable for the preponderance of regulations affecting transportation safety, occupational safety, and the environment. But what about valuing policies directed at populations with very short life expectancies, such as for drugs regulated by the Food and Drug Administration? Suppose an improved cancer treatment based on personalized medicine extends the life expectancy of lung cancer victims by an average of three months. Is it appropriate to apply an average society-wide VSL on the order of $10 million to value an extended expected life expectancy of three months? Wouldn't the overall VSL be an inappropriate reflection of patients' willingness to pay when the additional short-term survival period is severely truncated?

To address the valuation issues when there is a very small impact on expected longevity, one can construct the value of a statistical life year (VSLY), which is the counterpart of the VSL for a single year of life extension. Empirical estimates linked to the VSLY remain grounded in the theoretical framework for VSL but deal with more modest health impacts.[28] Based on empirical estimates using fatality rate data that varies by age, it is possible to estimate the VSLY, which can be derived from age-based estimates of VSL taking into account the additional life expectancy associated with each age. If the estimated VSLY is constant in each year, then the VSL will be steadily declining with respect to age since the number of years of remaining life expectancy declines. However, we know that the VSL doesn't decline steadily with age, as the VSL rises and falls over the life cycle. The VSLY pattern also rises and falls over the life cycle but declines less steeply than the VSL and peaks at a later age than does the VSL. Breaking down the contributory VSLY components of the VSL indicates that for empirical analyses in which the overall VSL peaks in the person's mid- to late 40s, the VSLY reaches its peak in the mid-50s. Based on one set of labor market estimates, the VSLY averages $411,000 (in 2015 dollars), rising to a peak of $545,000 at age 54.[29] What is also striking is that in terms of the VSLY there is very little drop-off with age, as the VSLY trajectory remains relatively flat. Whereas the VSL declines more steeply because people have fewer remaining years of life as they age, the value placed on each expected life year remains quite high so that the VSLY for those aged 62 exceeds that for those under age 40. The underlying economic intuition is quite consistent with age-related patterns of income and consumption in which older age groups continue to have substantial financial resources so that their willingness to pay for specific expected durations of life remains quite high.

These VSLY patterns have fundamental policy implications. It is not appropriate to assume that the value per statistical life year is constant. This value changes substantially over the life cycle. Since such quantity-of-life-adjusted values are most likely to be pertinent to valuing the lives of people in older age groups, it is especially important to take into account the relatively high value per expected life year in these age groups. One such application was in my analysis with Joni Hersch of the private cost of smoking to smokers. Previous analyses had used as a placeholder value that each year of life was worth $100,000, which might appear to be substantial if people were required to pay out of pocket for an additional year of life. Use of this value leads to a surprisingly small estimate of the personal health losses caused by smoking. Our analysis estimated the VSLY of smokers revealed in the labor market decisions of smokers, for whom we found that even this high-risk-taking group of smokers had a VSLY on the order of $539,000 for men and $386,000 for women (in 2015 dollars).[30] Workers who smoke have shorter life expectancies, but they nevertheless place a high value on their remaining life expectancy. These results also led to estimates that the private health loss, or "internalities," due to smoking are quite substantial and are several times greater than the levels implied by previous studies based on the arbitrary $100,000 figure.[31]

But are such VSLY numbers seemingly too large? In much the same way that people generally don't have lifetime financial resources to match their VSL, they also don't have annual income to equal their VSLY. Once again this disparity is not problematic because the analysis addresses statistical lives rather than certain prolongation of life. A VSLY of $400,000, for example, implies that a person is willing to pay $400 for a 1/1,000 chance of an additional year of life, not that the person can pay $400,000 for an additional year of life.

As in the case of the adoption of the VSL to replace the cost of death, the adoption of the VSLY will lead to much more protective policies. Consider the official health care guidance in the United Kingdom.[32] Expenditures per life year below £20,000 per expected life year are cost-effective, and expenditures may be worthwhile if they are as high as £20,000 to £30,000, or $25,800 to $38,700 in 2015 US dollars. Use of the VSLY as the reference value indicates that the UK guidelines undervalue years of life by more than an order of magnitude. Health care guidelines based on the VSLY would greatly expand the range of treatments and drugs that pass a cost-effectiveness test.

The valuation of each expected year of life by US agencies has also been too low, but nevertheless, much greater than in the United Kingdom. For many years, the FDA and the US Department of Health and Human Services used a VSLY of $116,000.[33] Subsequently, the FDA used values such as $300,000 and sensitivity analysis using values of different VSLY levels until adopting a $369,000 value in a 2016 regulatory analysis by the FDA in which it cited my early VSLY estimates with Aldy as the justification for the figure.[34] Adoption of the VSLY estimates derived from labor market evidence provides a solid empirical foundation for the valuation of modest gains in life expectancy for which application of the VSL would overstate the willingness to pay for the risk reduction. While the VSLY numbers are considerably below the overall VSL, the valuation approach leads to a much greater valuation of modest life-expectancy gains as compared with current practices.

Fairness Arguments Relating to Age

Thus far I have been concerned with society's willingness to pay for fatality risk reductions or matters of economic efficiency—whether the societal value of the benefits exceeds the costs. However, the age-related valuation question is often posed in terms of fairness. If we set aside considerations of economic efficiency, what is the fair or most equitable treatment of the benefits to different age groups? Should all lives be valued equally? Or, should all years of life be valued equally? Such questions don't have easy answers, and to the extent that there are meaningful answers, they hark back to concerns regarding the values implied by people's willingness to pay for risk reductions.

Consider an extreme case in which the comparison is between valuing the mortality risk reduction for a healthy 30-year-old with a remaining life expectancy of 49 years and an elderly individual with advanced emphysema and a life expectancy of one year. Using the same VSL in each case is equitable in the sense of using the same monetary value for each mortality risk reduction. However, the symmetric VSL approach is inequitable in terms of the quite different life expectancies that are being valued and the implicit VSLY reflected in these policies. The 30-year-old also has a one-year period of life expectancy at the end of life, but in addition also has 48 years of life expectancy before reaching that point.

An alternative perspective on the fairness approach is to value each life year the same irrespective of a person's age or remaining life expectancy. That formulation also has the semblance of being equitable, but the practical result of using a constant value per year of life is that the overall benefit value for mortality risk reductions will steadily decline with age.[35] Whereas the constant-VSL approach overvalues the risks to life for those with extremely low remaining life expectancy, the constant-VSLY approach also creates a bias by steadily reducing the total benefit value attached to the remaining years of life as a person ages. What this example illustrates is that it is usually impossible to achieve equity in both the VSL and the VSLY. If each year of life is accorded the same value for all, those with greater future lifetimes at risk will have a higher VSL because the VSLY is multiplied by a larger number of years of life being gained.

An alternative reference point for assessing fairness is to inquire how much the people whose lives are at risk value policies that reduce their mortality rate. The constant-VSL approach sometimes is inconsistent with these private valuations, as it leads to excessive valuation of the lives of age groups at both tails of the age distribution curve and an inadequate valuation of lives in the middle of the curve. Similarly, the constant-VSLY methodology falls short as a mechanism for valuing mortality reduction benefits in that it over-values the lives of very young age groups and places an inadequate value on the lives of the more senior age groups.

Pinpoint matching of the person's valuation of the risk reduction to particular policies is generally not possible, as it calls for greater precision than is feasible given the current state of the art. Moreover, for most policies, such controversial fine-tuning based on age and life expectancy is unnecessary. Application of a society-wide VSL for policies with broad impacts is efficient and embodies aspects of equity. In the special instances in which the policy delivers only a very minor effect on life expectancy, utilization of the VSLY approach retains a linkage to private valuations of risks, which are much greater than simple quantity adjustments to the VSL would suggest.

Failing to Learn from the Clear Skies Senior Discount Controversy

How the valuation issue is framed plays an instrumental role in governing the public's reaction. In the case of the senior discount for the Clear Skies Initiative, there was an established VSL amount that was being reduced in a manner that resulted in the senior discount. A similar framing issue arose with respect to a subsequent EPA devaluation of life unrelated to age. There was a major public outcry in 2008 after the EPA Air Office reduced the VSL used to assess air pollution regulations. Whereas previously the EPA Air Office used a VSL in 2008 dollars of $7.7–$7.8 million, in its analysis of the standards for industrial boilers and process heaters in 2004, it used a VSL of $7.0 million (in 2008 dollars). As in the case of the senior discount, once this reduction in the VSL level became public, this devaluation generated substantial critical media attention.[36] Since the new VSL level exceeded the value used by most other government agencies, it was not the absolute level of VSL that was the matter of concern but rather that lives were now worth less than before. The perception that something was being taken away combined with the powerful influence of loss aversion and the inherent sensitivity of VSL issues to generate another wave of controversy over VSL practices.

The situation was not helped by the failure of the EPA Air Office to provide a transparent rationale for the change.[37] To derive its new VSL estimate, the EPA Air Office relied on two meta-analyses of VSL in selecting the new VSL—a meta-analysis by Mrozek and Taylor and a meta-analysis by Viscusi and Aldy.[38] The preferred VSL was the midpoint of the 25th percentile value in the Mrozek and Taylor study and the 75th percentile in Viscusi and Aldy. While this odd formulation does have a semblance of scientific precision, there are many other seemingly less arbitrary estimates one could have constructed based on these studies. It would have been helpful had the agency provided a rationale for its approach and a sensitivity analysis using alternative procedures.

The resistance to this latest EPA devaluation of life in conjunction with the senior discount controversy led to a legislative proposal in 2008 by Senator Barbara Boxer, the "Restoring the Value of Every American in Environmental Decisions Act" (proposed in the 110th Congress, second session). Her unsuccessful legislative initiative led off with a general disavowal of the VSL approach, as it claimed that "using a dollar value to establish the worth of human life as the basis for making decisions . . . offends many deeply held religious, moral, and ethical beliefs of people in the United States." After inaccurately framing the VSL in terms of trading off certain deaths for money, the proposed legislation blamed the use of the VSL for the EPA's apparent failure to always adopt policies not necessarily even related to the VSL, including its purported failure to use "the latest science," failure to promote "technology-forcing standards," and failure to establish "right-to-know safeguards." The right-to-know safeguard critique was especially ironic in that the first major use of the VSL led to the adoption of the hazard communication standard for workplace exposures.

After completing this attack on the use of the VSL, the proposed legislation then sought to severely constrain the agency's ability to modify the VSL. Although the legislation did not propose any specific VSL number or a methodology for arriving at this estimate, it did want to prevent any downward adjustments in the VSL. Interestingly, the proposed legislation did not apply to all agencies, but simply required that EPA never reduce the VSL below the highest value used by the EPA before the act. As a practical matter, this would have entailed considering the VSL used by different program offices, as there was no official VSL mandated for agency-wide use. The proposal also would have prevented any downward adjustments in the VSL "based on age, income, race, illness, disability, date of death, or any other personal attribute or relativistic analysis of the value of life." The proposal would have mandated annual increases in the VSL based on changes in average income and related factors, though the nature and extent of the income adjustment was not specified. Finally, the proposal would have treated changes in the VSL as being similar to changes in regulatory proposals, with a required public comment period, a supporting analysis for any VSL change, and approval by the Committee on Environment and Public Works of the Senate and the Committee on Energy and Commerce of the House of Representatives.

Although this legislative proposal was not adopted, it is striking how an agency's changes in an economic parameter used in policy analyses—the VSL—were being treated as being tantamount to fundamental changes in actual policies. Agencies utilize a wide range of economic parameters in their analyses, such as the discount rate, the social cost of carbon, and dose-response relationships for chemical exposures. There is no comparable congressional review and public scrutiny for any of these other parameters. The prominence of the VSL in this discussion reflects the powerful influence the VSL has on a broad range of regulatory policies and the strength of the critical response that is stimulated by imposing apparent losses through policy procedure viewed as devaluations of life.

As in the case of the age adjustments to VSL, it was not the underlying intrinsic sensitivity of VSL issues that generated the controversy but rather the framing of the benefit assessment as a form of economic loss. What was particularly noteworthy about the EPA Air Office's 2008 reduction in the VSL is that the reduced VSL still exceeded the value used by most other government agencies. It was the direction of change rather than the level that was most problematic.

The downward shift in the VSL also was contrary to what one expects based on fundamental economic principles. As society has become more affluent, the VSL should presumably be increasing over time rather than decreasing. There is no clear economic rationale for why our lives should now be worth less. Unfortunately, the agency did not provide a detailed rationale for the change or explain why the VSL estimate should differ across different EPA branches. The EPA Air Office undertook a new literature review that gave rise to the lower VSL number, but there were not sufficient details regarding the assessment to identify a compelling rationale for a lower VSL. The EPA has been a leader in terms of applying the VSL methodology, but it and other government agencies could profit from framing policy changes more effectively and providing more transparent rationales for any controversial changes in VSL levels, particularly in instances where the applicable VSL is being decreased.

Practical Guidelines for Dealing with Age-Related Issues

Whether there should be age-related adjustments and how such adjustments should be calculated will vary depending on the risk context. In many situations, whether there should be an adjustment for age or for remaining life expectancy is simply a non-issue. Risk reduction efforts that deal with acute risks that cut across broad segments of the population would fit this characterization. Most job safety, transportation safety, and product safety efforts are of this type. Even in the case of mortality risks from illnesses such as cancer, the main adjustment will be in terms of taking into account the need to discount deferred benefits, but the value of the benefits in the future period can be obtained after applying the usual levels of VSL to this future context, as only major reductions in the length of life being saved are likely to be consequential.

Nevertheless, there will be situations in which risk reduction efforts generate very small increases in life expectancy for which application of a full VSL is not appropriate. Rather than do a brute-force quantity adjustment, the sounder approach is to return to first principles and inquire how the willingness to pay for risk reduction is affected by age or the shortened life expectancy. Before exhibiting a decline, the VSL increases with age, undermining the appropriateness of any simple reduction in the VSL based on the years of remaining life. The subsequent drop-off in the VSL that eventually occurs with age is much less than one would expect based on the decrease in the number of remaining years of life.

There may, however, be situations in which the remaining life expectancy is quite short. For these risk contexts, an applicable age-adjusted VSL may be appropriate. In the case of attaching benefit values to very small impacts, such as the additional life expectancy of several months or a few years resulting from an experimental drug treatment, use of the VSLY is the correct economic approach for promoting efficient risk levels as well as establishing a degree of fairness in terms of how we value quite different changes in life expectancy. While the shift to the VSLY generates a lower valuation amount than does use of the VSL, application of this approach more correctly reflects the value of modest risk reduction to those benefitting from the policies.

Any concerns about the use of the VSLY leading to a devaluation of policies generating small life-expectancy gains are misplaced. The adoption of the VSLY in the United States has boosted the assessed benefits of health-related policies associated with relatively small increases in life expectancy. If other countries such as the United Kingdom also used the VSLY as the guideline for small increases in life expectancy, there would be a huge increase in the economic valuation of such life-expectancy gains. The result would be much more protective, health-enhancing policies than under the current approach.

6

Should There Be Preferential Treatment of the Rich?

Inequality and the Value of a Statistical Life

Should risks to the lives of the rich be accorded a greater value than risks to the lives of the poor? Posing this question is not an entirely philosophical exercise. This issue arose in the early 1990s when I was advising the Federal Aviation Administration on the selection of the VSL for airline safety. Airline passengers are more affluent than the average victims of traffic accidents so that there is a potential rationale for assigning a higher VSL than is used by the US Department of Transportation generally. But is there a sound economic rationale for doing so, and if so, what should be the VSL premium for airline safety? What is the principle guiding such a premium, and is it generalizable? If lives of airline passengers should be accorded a higher value, is that also the case for all policies benefitting more affluent groups?

In this chapter, I explore these sensitive issues both for the United States and for the world. Income differences play a particularly critical role in the establishment of appropriate international VSL levels derived when policy analysts transfer US estimates to other countries. Perhaps somewhat surprisingly, the downward adjustment of US VSL numbers to reflect the lower income levels elsewhere does not lead to less protective policies in poorer countries but instead boosts the value of safety above the levels currently used in international policy settings.

It is useful to begin our inquiry by returning to the fundamental economic principle for assessing policy benefits. The value of policy benefits is governed by society's willingness to pay for the benefits. In the case of policies that impose losses, the counterpart benefit value is the amount people require to be compensated for incurring the loss, which is also termed the willingness-to-accept value for the harm being inflicted. In each instance, the valuation is likely to depend on the person's financial resources and to vary in ways that accord with usual expectations. One might expect that richer people will value changes in risk levels more highly, just as their financial resources bolster their valuations of other normal economic goods. If such a relationship is borne out empirically, it would lead to a higher VSL based on one's income.

An underlying assumption of this economic approach is that policies should be preference-based and linked to society's willingness to pay for the benefits. This reasonable assumption underlies the entire benefit-cost analysis framework used for policy evaluation as well as economic analysis generally, but it is possible to advance other policy evaluation criteria. For example, one might advocate the use of a social welfare function that places additional emphasis on advancing the well-being of the disadvantaged.[1] Here I will outline the implications of a standard economic efficiency approach and then indicate how it can accommodate distributional concerns.

Making income-based distinctions in establishing the values placed on health and safety risks has precedents in terms of the structure of court awards after fatalities. The largest component of compensation in personal injury cases, including wrongful death cases, is payment for the present value of the lost earnings of the injured party. This amount varies proportionally with income. Similarly, life insurance policies provided by employers are typically tied to the worker's salary. Workers' compensation payments are based on the value of the worker's wages before the injury, subject to upper benefit limits that vary by state. These programs, however, have a different purpose than does the VSL. Court awards, life insurance, and benefit programs for injuries are targeted at addressing losses suffered by injured parties and their survivors rather than the value to the person at risk of preventing such injuries.

A more instructive parallel to ascertain whether variations in VSL with income are reasonable is to consider the expenditures that people make to enhance aspects of their lives that influence their health and safety. Automobile companies generally introduce new safety devices first for luxury vehicles for which a low price point is not an essential aspect of the vehicle marketing. Thus, within the GM product lines, Cadillac, Buick, and Oldsmobile had airbags before the lower-priced Chevrolet and Pontiac lines. Similarly, more affluent households are more likely to purchase residences in safer, less polluted neighborhoods. Access to better nutrition and health care also increases with income. The benefit valuation question being addressed in this chapter is whether the VSL also increases with income, to what extent, and whether these variations have any legitimate policy role.

The political and moral sensitivity of these income-related issues is perhaps even greater than the concerns with respect to age adjustments. In the case of age variations in the VSL, the equity aspects are unclear since equalizing the VSL across all people creates inequities across the population in the VSLY due to the differences in the quantities of life at risk. For income-related adjustments, the equity issues become more pronounced, as valuing lives of the rich more highly is always unfair to the poor. Making distinctions based on income also might be particularly sensitive in the current era in which rising income inequality has become a salient political issue. Nevertheless, I will suggest that while recognition of income-related differences in the VSL is not likely to be a routine procedure, such differences in willingness to pay for safety exist, and there are situations in which such variations should be recognized. Moreover, for adjustments of the VSL across time and across countries, such adjustments play a particularly valuable role.

Income-Related Variations in the VSL

Economic analyses of the effect of income on the VSL focus on the income elasticity of the VSL, which is defined as the percentage change in the VSL with respect to a 1 percent change in income. The focus on elasticities converts the analysis into percentage terms rather than absolute terms, facilitating both the empirical analysis and the policy application of these estimates. There have been three principal sources of revealed-preference evidence on the income elasticity of VSL—estimates based on meta-analyses of VSL, estimates across different meta-analyses corrected for publication selection bias, and estimates across different components of the wage distribution at a point in time or for labor markets over time.

Meta-analyses involve a synthesis and pooling of the VSL estimates from a series of studies of VSL. It is then possible to estimate the effect on the estimated VSL of differences in worker income levels across studies, controlling also for other key variables that are likely to influence the study's VSL estimate. Here I will review the estimates in my meta-analysis with Joseph Aldy in which we presented income elasticity estimates using a sample of forty-nine different VSL labor market studies for which we estimated our own equation specifications as well as replicating the results of four other meta-analysis estimates of the income elasticity of the VSL using our sample but the previous studies' statistical specifications.[2] Using our dataset and the different equation specifications from these four articles, we estimated income elasticity of VSL values of 0.51 to 0.61. Thus, a 10 percent increase in income leads to a 5–6 percent increase in the VSL. Examination of six other model formulations that we developed produced income elasticity estimates in a similar range, as they varied from 0.46 to 0.60. In all instances, the income elasticity of VSL is positive and substantial but less than proportional.

An alternative approach is to examine a meta-analysis of the income elasticities found in previous meta-analyses.[3] However, rather than simply averaging the studies, this meta-analysis of income elasticity estimates also accounted for the possibility of publication selection bias. In particular, there may be a bias toward publishing income elasticity estimates that are consistent with the theoretical predictions regarding the income elasticity or are consistent with other previous empirical work.[4] The procedure used in this study utilized a sample of 101 estimates drawn from fourteen published meta-analyses in a meta-regression equation that purges the estimates of the influence of publication selection bias. The ten most precisely estimated VSL income elasticity values and the overall meta-regression estimate were both in the narrow band of 0.61 to 0.62, which is a range similar to that in the first approach discussed above, using separate meta-regression analyses of individual VSL estimates.[5]

A third approach is to examine the income elasticity across a particular sample rather than a meta-analysis of the average elasticity values across different studies. Examination of the income elasticity across a wage distribution in a single year generates an average income elasticity of 1.44.[6] What is particularly striking is that the income elasticity is very large at the bottom of the wage distribution, reaching a value of 2.2 at the 10th percentile, after which it declines to an elasticity of 1.2 beginning at the 75th percentile and above. The greatest income-related responsiveness to the valuation of risks is at the lower end of the wage distribution. Put somewhat differently, for workers with very low wages, small differences in financial well-being have relatively large effects on their willingness to boost their income through work on hazardous jobs. It is also feasible to estimate the income elasticity using a sample that spans multiple years. An analysis by Costa and Kahn of long-term historical trends in VSL based on labor market estimates from 1940 to 1980 yields an income elasticity of the VSL of 1.5 to 1.7.[7]

As these estimates using several different approaches indicate, regardless of the methodology used, the overall result is that higher income levels raise the VSL. Although the studies differ in terms of the magnitude of the relationship, the floor on the elasticity value across these different studies is positive and at least 0.5.

For the most part, these income elasticity estimates are based on US VSL studies. International estimates of income elasticity may be different because these countries often have quite different income levels. Recent empirical estimates suggest that the income elasticity estimate for countries outside the United States is around 1.0 so that a percentage change in income leads to identical percentage change in the VSL.[8]

Dealing with Contemporaneous Income Differences

Incorporating contemporaneous income differences in policy assessments for risk exposures has an economic efficiency rationale. The willingness to pay for benefits of policies that reduce fatality risks increases with the income level of those being protected by these policies. Based on the usual economic efficiency criteria underlying benefit-cost analysis, recognition of such income-related differences is quite pertinent. However, whereas accounting for income differences across time is viewed as being innocuous, adjustment for contemporaneous income differences in the VSL has generated strident policy debates.

To frame the subsequent discussion, let me summarize my policy perspective. From the standpoint of economic efficiency, recognizing income-related variations in the VSL has a strong economic efficiency justification. In situations in which the beneficiaries of the government policy are paying for the cost of the policy, having the VSL reflect their income levels also should have broad appeal. Use of an income-adjusted VSL will match the stringency and costs of safety policies with the preferences of the beneficiary income group within a country or when transferring VSL estimates across countries. In each instance, those benefitting from the policy are footing the bill, and the VSL is adjusted to reflect their preference.

When the policies are funded more broadly, income-based VSL levels may lead to the poor subsidizing policies for the rich. Doing so may be efficient but also is politically controversial. Whether it is worthwhile to make such distinctions depends on the extent of the efficiency gains and income inequities created by the policy funding. If the policy is funded by general revenues and the income tax structure is progressive, the net result may not be redistribution to the more affluent. Nevertheless, there may be substantial opposition to making such distinctions.

A politically expedient approach is to use a single VSL across all income groups when the beneficiaries of the policy are not paying for the improved safety. Doing so in effect serves as an implicit form of income distribution toward the poor. As I will indicate in the subsequent discussion, the critical context for which income-based distinctions are needed is not so much for domestic policies but for international applications of the VSL.

The most frequent counterargument to accounting for income variations in the VSL is that lower-income people are willing to pay high amounts for improved safety, but they lack financial resources and simply don't have the ability to pay. According to this line of argument, if the ability to pay were equalized across the population, they too would value risk reductions quite highly. Unfortunately, such income-equalization thought experiments do not reflect the world in which we live or citizens' preferences across a broad range of matters. Nor would it be sensible to shape policies from the vantage point of assuming that everyone had the preferences of more affluent citizens. If everyone had financial resources equal to those of Bill Gates, there are many choices that would be altered, including whether it was worthwhile to earn income through potentially dangerous employment. Nobody with such financial resources would be willing to work at any jobs posing even minimal risks or that on balance were unpleasant in any respect. Making policies based on the assumption that everyone was endowed with the assets of a billionaire would lead to bizarre policy prescriptions that would not be consistent with the preferences of lower-income citizens who must make political and private choices based on their current financial situation rather than mythical alternatives. Even assuming that everyone was endowed with average income would make many risky pursuits unattractive, such as commercial fishing operations and high-rise construction work. Policies that are based on preferences that people would have if they had different resources than they currently do will lead to policy outcomes that don't enhance their welfare as they perceive it based on the resources they currently have at hand.

Targeting policies to benefit the rich also would generate substantial resistance. Should, for example, government agencies be more concerned with pollution that affects more affluent neighborhoods than poorer sections of town? In situations where the funding for such efforts is publicly provided, such distinctions may not appear to be compelling. However, policies that reflect the preferences of the more affluent citizens but are valued less by those with lower income levels may not mirror the choices that the less-affluent citizens would prefer to make if they could reallocate public funds. Forward-collision warning systems, automatic emergency braking, and lane-keeping assist emerged as standard features or options in higher-end vehicles, not entry-level cars. Just as not all car purchasers want to pay for every safety device upgrade that is included in luxury cars, they similarly would prefer to have government policies that better address their preferences. Using general revenues to confer targeted risk reduction benefits on more affluent groups represents a situation in which the gainers could potentially compensate the losers. Once compensation is actually paid and is not simply a potential payment, the process of making income-related distinctions becomes more compelling. Developing a policy portfolio in which there are multiple components may facilitate the compensation of losers so that everyone can benefit from the entire menu of policies. Fortunately, government officials don't routinely deal with policies in which there are considerable income-group disparities in their risk impacts. Most policies, such as environmental standards and regulations that improve transportation networks, have effects that cut across society.

A prominent situation in which there is such targeting and where I advocated recognition of income differences is that of airline safety.[9] The impetus for my recommendation in the 1990s that the FAA be permitted to use higher VSL estimates than the rest of the DOT was twofold. First, the VSL used by DOT was well below a reasonable value, but branches of the DOT dealing with auto safety standards were under pressure from the automobile industry to maintain a low VSL to discourage additional government regulation. If these other branches were going to adhere to arbitrarily low values because of branch-specific political pressures, then it made no sense to constrain the FAA to undermine its regulatory efforts by using an inadequate VSL. Second, even if a lower VSL for matters such as auto safety were well founded, the VSL valuations of airline passengers merited an upward VSL adjustment, which did not pose equity concerns given the nature of the regulatory costs.

The rationale for a higher VSL for the FAA did not appear to be controversial. The average airline passenger has a higher income level than the average person protected by improved guardrails on highways. Based on these differences, in my work for the FAA, I calculated an income-adjusted VSL and advocated that the agency be permitted to apply a higher VSL than did the other branches of DOT to reflect airline passengers' greater VSL. The airline regulation situation was one in which regulations did not entail public funds being expended to subsidize the well-being of airline passengers. Rather, the regulations establish requirements that will affect the costs incurred by the airlines, which in turn will raise ticket prices. In effect, the passengers will be paying for the improved safety. Though airline profitability may also be affected by the regulatory requirements, setting these regulations based on the VSL levels pertinent to airline passengers will simply replicate the levels of safety that the airline should provide based on passengers' valuation of the safety. What is perhaps most pertinent is that none of the regulatory costs are shifted to the non-airplane-passenger segments of society. Consequently, concerns about the policies generating income inequities are irrelevant. However, failing to have policies that reflect the higher value of safety of airline passengers does them a disservice, does not benefit the citizenry at large, and will fail to deliver the safety levels that airline passengers are willing to pay for.

A similar kind of rationale applies to companies selling products targeted to high-income groups. Producers of luxury automobiles are selling their products to consumers who have very high income levels and much greater VSL levels. When assessing whether the company has met its obligation to manufacture a product that strikes a suitable balance between safety and risk, the applicable VSL should be the income-adjusted level as that value reflects how much the consumers of that product would be willing to pay for safety improvements if they were cognizant of the car's safety features. In the case of cars marketed to a broad consumer base, the pertinent VSL would be the average VSL across the population, just as in the case of government regulations that have widespread impacts.

What if instead a company marketed its cars to lower-income consumers? Would the company then be justified in using a below-average VSL when deciding on the safety measures for the cars? Mass-marketed products such as cars are not produced for particular individuals but are sold to the general public and are subject to re-sale, including potential purchasers with higher income levels. They might reasonably expect that all cars meet the usual government safety standards and that firms incorporate safety features consis-tent with the levels of safety provided by that country's government regulations, which are based on the average VSL for the population. Reducing the VSL below the average VSL when making automo-bile safety decisions consequently would be inconsistent with these expectations.

Dealing with International Differences

Income levels play a central role with respect to international com-parisons. Would we expect the VSL to be the same in India, Taiwan, Chile, and Poland as in the United States? Of course not. Some labor market estimates of the VSL for India, for example, are in the range of $1.4–$1.9 million (in 2015 dollars).[10] Even within the United States, the VSL has risen over time as society has become more affluent. The VSL is not a universal constant but will vary across countries based on differences in income levels and risk-taking proclivities.[11] Following the US reliance on labor market estimates, one might also turn to country-specific labor market estimates of the VSL. There has been an increasing number of such studies across the world, generally yielding estimates that are broadly consistent with overall expectations that the VSL levels should exceed the present value of lost earnings. These studies are subject to two potential shortcom-ings that impede such efforts to use country-specific empirical es-timates. First, the fatality risk and employment data used to derive market-based estimates in these other countries are not as reliable as are US data series. If the data are particularly inadequate, it may be preferable to utilize well-run stated-preference survey valuations of VSL in the absence of appropriate country-specific estimates. Second, the existence of relatively high US estimates frequently leads to publication selection biases in which researchers in other countries may use the US VSL levels as a target that their estimates should meet, leading to the possibility of upwardly biased estimates. We explore these issues in chapter 8. As a result, extrapolation of VSL estimates using US estimates coupled with income adjustments is a sounder approach.

An excellent starting point for estimating the VSL in other countries is to apply the US VSL internationally after making an income elasticity adjustment. This adjustment might not be an adjustment based on the average income elasticity across the population, but may be tailored to the income elasticity at the income level that is pertinent to the population of interest. Recognition of income elasticity differences is particularly pertinent for countries with very low levels of income, for which empirical estimates suggest that the elasticity may exceed 1.0.

Here I will use an average estimate of the income elasticity of the VSL outside the United States, which is about 1.0. What would extrapolation of these US estimates to project the magnitudes of the VSL in other countries imply both about the VSL levels in these countries and the appropriateness of the VSL estimates that these countries use in policy analyses? While one might expect that such downward income-based adjustments in the US VSL would greatly undervalue fatality risks to those outside the United States, compared to the values these countries currently use, the opposite pattern is observed. Figure 6.1 summarizes the estimates for fifteen countries, using an income elasticity of 1.0 and a baseline VSL of $10 million. The projected VSL estimate for the United Kingdom would be $7.1 million, which is much greater than the $2.4 million UK policy value for fatality risks addressed by transport regulations and the $2.1 million UK policy value for fatality risks reduced for floods.[12] The VSL estimate for Canada of $7.6 million also exceeds a

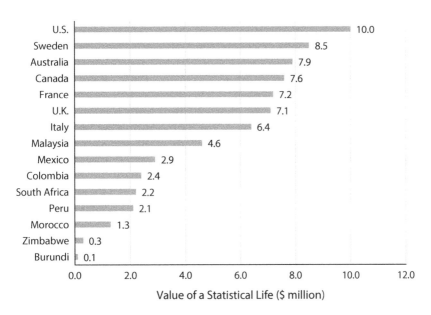

FIGURE 6.1. International Estimates of the VSL

recent policy value of $5.6 million, and there is a greater discrepancy for Australia, which has a projected VSL of $7.9 million as compared with a current policy value of $3.5 million. There is also an especially large discrepancy for Mexico. While Mexico's comparatively lower income levels lead to a projected VSL of only $2.9 million, a recent policy application in Mexico used a VSL of $0.9 million. Similarly, the estimated VSL of $4.6 million for Malaysia exceeds the policy value of $1.0 million, the $2.4 million figure for Colombia exceeds the policy value of $0.9–$1.0 million, and the $2.1 million value for Peru exceeds the policy value of $1.6 million. Other VSL estimates in figure 6.1 reflect plausible patterns with very high VSL levels in countries such as Sweden. There are very low VSL levels in extremely poor countries such as Burundi, where the gross national income per capita is $730, as compared with $57,540 in the United States. While income-based differences make the projected VSL lower in countries outside the United States, there is strong evidence that countries outside the United States greatly undervalue risks to life.

International VSL estimates are often derived from stated-preference studies, which as chapter 2 observes, generally lead to lower values. The extent of the differences are apparent when examining the VSL estimates for the World Bank income groups.[13] Low-income economies with a gross national income (GNI) per capita of $1,026, such as Malawi, have a VSL of $0.18 million based on my estimates and values ranging from $0.05 million to $0.10 million using OECD and World Bank estimates. For lower-middle-income economies with GNI per capita of $4,036, such as Ghana, my VSL estimate is $0.70 million, whereas the OECD and World Bank range is $0.27–$0.38 million. For medium-income countries with a GNI per capita of $12,476, such as South Africa, my VSL estimate is $2.17 million, as compared with an OECD and World Bank range of estimates from $1.16 to $1.65 million. Even with substantial adjustments for international income differences, use of the $10 million baseline US figure from the CFOI labor market estimates coupled with an income elasticity of 1.0 generates consistently higher VSL estimates throughout the world.

The lower levels of the VSL in other countries have additional implications as well. In particular, one would not expect these countries to have the same rigorous health, safety, and environmental standards as does the United States. Former Secretary of the Treasury and Harvard University President Larry Summers famously generated controversy by suggesting in a memorandum that was intended to be sarcastic that toxic wastes should be unloaded to the lowest wage countries because they are most willing to bear such risks.[14] His fundamental point that there are legitimate differences across countries in their valuations of safety is certainly on target, if excessively blunt. How policies should incorporate such concerns becomes more nuanced than simply exporting all the hazards to less advanced countries.

Are there reasonable ways by which US policies might recognize the potential differences in VSL across countries? A protectionist position would be to ban all imports not produced in a manner that is in compliance with US health, safety, and environmental regulations or perhaps the regulations of other more advanced economies, such as the European Union or OECD nations. These proposals serve largely to maintain the wages of the more affluent workers whose interests are being protected by the restrictions but may do little to advance the well-being of those in very low-income countries for whom the basic aspects of survival are at risk. The more appropriate standard for judging the acceptability of risk standards in other countries is whether the current policies are consistent with efficient regulatory policies that would emerge if safety standards reflected that population's VSL. It is highly likely that many of the extreme hazards, such as the textile factory fire in Bangladesh that killed 112 workers, may violate safety norms there as well as the standards that would emerge if their regulatory policies reflected the VSL in more affluent countries.[15] Such extreme violations of safety standards that are clearly inconsistent with that society's VSL levels are a more compelling basis for putting pressures on these countries than making judgments from the US perspective of a richer foreign country. In this as in all other instances, the task is to respect the preferences of those directly affected by the safety standards rather than to impose our perhaps quite different preferences.

Dealing with Income Differences over Time

Income differences across time have created fewer challenges for policy. The temporal increase in societal income levels coupled with the positive income elasticity of VSL have contributed to the increased valuation of safety over time. The emergence of health, safety, and environmental regulations in the 1970s in the United States rather than in less developed countries was a reflection of the higher levels of affluence in the United States, which in turn boosts societal valuations of risk and the demand for greater levels of safety. Safety improvements are not simply the result of exogenous regulatory policies or technological innovations that are on automatic pilot. Consumer and public pressures for greater safety levels will accompany increases in societal income levels over time.

Taking into account the temporal variation of the VSL with income levels has become a standard practice at government agencies.

Rather than continually updating estimates of the VSL based on new labor market estimates of the VSL, agencies primarily rely on selected historical sets of VSL estimates and meta-analyses of the VSL. Agencies, such as the EPA and DOT, then update these estimates for changes in societal income levels.[16] The EPA updates the VSL based on the growth in real (inflation-adjusted) income and assuming an income elasticity of the VSL of 0.5, while the DOT bases its updates on real income growth in median weekly earnings and currently assumes an income elasticity of 1.0.[17] Although worker wages can fluctuate downward during recessions, the long-run temporal trend has been that of rising wage levels, which government agencies have taken into account by boosting the agency's VSL upward over time. It was in part because of the general practice of consistently raising the VSL with rising societal affluence that the 2008 reduction in the VSL by the EPA Air Office was such an unexpected government action.

While these adjustments in the VSL to account for changes in societal income levels entail only short-run updates, it is also possible to undertake longer-term adjustments as well. How, for example, should we value risks to lives in future generations? This type of question often arises with respect to policies with very long time horizons, such as policies directed at global climate change. But they are also quite pertinent to evaluation of capital investments with nearer-term payoffs that extend over several decades, such as dams and other flood prevention structures. The application of societal discount rates to future benefits can greatly diminish the present value of the benefits of future mortality risk reductions. Taking into account the offsetting influence of the growth in the VSL dampens this depressing effect by applying a net discount rate equal to the interest rate less the annual growth rate in the VSL.

Consider the following two examples based on a government discount rate of 3 percent. For a contemporaneous VSL of $10 million, the present value of a single expected life that will be saved is $4.1 million if the policy effect is thirty years away and only $520,000 for policies with impacts that are one hundred years in the future. However, the use of a discount rate embodies an assumption that there is some underlying rate of economic productivity, where a large component is the increase in labor productivity. If the VSL is increasing over time by 2 percent annually because of increased societal affluence, the net effective discount rate to be applied to future VSL values is 3 percent minus the 2 percent growth in the VSL, or a discount rate of 1 percent. Using a 1 percent discount rate rather than 3 percent leads to a VSL in thirty years that has a present value of $7.4 million and a VSL in one hundred years with a present value of $3.7 million. Accounting for the growth rate in the VSL that is implicit in the same assumptions that give rise to the discount rate greatly boosts the value of deferred risk reductions. In the extreme case in which the VSL is rising at a rate of 3 percent annually, the role of any discounting drops out of the analysis, as the present value of the applicable VSL at a point in the future is a value of $10 million irrespective of the time of the mortality risk reduction.

Nuclear Waste Storage and the Very Distant Future

The powerful influence of discounting is evident with respect to assessment of the long-term risks averted through nuclear waste storage efforts. Time horizons such as one hundred years are not entirely hypothetical when dealing with long-term risks such as global warming, but a century may be just the beginning of the pertinent time range government analysts considered for nuclear wastes. The United States embarked on an effort to promote safer nuclear waste storage in a central location rather than having this waste dispersed throughout the country in less secure, decentralized locales. The proposed site the EPA analyzed for nuclear waste storage was Yucca Mountain, Nevada, which is located about one hundred miles northwest of Las Vegas.[18] The risk to residents and visiting tourists would be negligible, as the nuclear waste depository would be 300 meters underground, leaving 350 meters between the water table and the repository. The focus of the EPA's analysis was on the risk that the site would pose to a hypothetically exposed individual in the next 10,000 years or possibly even further in the future. This time frame exceeds all of recorded human history and will certainly include substantial unforeseen technological progress that would reduce any risk. Despite this incredibly long-term perspective, the US Court of Appeals for the DC Circuit ruled against the agency with respect to the time frame, claiming that 10,000 years was too short a period to consider.[19] The EPA's policy analysis considered Yucca Mountain in the abstract and completely ignored the reduction in risk levels that would result from Yucca Mountain storage. The current decentralized storage approach poses much greater risks than does Yucca Mountain. Setting aside this oversight in the analysis, what is the present value of a case of cancer to someone exposed at Yucca Mountain in 10,000 years? Based on a 3 percent discount rate, the present number of cases corresponding to a discounted case of cancer in 10,000 years is $(1/1.03)^{10,000}$, or 4.2×10^{-129}. If a case of cancer is valued at $10 million, the present value of a case of cancer in 10,000 years would only be 4.2×10^{-122}. Even if the entire current US population was crammed into Yucca Mountain and exposed to a lethal level of risk, the present value of the mortality reduction benefits would be negligible. Making an adjustment for hypothesized income growth of 2 percent over time, which in turn dampens the discounting effect, boosts the present value of the VSL but not enough to generate nontrivial benefit values. When valued at a VSL of $10 million, the discounted value of a case of cancer in 10,000 years is only 5.5×10^{-30}. Effects more than 10,000 years away drop out of any analysis based on present values.

Rather than attempt a meaningful assessment of the benefits and costs, the EPA took a different approach divorced from any concern that the benefits should bear some relation to the cost. Even though the agency made no claim that people would actually be exposed to the risk or have a significant probability of exposure to the subterranean waste, it based the analysis instead on exposure levels of people who might hypothetically be exposed in the distant future. The EPA standard that they wanted Yucca Mountain to meet was a maximum hypothetical exposure of 15 millirems per year for the next 10,000 years and a maximum dose of up to 350 millirems from 10,000 years to 1 million years. These were entirely arbitrary technological targets. There was no analysis indicating that ensuring that nobody had exposure levels in excess of these amounts made economic sense. To put these hazards in perspective, the average background radiation risk from residents in the high altitude state of Colorado is 700 millirems per year, which is double the radiation level EPA regarded as permissible after at least 10,000 years.[20] While it is likely that political opposition to the Yucca Mountain storage approach was the driving force that led to this effort being stymied rather than any meaningful attempt to balance benefits and costs, examination of this policy effort brings to the forefront the potential importance and long-term intergenerational perspectives that may influence policy decisions. Unfortunately, the centralized nuclear waste storage possibility still languishes, with the results being that nuclear waste is being stored throughout the country at sites posing risks that dwarf those that would ever be posed by Yucca Mountain.

When agencies contemplate policies with impacts extending hundreds and thousands of years into the future, intergenerational benefit valuation procedures become critical matters of concern. Dealing with such complications need not paralyze attempts at systematic analysis. Application of the fundamental principles for assessing the VSL clarifies these aspects of the analysis. Sensitivity analyses can examine how different assumptions regarding discount rates, income growth, and income elasticities come into play. A potentially greater danger than an imperfect analysis is that the intergenerational component of the analysis will either lead to a disregard of long-term effects or the paralysis of all meaningful attempts to take action to address risks that have a long-term component.

Limited Policy Application of Intertemporal Updates

Interestingly, the application of intertemporal adjustments to the VSL based on changes in income levels has not generated policy controversies, perhaps because all the changes are positive and also tend to be short-term adjustments to current VSL levels rather than projections into the distant future. Routine updates to make the currently applied VSL estimates reflect the values of the population that now has a higher income level than before are a fairly innocuous change. Updating future values of VSL to reflect how their VSL levels will differ simply applies the same principle. The economic task is to ensure that the levels of VSL in the benefit-cost calculation reflect the preferences of the population being protected, whether that population is the current population, a population thirty years from now, or a population a century or more from now.

However, the adjustment that updates the VSL for future generations also implies that the inflation-adjusted income levels in the future will be greater than today, which has implications regarding the perceived equity of the benefit assessments. If a 2 percent annual growth rate in both income levels and the VSL is assumed based on an assumption that the VSL is proportional to income, then the projection of VSL into the future implies that income of the population in one hundred years is 7.2 times greater than it is today. As a result, if policymakers are asking the current generation to pay for these programs, then in effect, the relatively poor current generation will be making sacrifices to benefit a much more affluent future generation. In much the same way that it may seem bizarre to have asked late-nineteenth-century citizens who didn't have indoor plumbing, paved roads, or long life expectancies to sacrifice their welfare to promote our well-being, an outside observer might view it as inequitable that our current generation sacrificed their well-being to promote that of much wealthier future generations.[21]

Opponents of these lines of argument have suggested that future generations really won't be better off because of the depletion of natural resources and the adverse long-term impacts on the environment resulting from choices made by the current generation, such as global climate change. Economic analyses that hypothesize that long-run productivity will decline because the rate of innovation will diminish are in a similar spirit.[22] If these changes do in fact dampen future income growth, then it would be inappropriate to assume an annual growth rate in the VSL such as 2 percent, which would reduce the role that the VSL plays in analyses of longer-term impacts unless one also reduced the discount rate to reflect the decline in productivity.

As in the case of age adjustments in the VSL, the tailoring of the VSL to the preferences of future generations may involve equity issues as well as efficiency concerns. Adopting an efficiency-based approach tied to the willingness of the policy beneficiaries to pay for the benefits is most straightforward and easiest to implement. Once the focus turns to equity, the nature of the equity discussion is less compelling and brings the discussion back to the first principles of benefit-cost analysis, which is that policy benefits should be tied to the willingness of beneficiaries to pay for the benefits.

Being Richer Is Safer

That people who are more affluent are generally healthier and have longer life expectancies is well established and has additional implications for policy evaluation criteria. The relationship between income and life expectancy has bearing on income-related ramifications of regulatory expenditures. The imposition of regulatory costs in effect will make people poorer by diverting funds that could have been used for other purposes, such as better housing and health care, to support the costs of the regulatory policy. There is an opportunity cost associated with regulatory expenditures. Regulatory initiatives also have beneficial effects on health and safety, as that is their intended objective, but the associated opportunity costs have an adverse effect by diverting funds that could be used for welfare-enhancing purposes.

Consider the extreme case in which the regulation imposes costs but yields zero benefits. No health and safety benefits are derived from this activity, but the cost of the zero-benefits regulation diverts funds from more productive forms of expenditures. Because of the positive relationship between wealth and health, this loss of financial resources has an adverse health effect on society. There are no offsetting health benefits from completely worthless regulatory efforts, so that on balance the purported health and safety regulation will have adverse health impacts.

While the zero-benefits regulation example is not among government agencies' regulatory initiatives, many regulatory policies are not far removed from the zero-benefit level, as they have only minimal direct beneficial risk impacts. Due to restrictive legislative mandates that limit agencies' ability to strike a balance between benefits and costs, the regulatory costs per expected life saved sometimes exceed $100 million, $1 billion, or more. Interestingly, extremely ineffective regulations that do little to save lives on balance may have a counterproductive impact, even if fostering health irrespective of cost is our policy objective. The analyses that address this linkage have received designations such as health-health analysis and risk-risk analysis, in recognition that what is at stake is the net safety-related consequences of policy.

The initial policy applications of this exploration of counterproductive risk effects were in two different venues. In a court case involving Occupational Safety and Health Administration regulations, DC Circuit Judge Stephen Williams speculated that the net effects of the regulation might be adverse based on the counterproductive health impact of ineffective regulatory expenditures.[23] A second context in which the counterproductive risk effect was raised was in a letter from the administrator of the US Office of Management and Budget to OSHA.[24] The press accounts regarding this exchange failed to appreciate the underlying soundness of the OMB arguments but instead characterized the OMB concerns as making the seemingly bizarre argument that health and safety regulations kill people.

Unfortunately, there is considerable truth to OMB's seemingly misguided concern. The fundamental question is what level of cost per expected life saved will lead to a net counterproductive effect of the regulation. Is it $10 million, $50 million, $100 million, or some higher number? The counterproductive level of expenditures depends on how effective increases in income are in reducing mortality rates. If there is substantial responsiveness, the counterproductive expenditure level will be much lower.

The practical difficulty is that getting a handle on this relationship is not straightforward. More income may buy better health, but improved health status also boosts one's income. Disentangling the interdependence of these relationships has created empirical challenges. As a result, early estimates of the cost-per-life-saved cutoff before expenditures became counterproductive were often relatively low, on the order of $5 million to $20 million.[25] These fairly low values had the quite stunning implication that with the exception of DOT policies and a small group of other very effective regulations, the net health effects of the regulatory policies would be counterproductive. Well-intended health, safety, and environmental regulations on balance were killing more people than they saved because they were so ineffective.

This startling result hinged on the relatively low cost-per-life-saved threshold after which expenditures became counterproductive. The low cost-per-life-saved level at which counterproductive impacts would occur struck me as implausible in that some of these estimates were not dramatically different from the estimates of VSL. The study cited by Judge Williams indicated that expenditures with a cost per life saved of at least $21.1 million (in 2015 dollars) would have a counterproductive effect. Was it really the case that spending about double the level of VSL would induce adverse health effects so that on balance the policy would be counterproductive? If that is the case, even at cost-per-life-saved expenditures below that level, there is a substantial risk-increase offset that diminishes the beneficial consequences of any mortality risk reduction efforts. Such counterproductive effects would mean that for the entire range of risk reduction choices that people make, the efficacy of such expenditures is much less than they think based on their direct effect. The result may be that safety efforts at best may be a breakeven proposition.

But how could it be that the true VSL for saving lives is similar to the value that leads to the loss of a life? Resolving this apparent contradiction requires a different conceptual approach. Somewhat surprisingly, the level of the VSL played no role in early conceptual approaches to ascertaining the level of expenditures that was counterproductive, as these relied on brute-force direct estimates of the health-income relationship. It is more instructive to develop a theoretical relationship that specifies the linkage that the VSL and the cost-per-life-saved counterproductive cutoff should have. This linkage is quite direct. The cost-per-life-saved amount that will lead to a counterproductive effect equals the VSL divided by the marginal propensity to spend out of income on health.[26] Based on a marginal propensity to spend on health of 0.1, the counterproductive cutoff value is simply ten times the value of the VSL. With a VSL estimate of $10 million, at expenditures of $100 million or more per expected life saved, the net health effects of the regulation become negative. Other refinements of this approach suggest that the cutoff could be somewhat lower.[27] Counterproductive expenditure levels such as this are more plausible in that they are sufficiently higher than the estimated VSL so that not all safety-enhancing efforts are worthless from the standpoint of promoting health.

As a rough rule of thumb, expenditures of $100 million or more per expected life saved are in the zone of regulatory expenditures that do more harm than good even if all that matters are the health effects of the regulation. Having such a cutoff may appear to be unnecessary. If policies were subject to any kind of reasonable benefit-cost test, we would never see any regulations that were so ineffective that the cost per expected life saved reached such values. Recent regulatory initiatives have sought to strike a more sensible benefit-cost balance than the earlier regulatory cost outliers. However, some of the most costly regulatory policies are not bound by the executive order that benefits exceed costs for all major regulations because the existence of restrictive statutory mandates exempts them from this test. In addition, many government policies do not involve the promulgation of any new regulations but instead deal with the implementation and administration of existing policies, such as choosing which hazardous waste sites merit cleanup.

Policy Prognosis

There is considerable empirical evidence that the VSL increases with income, possibly less than proportionally, but still to a substantial degree. What to do with this body of literature is not as well defined. Applying the VSL estimates in any policy context is intrinsically controversial so that it is understandable that policymakers are often reluctant to fine-tune the VSL for different income levels. The principal context in which this approach has been adopted without much fanfare is with respect to updates to the VSL in which past estimates are brought forward to the present time to account for increases in income levels over time.

Just as in the case of dealing with age-related sensitivities for which using the average VSL for the population is often a reasonable approach, it is likely that broadly based policies and products can be assessed using an average VSL for the population rather than making the VSL income-specific. Those with higher than average income will value the risk reduction by more than the VSL, and those with lower than average income will value safety by less than the VSL. Mass-marketed consumer products that are sold to diverse population groups and government policies with broad impacts typically can do no more than promote societal well-being on average.

There may, however, be some unusual situations in which efforts to alter the risk levels will have quite different effects across the population. As unpleasant as the task may be, it is inevitable that some decisions may have to be made with respect to income-related differences. Contexts in which the beneficiaries are paying for the risk reduction, such as airline passengers and purchasers of luxury vehicles, are those for which there is a compelling rationale for incorporating any differences in preferences based on income.

Even when beneficiaries are not paying for the policy, when policies affect different income groups disproportionately, the efficient valuation approach is to use the income-adjusted VSL. However, political expediency may require use of an undifferentiated VSL, thus providing a form of income redistribution to the poor.

Coupling the US VSL estimates with income adjustments to establish international VSL levels might seem to raise similar equity concerns. However, the policy impact of such a procedure is to raise the VSL throughout the world. As was previously the case for the United States, there is a systematic international tendency to undervalue lives. Coupling my VSL estimate with income adjustments leads to higher VSL estimates and more protective policies than under current government practices in other countries, such as the United Kingdom, or the VSL levels following guidance from international bodies, such as the OECD and the World Bank.

How we should address VSL levels for impacts in the future also raises income-related concerns as society continues to become richer. Government agencies routinely update the VSL to account for increases in income levels, and assessment of policy benefits in the distant future reflect the policy benefits that will be derived by these people. Even though such boosting of the VSL for temporally remote benefits represents a transfer to more affluent future generations, there is a strong efficiency rationale for doing so. Moreover, unlike contemporaneous income differences, placing a high value on future benefits may encounter less political opposition.

The choice of the VSL for valuing distant future impacts and international safety standards also is tied to the income-VSL relationship. Because the VSL of future generations is greater than that today, and the applicable VSL in other countries typically would increase the value currently placed on safety in these countries, the well-established aversion to decreases in the VSL does not enter as a barrier to applying an appropriate VSL across time or across countries. Doing so will, however, raise other equity concerns, such as whether the current generation should provide benefits to the more affluent future generations. Whether efficiency-based policies accord with notions of fairness and risk equity requires a broader exploration of equity concerns, which is the focus of the next chapter.

7

Promoting Risk Equity through Equitable Risk Tradeoffs

Equity as a Policy Concern

Policy debates often frame regulatory issues in terms of equity rather than efficiency. Is it fair to value the lives of older people less than the lives of their younger counterparts? Is it fair to value the lives of the rich more than the lives of the poor? The role of such equity issues has been particularly prominent with respect to environmental equity. As the discussion in the previous two chapters indicated, resolving these equity considerations is often problematic since there may be no clear-cut solution to deciding what is fair. And conceptualizing the issue in terms of fairness may obscure the more fundamental safety objective of matching policies with the preferences of those affected by the policies. This chapter provides a different equity approach grounded in equitable risk tradeoff rates. This policy framework is a more compelling conceptualization of what it means for risks to be equitable.

My first encounter with environmental equity concerns occurred when I lived in North Carolina in the early 1990s. Orange County, North Carolina, was searching for the site of a new landfill to serve as the county garbage dump. The existing landfill, which was located in a rural area, was becoming full so a new site was needed. Rather than continue to use farmland as the site for landfills, the avowed objective was to promote environmental equity by siting the new landfill outside of rural areas. The first recommended site for the landfill was an undeveloped area adjacent to one of the most expensive subdivisions in Chapel Hill, NC. I had a personal interest in the proposed site since the landfill would have been located less than 500 yards from my house. The landfill site would have depressed neighborhood property values and, in turn, would have diminished property tax revenues for the county. After a local real estate agent and I prepared an analysis that showed the substantial loss in property taxes that the county would experience by locating the landfill in this area, the county sought an alternative site. However, rather than utilize low-valued farmland, the choice was to designate a section of Duke Forest for the landfill. This forest was a pristine research preserve of the Duke University School of the Environment. Seizing this land as the site was an environmental atrocity, but purportedly equitable from a county-level perspective, as no farmland in the county would be affected. The politically expedient selection avoided the property tax loss and had no significant effect on Orange County residents but disadvantaged Duke University, which was an educational institution based in the adjacent Durham County.

Concerns with respect to equity have led to national policy mechanisms intended to promote health and environmental equity in federal policies but which often have not been more effective than this North Carolina landfill experience. In 1994 President Clinton issued Executive Order No. 12898—Federal Actions to Address Environmental Justice in Minority Populations and Low-Income Populations—which required agencies to achieve environmental justice by "identifying and addressing as appropriate, disproportionately high and adverse human health or environmental effects of its programs, policies, and activities on minority populations and low-income populations."[1] The executive order also established the Federal Interagency Working Group on Environmental Justice. The Office of Environmental Justice was subsequently established as a branch of the EPA to promote recognition of equity considerations and to monitor the equity-related impacts of environmental policies. A considerable academic literature also emerged dealing with these concerns under headings such as "environmental justice," "environmental racism," and "environmental equity."[2]

Equity concerns pertaining to risks are not limited to environmental policies. Population groups differ considerably in terms of the risks that they face. In some instances, the differences may be a direct consequence of risk-related threats, such as the mismanaged water treatment facilities in Flint, Michigan. In other cases, the difference in personal risks may stem from factors not directly tied to the risk exposure, such as poor education or bad nutrition. Should we give these people who are exposed to inordinate overall risks preferential treatment in other risk regulation policies to compensate for the disadvantaged status that stems from these broader influences? Or should the judgment of what is equitable be framed more narrowly? Which factors should count and which factors should not in assessing what is equitable? Does the level of risk matter, the reason why the risk level is that great, or the cost of reducing the risk?

Unfortunately, there is a myriad of possible conceptualizations of what is equitable. The purported equitable outcome will vary depending on how the equity issue is framed. The introduction of equity concerns into policy debates almost invariably pushes policies away from more sensible risk-cost balancing and is harmful to public welfare. Risk regulation efforts are similar to government expenditure programs in that there are often substantial income transfers that result from these efforts. Because there are always gainers and losers from government policies, it is usually possible for the potential gainers to advance the argument that providing special benefits to their group is equitable. The potential for such gains gives rise to rent-seeking behavior, as the parties who will be affected by policies expend resources to direct the impact of these policies to advance their own interests.

This chapter examines a variety of equity concepts that have been suggested and establishes a more principled methodology for addressing risk equity. In particular, I propose that risk equity be framed in terms of equitable risk tradeoffs whereby the expenditures per unit of risk reduction are equalized across the population. The focus on equitable risk tradeoffs includes recognition of both the level of the risk and the amount of total costs that is being allocated to reduce the risk. Application of the equitable risk tradeoffs approach to several of the most prominent alternative approaches to equity will demonstrate the ability of this conceptualization of equity to avoid the pitfalls of more narrowly framed notions of equity and to do more to advance conventional notions of environmental equity than do current policies.

The Equitable Risk Tradeoffs Approach

As a starting point, it is instructive to consider the situation in which everyone has an identical tradeoff between cost and risk. In the case of mortality risks, let everyone have the same VSL so that, for example, all people have a VSL of $10 million and, as a consequence, would be willing to pay $1,000 for a mortality risk reduction of 1/10,000. Individuals seeking to maximize their welfare when facing a continuous set of choices will have identical risk-cost tradeoffs across all different domains of choice—as reflected in the wages that they are paid for risky jobs, the additional price they are willing to pay to live in a safer neighborhood, and the health care expenditures they are willing to make to increase longevity. Otherwise, they could promote their health more effectively by boosting the efforts that deliver larger mortality risk reductions for less cost. In effect, individuals set their own price for safety based on their willingness to bear risk, and seek to equalize the risk tradeoff rate across all activities. The VSL establishes the price level for which safety measures make sense and which do not. If a worker is offered a wage for a risky job that implies a VSL of less than $10 million, it is not worth doing, and if the cost of producing a safer product exceeds $10 million per expected life saved, then that product is not desirable from a safety standpoint. Informed consumer decisions in well-functioning markets lead to appropriate matching of risky prospects with individuals' willingness to bear risk.

Whereas private decisions seek to align risky opportunities in a consistent manner, the cost per expected life saved for government policies ranges quite widely. Consider a set of 53 government risk regulations based on the cost per life saved.[3] For purposes of this discussion, let us assume that the pertinent VSL is $10 million in 2015 dollars. Note that the same results with respect to the efficiency of regulations also hold using somewhat different VSL estimates, such as a VSL of $9 million. For a cost-per-life-saved cutoff of $10 million, 25 of the 53 programs would have a cost per life saved that would pass an equitable risk tradeoffs test, and 28 of the 53 programs have a cost per life saved that exceeds $10 million. The sometimes-wide disparities in the regulatory costs per life saved create clearly inequitable tradeoffs. The groups that are the beneficiaries of government regulations that, for example, entail a cost of $100 million or more per expected life saved are being accorded a much more stringent level of protection than the typical motor vehicle passenger, as all twelve transportation regulations in this sample of regulations have a cost per expected life saved under $10 million.

To establish equity in regulatory protections, the objective should be to promote equitable risk tradeoffs across policies. Very cost-effective regulations should be strengthened to the point at which the cost per additional life saved reaches $10 million. There may, of course, be some situations in which the protections are lumpy so that marginal increases in stringency are not possible. For example, once aircraft floor emergency lighting has been installed, adding additional lighting may not enhance safety. But in other situations, such as automobile side-impact standards, recognition of a higher risk-cost tradeoff value could make doors with more structural integrity desirable. Similarly, application of a higher VSL might have led to earlier adoption of electronic stability control systems for autos. For policies at the upper end of the cost-per-life-saved distribution, a concern with promoting equitable risk tradeoffs will not necessarily mean that dangerous health exposures go unregulated. Rather, the permissible exposure limits for dangerous chemicals can be set at a less stringent level to be better aligned with the pertinent VSL. When there is such flexibility to adjust the stringency across policies, failure to promote equitable tradeoffs that seek to equalize the cost per life saved across policies will save fewer lives than would have been saved if these funds had been allocated in a cost-effective manner. Using the VSL as the reference point for the equitable risk tradeoff rate ensures that the policies will be in line with the expenditures that consumers would make if they were allocating their own funds.

Although one can envision refinements in the equitable risk tradeoffs approach, application of a uniform society-wide VSL is an excellent starting point for assessing most government policies. Public policies by their very nature tend to affect broad population groups. Consequently, utilization of an average VSL estimate from the literature is often very reflective of the average VSL that one would compute based on the distribution of risk preferences across the population affected by the regulation. In the following discussion, I will treat the average VSL in which the same risk-cost tradeoff is used for all members of society and all regulations as the presumptive reference point for establishing equitable tradeoffs. To justify departures from this symmetric situation, there must be a compelling rationale for doing so, such as those discussed below and in the previous chapters.

Legitimate Sources of Heterogeneity that May Matter

Age-related differences in VSL often figure prominently in discussions of heterogeneity because the duration of life at risk decreases with age. Based on the anticipated gains in life expectancy that the government is purchasing through risk reduction policies, there is a smaller benefit from reducing mortality risks to older populations. As the discussion in chapter 5 indicated, whether the issue is framed in terms of the value per statistical life or the value per statistical life year may affect how one's age affects the benefit assessment. But within the framework of relying on equitable risk tradeoffs, all that matters is the private valuation of risk, which need not be broken down into the cost per life year. If the person's VSL remains steady over the life cycle, then the policy-relevant VSL should also remain stable irrespective of the length of remaining life. The adjustments that one might make for age, with lower VSL levels at the upper end of the age distribution and even lower VSL levels for people in their late teens and early twenties, are more modest and may be in the opposite direction of what one would do based on a crude years of remaining life adjustment.

The other well-documented source of substantial heterogeneity in VSL is with respect to the income-VSL relationship. As the discussion in chapter 6 indicated, the low estimates of the income elasticity of VSL are in the range of 0.5–0.6 or greater, with international estimates being around 1.0, and some estimates of the income elasticity being even higher. If there are substantial differences in income levels across different regulatory policies, then it is likely that the pertinent VSL levels will differ as well. However, most regulations affect societal income groups broadly, and there is only a fairly small set of risk regulation efforts that have differential effects across income groups.

Airline safety regulations serve as noteworthy regulations with impacts that are targeted toward specific income groups. My analysis of the VSL for the FAA proposed an adjustment to the VSL estimates to account for the above-average income levels of airline passengers.[4] In situations where the regulatory costs will be borne by the program beneficiaries, such as through higher prices as in this case, I have proposed that income-related differences in valuation should be taken into account.[5] This approach does little more than ensure that government regulations achieve the same kind of equitable risk tradeoffs that would result if the passengers had the opportunity to purchase safety in a well-functioning market. Recognition of the higher VSL levels when beneficiaries are paying their own way may have broad political appeal, as the former administrator of OMB's Office of Information and Regulatory Affairs, Cass Sunstein, views these as the simple cases.[6] As discussed in chapter 6, matters become more complicated when the beneficiaries are not paying their own way but, instead, public funds are being used to finance the risk reduction.

What if the proposed policy will disproportionately affect the poor, who have below-average VSL levels? Is it equitable for the government to ignore their lower VSL and promulgate regulations that the poor cannot afford but will impose costs that they will be forced to incur? Prominent examples of this phenomenon involve the proposed application of US VSL levels and US safety standards to less-developed countries. The overall objective of policies should be to promote the expected welfare of the citizenry based on their preferences, assuming that they are cognizant of the risks. Mandating safety measures that impose costs on the beneficiaries that they would not choose to incur on their own will make them unambiguously worse off as they perceive their welfare.

While it may be interesting on a conceptual basis to explore income-based targeting of safety policies, in practice there are very few instances in which uncomfortable income-based distinctions must be made. Consider the quintessential example of environmental equity—people exposed to hazardous waste sites near their homes. Residential hazardous waste exposures have served as the most prominent case studies in the environmental justice literature. Interestingly, based on the effects of hazardous waste sites on property values, the average VSL for the cancer risks posed by these sites is not substantially lower than for the economy as a whole, but is in the same general range as labor market estimates of VSL.[7] Although one might expect that the people who live in these higher-risk neighborhoods would have a lower VSL, the empirical evidence fails to suggest a substantial discrepancy. Even applying the equitable risk tradeoff approach based on the target beneficiaries' VSL, there would be no rationale for departing from the use of average population VSL levels when valuing these cleanup efforts. Risk reduction policies should be equally aggressive in addressing hazardous waste risks as other targets of government regulation.

Other risk-taking behavior similarly indicates that there may be differences in the VSL across the population based on risk propensities, but they do not appear to be so great that these groups should be singled out for devaluing the risks to their lives. The greatest health risk that consumers incur on a large scale is that associated with smoking cigarettes, which poses a lifetime risk of death of 0.26, which is 2,600 times as great as the risk needed to trigger the cleanup of a hazardous waste site.[8] If smokers are in fact more willing to incur risks, as this behavior suggests, then one would expect their risk-taking decisions to differ in other substantial ways. In research with Joni Hersch, we found fairly consistent patterns in risk-taking behavior: "Compared to nonsmokers, male smokers are 16 percent less likely to wear their seatbelts, five percent less likely to check their blood pressure, and nine percent less likely to floss their teeth. They also are more likely to work on hazardous jobs and, for any given level of job riskiness, are more likely to be injured on these jobs. Moreover, they are more likely to be injured at home as well, incurring roughly double the home accident rate of nonsmokers. Quite simply, smokers are greater risk takers than are nonsmokers, and this willingness to bear risk is manifested across a wide range of personal activities."[9] Smokers also work on risky jobs for less additional compensation for nonfatal injury risks.[10] However, as is also the case for residents living near hazardous waste sites, there doesn't appear to be a stark difference in the labor market estimates of the VSL for smokers and nonsmokers.[11] Until there is more refinement in both the estimates of the VSL and the identification in regulatory impact analyses of populations with possibly different VSL levels, relying on average VSL estimates may remain a reasonable policy approach rather than trying to fine-tune the VSL based on the risk-taking propensities of the affected population.

Missing in Action: Situations in Which Markets Don't Provide Guidance

The economic theory underlying labor market estimates of the VSL assumes that workers have a broad set of available options and are cognizant of the risks. If, however, there are impediments to such decisions, such as labor market discrimination, then using the VSL based on the person's labor market decisions as the equitable risk tradeoff value does not provide appropriate guidance. In particular, the evidence suggests that there is frequently market segmentation in which disadvantaged groups do not have access to the same jobs as do other workers. A principal test for this phenomenon is whether the disadvantaged workers are incurring greater risks for less additional hazard pay than the additional risk premium amounts that more advantaged workers receive for lower risk levels. This test is met in the case of African American workers who incur higher job risks than do whites but receive less compensation for these risks, resulting in a lower implied VSL.

Detailed examination of the labor market treatment of immigrants demonstrates the potential shortcomings in market behavior.[12] Non-Mexican immigrants face fatality risks that are almost the same as those of native US workers. However, Mexican immigrants incur job-related fatality risks that are about 1.4 times as great as the risks faced by the average native US worker. The stylized image of immigrants taking on the most unattractive jobs in society is consistent with these statistics. However, while native US workers are compensated at a level that yields a VSL in a familiar range of $9–$10 million per statistical life, the estimates for Mexican immigrants show much less wage compensation for risk. The problems are especially acute for Mexican immigrants who are not fluent in English, as they receive no evident wage premiums for the substantial additional hazards that they face. While the government recognizes that non-English-speaking immigrants may face potential labor market problems in terms of occupational safety,[13] efforts to address these shortcomings have not yet been successful.

In instances such as these, utilization of the VSL methodology makes it possible to identify the profound failures of the labor market. Consequently, it would not be appropriate to use such misleadingly low estimates of the VSL as the equitable tradeoff rate for these groups. Instead, the market evidence provides a signal that there is a market failure and a government failure to adequately protect these workers.

Absolute Risks as the Risk Equity Measure

Discussions of risk equity may focus on whether the overall risk levels are equitable. Should all people face the same absolute risk level or some risk level below a target upper limit? Individuals differ in their susceptibility to disease and in their risk-related skills. The

lack of physical strength makes jobs with heavy lifting a more hazardous pursuit, and poor hearing and eyesight raise the risk of motor
vehicle injuries. Some risks vary systematically by gender.[14] Men face
higher risks of death from accidents and homicides, while women
are more susceptible to fatality risks from Alzheimer's disease, as
well as influenza and pneumonia. Other risks vary with age, as risks
of accidental drowning and mechanical suffocation are concentrated
among those aged 0–4, and people aged 75 and older are prone to
fatalities from falls. Sometimes assessments of risk equity are refined
to take into account factors such as gender and age. One might want
to inquire if people have the mortality risk that is expected based on
their gender and age, or if they are exposed to especially large risks.

Equalizing risks for all people even after making the risk assessments conditional on gender and age is not feasible or desirable. In
addition to genetic differences in physical characteristics and susceptibility to illness, people take numerous actions that influence
their mortality risks. These factors include where they choose to live,
whether they smoke, whether they engage in excessive drinking,
and what their dietary habits, exercise regimens, and occupational
risks are. Most of the resulting hazards are the consequence of individual choices. Presumably the quest for risk equity should be
accompanied by encouraging people to avoid high-risk exposures,
not to penalize people with particularly healthy lifestyles. We could
choose to promote the reduction of high-risk exposures by banning
or limiting risk-related activities, but doing so will often reduce the
intended beneficiaries' welfare as they perceive it.

The fundamental problem is that basing risk equity on an objective of equalizing absolute levels of risk is not a sensible basis for
policy. Focusing on a person's overall risk level is an entirely different
approach than a benefit-cost framework that inquires how a policy
can alter the risk, what it costs to reduce the risk, and whether that
cost is in line with the equitable risk tradeoff rate. Costs and preferences do not play the critical role that they should when the objective is to equalize absolute levels of risk. Rather than focusing on the
risk reduction gains that are achievable through policies, seeking
equity in absolute risk levels addresses the total magnitude of the

risk, which may bear little relation to what the policy achieves. Identifying particularly high-risk groups is sometimes useful in helping to locate problems that can be addressed through well-formulated policies, but basing policies on the absolute risk alone is not an appropriate guide to where we should spend our risk reduction funds.

Incremental Risks as the Equity Measure

Rather than focusing on absolute risks levels, policies often address incremental risks from a particular class of hazards or source of risk, such as radiation exposures for nuclear power plant workers. Even if we restrict our policy focus to incremental risks, it is not feasible to equalize these risks across the population. Floods are much more frequent in eastern, northeastern, and midwestern states, as compared with the relatively arid western states. Would it really be sensible to try to equalize the flood risk to residents of Arizona with homeowners near the banks of the Mississippi River? Similarly, the hazards from hurricanes are greater in New Orleans than Minnesota, and California is more prone to earthquakes. The greater risk of tornadoes in Kansas and other states located in Tornado Alley is a real phenomenon, not simply a fictional invention of *The Wizard of Oz*. Alaskans are less concerned with the risk of death from heat waves than Chicago residents, who experienced over 700 deaths in the heat wave of 1995. Equalizing these and other classes of risk that vary geographically is not feasible.

Similarly, equalization of incremental risks across all products and jobs is not a sensible basis for policies. Driving motor vehicles, downhill skiing, smoking tobacco products, scuba diving, playing football, and hang gliding all pose inherent risks. Similarly, high-rise construction work and coal mining are always going to pose greater hazards than more sedentary occupations. Seeking to achieve such equalization in incremental risks would be inordinately costly and ultimately futile.

Nevertheless, equalization or regulation of incremental risk levels often serves as the policy approach. Workers in nuclear power plants are limited to radiation exposures of 20 milliSieverts per year, and the

EPA sets the trigger for cleaning up hazardous waste sites at a lifetime cancer risk of 1/10,000. Similarly, the policy debate over storage of nuclear waste at Yucca Mountain focused on the increased risk from radiation exposures more than 10,000 years in the future rather than on the costs and the overall value of the total number of cancers that would occur with and without the Yucca Mountain facility.

Wholly apart from concerns relating to monetization of benefits, focusing on incremental risk probabilities rather than benefits is a misguided approach. What is missing from such a policy targeting strategy is any concern with the extent of the population at risk. The risk probability does take into account some influences such as the frequency and duration of exposure, as well as the nature of the dose-response relationship. But the total harm from any risk depends on the size of the population exposed to the risk. The total adverse health impact is based on the risk probability multiplied by the number of people exposed to that risk. That amount serves as the core of any benefits calculation, which can then be monetized using the VSL.

Equalizing Real versus Imaginary Risks

When policies are based on risk levels, should the focus be on the best scientific estimates of the risk or on the public's perception of the risks? If these public perceptions are the result of misplaced fears and alarmist responses, should they nevertheless serve as the policy guide? Public fears of plane travel, pesticide residues on produce, and low-probability events such as the risk of being killed in a terrorist attack often lead to exaggerated perception of the risks. Although I believe the emphasis should be on actual risks, there are advocates of respecting the public's risk beliefs in much the same way that economists generally advocate respecting the preferences of consumers.

Consider the following example based on an American Economic Association conference panel in which I advocated the reliance on actual probabilities, and Paul Portney made the case on behalf of perceived risks.[15] Suppose that the government faces the decision of which chemical waste site to clean up. The cost of cleanup is the same in each instance. In Portney's town of Happyville, the waste site poses no real risks but the population believes that one hundred people will die because of the chemical waste. In my neighboring town of Blissville, there is no public awareness of the risk, but in fact there will be one hundred cases of cancer that will occur if the site is not cleaned up. Cleaning up the Happyville site will create substantial perceived benefits, but no real health benefits, whereas cleaning up the Blissville site will create real risk reduction effects that will not be valued by the residents because they do not believe that the site poses any risk.

Pandering to fears of imaginary risks will not produce any actual health benefits but will squander societal resources, lending to the counterproductive risk effects predicted by the analyses relating to the "richer is safer" phenomenon. Advocates of cleaning up the Happyville site include not only some academics but also many government officials with whom I've discussed this approach. Giving priority to imaginary risks over real risks is not innocuous. It leads to a policy strategy that is a form of what I have called "statistical murder," as lives are being sacrificed to address mythical risks.

But shouldn't government policies nevertheless place substantial weight on the public's preferences and beliefs since in a democratic society the government should be responsive to the preferences and beliefs of the citizenry? EPA officials offered this justification to me when I criticized the focus on imaginary risks. These types of civics lesson rationales are not compelling. The government frequently makes decisions that override inaccurate risk beliefs of the citizenry. A principal rationale for much occupational safety regulation, product safety regulation, and consumer protection regulation is that people often underestimate the risks they face, and it is the task of government policy to address these inadequacies that will result. We should not refrain from intervening in these instances when people underestimate the true magnitude of the risks simply because they are ignorant of the hazards. Similarly, we should also target other interventions that will be the most welfare-enhancing based on an equitable risk tradeoff approach that is based on actual risks rather than perceived risks.

Equitable Hazardous Waste Policies

Consideration of the policy area where risk equity discussions have been most prominent—the cleanup of hazardous waste sites by the EPA Superfund program—illustrates the substantial pitfalls of departing from equitable risk tradeoffs coupled with a benefit-cost approach. There are many layers of flaws in the policy approach embodied in the EPA practices, so it is worthwhile to consider some of the most critical components and why the agency's risk-based approach is less protective and less equitable than the equitable tradeoffs approach.

> Lesson 1. Current policy priorities are less protective because they are based on calculated risk levels rather than comprehensive benefit assessments.

The trigger for hazardous waste cleanup is tied to incremental risk levels. Consideration of risk levels alone is an inadequate basis for targeting cleanups. Sites with an assessed individual lifetime cancer risk of 1/10,000 or greater merit cleanup based on agency criteria, and sites posing a lifetime cancer risk between 1/10,000 and one million are in the discretionary range. These probabilities do not in fact represent the actual risks but instead are the result of agency calculations in which the upper-bound values of various components of the calculation are used in estimating the risk levels.[16] However, for purposes of this discussion, let's set aside the upward biases in the risk assessments and assume that these probabilities do correspond to actual risks of cancer. What is missing from this policy approach other than a failure to also consider costs? Somewhat surprisingly, the number of people exposed to the risk never enters the policy assessment, whereas a benefit-cost approach would incorporate the impact on the exposed population in any benefit assessment.

The failure to incorporate the size of the population exposed to the risk is not an oversight, but is a conscious policy choice. EPA risk analyses are based on what officials call an "individual risk approach" in which the concern is whether there may be a risk exposure above the cutoff either now or in the future to any particular individual. In a study of Superfund that James T. Hamilton and I prepared for the EPA economic policy office, we advocated an approach incorporating the size of the population exposed to the risk.[17] However, the Superfund officials explicitly dismissed our benefit calculation procedure in which the number of people harmed mattered. They termed this the "population risk approach." One possible rationale for their individual risk approach is that they believe that providing protections for any single individual exposed to the risk is more protective than accounting for the scope of risk exposures. However, assessment of the total number of cases of cancer that will be averted should be quite pertinent to which sites most merit prompt cleanup. It surely matters if 1,000 people are exposed to a given risk or if only one person is exposed. For any given cleanup cost level, the greatest gains in expected welfare will accrue from cleaning up the sites that pose substantial risks to large exposed populations. Failure to consider population exposures leads to the prevention of fewer cases of cancer than would result from a more comprehensive methodology.

> Lesson 2. Agency practices that give equal weight to real and hypothetical future risks disadvantage current populations facing actual risks.

The second critical deficiency in the EPA policy is that real and hypothetical people count equally. A risk that might occur at some time in the future receives the same weight as a risk that actually affects current populations. This failure to focus on actual risks is a different variant of the Happyville residents being deluded by exaggerated perceived risks. In this instance, the problem is not that EPA has exaggerated perceptions of a risk, but rather that nobody may ever be exposed to the risk, either now or in the future. Real and hypothetical risks count equally in the agency's methodology. While these hypothetical risks are termed "future risks," they may not ever emerge as risks at all, even in the distant future. The presence of a calculated future risk does not assume that there will be an actual risk to some exposed population. Rather, the assessment of the site can include a future risk assessment if the analyst can envision some hypothetical future use of the land that might lead to future risk exposures. These so-called future risks, not current risks, comprise the dominant risks that are identified in the agency analyses and that serve as the principal basis for cleanup decisions.

Outsiders to the agency's practices might view the agency's analytical assumptions to be bizarre. Justice Breyer confronted a noteworthy example of mythical future risks in a hazardous waste case:

> Let me provide some examples. The first comes from a case in my own court, *United States v. Ottati & Goss*, arising out of a ten-year effort to force cleanup of a toxic waste dump in southern New Hampshire. The site was mostly cleaned up. All but one of the private parties had settled. The remaining private party litigated the cost of cleaning up the last little bit, a cost of about $9.3 million to remove a small amount of highly diluted PCBs and "volatile organic compounds" (benzene and gasoline components) by incinerating the dirt. How much extra safety did this $9.3 million buy? The forty-thousand-page record of this ten-year effort indicated (and all the parties seemed to agree) that, without the extra expenditure, the waste dump was clean enough for children playing on the site to eat small amounts of dirt daily for 70 days each year without significant harm. Burning the soil would have made it clean enough for the children to eat small amounts daily for 245 days per year without significant harm. But there were no dirt-eating children playing in the area, for it was a swamp. Nor were dirt-eating children likely to appear there, for future building seemed unlikely. The parties also agreed that at least half of the volatile organic chemicals would likely evaporate by the year 2000. To spend $9.3 million to protect non-existent dirt-eating children is what I mean by the problem of "the last 10 percent."[18]

Other examples of future risks that I have encountered were equally far-fetched. The risks that were hypothesized for one North Carolina site that we analyzed involved the possible construction of a factory on currently vacant land. If such a factory was built, might there be risks posed by the chemical waste? The analysts hypothesized that the waste could potentially contaminate a nearby creek and that during their breaks the workers at this hypothetical factory would go swimming in the creek and be exposed to the chemicals. Although I was on the Duke faculty in North Carolina for just over a decade, including some very hot days, I don't know of any workers who went swimming in nearby creeks to cool off.

> Lesson 3. Ignoring the size of the populations exposed to the risk disadvantages large exposed populations, including minorities and low-income groups.

The third problem with the current policy approach is that ignoring the size of the population actually exposed to risk leads to an evaluation approach that is inimical to any concern with environmental equity. Failing to place adequate weight on the populations currently exposed to the risk disadvantages minorities and the low-income groups that are the intended beneficiaries of the environmental equity movement. Who is most likely to have current hazardous waste risk exposures and to be exposed in close proximity to such risks in large numbers? Minorities are not disproportionately represented in a sample of populations in the general vicinity of the 150 Superfund sites that Hamilton and I examined.[19] However, minorities are much more likely to be exposed in close proximity to the risk, such as living within a mile of the site, and to more severe risks. Their exposures also are most likely to be in residential areas in which both children and adults are exposed to the risk daily. Disadvantaged residents are much more likely to be exposed to these serious risks than are more affluent citizens. Ignoring the size of the populations exposed to the risks discounts the benefit value of protecting these disadvantaged groups by equating the importance of protecting large numbers of people actually exposed to the risk with a single hypothetical future individual who may never face real risks.

> Lesson 4. There may be no efficiency-equity dichotomy for risk regulations. Efficiency can promote equity.

Current practices based on avowed commitments to environmental equity shortchange disadvantaged populations at risk. But if we relied instead on a benefit-cost approach, wouldn't matters be

even worse because of a presumed conflict between equity and efficiency? To address this issue, Hamilton and I calculated the risks,
expected cancer cases, and costs for 150 hazardous waste sites.[20]
What we found is that cleaning up the sites based on their cost-
effectiveness would save many more lives at substantially lower costs
than the current policies. Even very stringent limitations on how
much is spent on cleanup could generate tremendous gains if resources were allocated more effectively. If the EPA only addressed
those sites with a cost per case of cancer averted of $8.2 million or
less (in 2015 dollars), it could eliminate 97 percent of the cancer
cases that could be addressed by cleaning up all 150 sites, and do
so at 3 percent of the total cost.[21] And if priority was given to the
most cost-effective cleanups, policies would prevent more cancer
cases in the near term rather than perhaps decades from now when
all sites on the agency's long-term cleanup agenda are addressed.
Given the glacial pace of remediation efforts, being a high priority
for cleanup is pivotal.

In this instance, making policies more efficient also promotes
equity because the less affluent members of society have greater risk
exposures. The irony is that the agency has made an avowed commitment to promote equity consistent with a presidential directive, and
it has adopted a series of policies intended to be extremely protective, such as making any actual or hypothetical future risk to a single
individual a sufficient basis for moving forward with hazardous waste
cleanups. However, the preponderance of risks being addressed are
the hypothetical future risks, while actual risks affecting large populations remain after being given lower priority for cleanup.

> Lesson 5. Bureaucratic practices that implicitly undermine
> equity are more influential than symbolic institutional com-
> mitments to environmental equity.

Despite all of the risk analysis biases that make risks to minorities and low-income groups count for less in the assessment of site-
specific risks, the EPA nevertheless could target its policies so that
it gave equal or greater weight to the risks to disadvantaged citizens. There unfortunately is no such compensation for the biases

incorporated in the calculated risks. An instructive measure of policy emphasis is the cost per expected case of cancer that is expended to reduce Superfund risks. If there is environmental equity in terms of equitable risk tradeoffs, the government would spend as much per case of cancer averted when minorities are present as when they are not. However, particularly when large minority populations are present, the government selects the least expensive cleanup alternative. The sites where white residents are present are targeted for cleanup and with much more vigilant cleanups and a higher cost expended per expected cancer case avoided. The cost per life saved that the agency incurs for these sites is higher than at the sites with substantial minority populations.

Consideration of whether there is an equitable risk tradeoff rate makes it possible to cut through the vagaries of the different components of the analyses and focus on their net impact when incorporated in policy decisions. On balance, the government's commitment to environmental equity is symbolic, not real, as agency practices systematically undercut the well-being of those whom they have an avowed commitment to protect.

Making Equitable Risk Tradeoffs the Policy Guide

Exploration of different approaches to risk equity suggests that most notions of risk equity are not sensible concepts. Achieving equity in terms of the absolute risks or incremental risks that people face typically is not feasible. Closer examination undermines the superficial appeal of having people face the same risks or the same incremental risks, many of which are the result of voluntary decisions or risk heterogeneity that is very costly to alter.

The equity concept I have advocated is that of equitable risk tradeoffs. Policies should reflect the VSL tradeoffs of the affected citizenry and, except in unusual situations, should equalize these tradeoffs across different interventions. There currently is a substantial policy imbalance, with some hazards being addressed through stringent policies and others being less vigilant. Linking the equity concept to the affected parties' tradeoffs between risk and cost enables individuals' risk preferences to be included in the policy assessment. In most instances, the pertinent equitable tradeoff value will be an average VSL. The most notable exception is the small group of policies targeted at specific income groups. But for these, it is often the case that the costs of the regulatory intervention will be borne privately, as in the case of safety standards for air travel.

Failure to adopt an equitable risk tradeoff approach in conjunction with ranking policies based on their cost-effectiveness can lead to wildly ineffective policies. Current hazardous waste cleanup policies provide a cautionary tale of how well-intended efforts at protecting disadvantaged groups serve as very poor vehicles for promoting equity once the government is oblivious to fundamental components of a sound risk analysis. The level of the risk, the size of the exposed population, and the cost of reducing the risk all are essential ingredients to applying my proposed equitable risk tradeoff approach. The traditional economic dichotomy between equity and efficiency is a false dichotomy for risk regulations. Equitable risk tradeoffs can promote equity.

8

Fine-Tuning the Selection of the Pertinent VSL

Why Off-the-Shelf VSL Estimates Could Be Inappropriate

What is the right VSL number to use? I am frequently asked this question, usually in terms of asking me the level of "the current number." But even posing such a question implies that there is one VSL number and that it is transferable across different contexts so that job-related VSL estimates also pertain to auto accident deaths, cancer, and other risks. This chapter examines whether a one-size-fits-all approach is warranted, as well as other refinements in the selection of the VSL.

Choosing the VSL for a particular situation seems straightforward. If the task is to value fatalities from motor vehicles, then one might simply turn to the US Department of Transportation's guidance document for valuation of mortality risks.[1] Other agencies, such as the US Environmental Protection Agency, may have similar internal guidelines that can be used to evaluate those policies,[2] and there are broader VSL range guidelines from the US Office of Management and Budget.[3] In the absence of specific governmental guidance, one can turn to various surveys and meta-analyses of the VSL in the literature.[4] Grabbing an off-the-shelf estimate of the VSL, such as the $10 million figure that has been the focus of my discussion, is often an expedient solution to the benefit valuation task. But using an average VSL estimate sometimes involves strong assumptions, which we will explore in this chapter.

Drawing on estimates from the literature assumes that the published estimates reflect the population's VSL. If there are biases in terms of which estimates are submitted for publication and ultimately published and which are not, then simple averages from the literature may be a misleading measure of the affected population's VSL. These difficulties first gained attention in the medical literature with respect to biases in the reporting of the results of clinical trials for drugs, but there is evidence of publication biases in the economics literature as well. Although reported estimates of the VSL are subject to significant publication selection effects, available statistical methods make it possible to derive bias-corrected estimates.

There also may be valuation issues regarding the application of VSL estimates from one market context, such as fatality risks for jobs, to situations in which the mortality risks are quite different. A modest extension of the generalizability of labor market VSL estimates would be to apply these values to other traumatic injuries, such as those resulting from motor vehicle accidents. There also could be differences in terms of the nature of the health impact or the risk event. Illness risks, such as cancer, do not involve traumatic injuries and may be associated with different valuations than occupational accidents. Risks from terrorist attacks that kill large numbers of people in a single event also may generate different benefit valuation amounts than fatalities involving only a single person. Nevertheless, the labor market VSL can serve as the baseline for assessments in a broad range of situations, where the key concern becomes whether these other hazards merit a premium relative to the labor market VSL.

Other potentially influential determinants of people's valuation of the risk is the risk level and the direction of change in the risk. Are we in a statistical lives situation or an identified lives situation in which people face certain death? Is the policy addressing the valuation of an effort that reduces the risk, or has the risk been increased so that the inquiry is with respect to the amount people require in order to accept the risk, as in the case of valuing product defects? A considerable literature has documented discrepancies in valuations when people are considering risk increases rather than risk decreases. Application of these findings to adjust the VSL may affect the appropriate level of the VSL that should be applied in a particular situation. Whether and to what extent these types of concerns alter the choice of the pertinent VSL is examined in this chapter.

Publication Selection Bias

Researchers do not submit all of their VSL estimates for publication, and journals do not publish every article that is submitted. Is it reasonable to rely on various average VSL estimates from the literature as a guide to the public's preferences with respect to mortality risks? Or is there a potential bias that arises in terms of which estimates are submitted for publication and published? If there is such a bias, can the published estimates be adjusted to account for it?

The influence of potential publication selection effects initially became prominent in the medical literature. Researchers undertaking randomized control trials of drugs may choose to not report or publish results that are unfavorable for the drug or are statistically insignificant.[5] The researchers, the sponsoring drug companies, and journals may lack interest in publishing seemingly unproductive lines of research. This kind of outcome reporting bias leads many researchers to never publish the results of some clinical trials. Studies demonstrating statistically significant results are more likely to be submitted for publication than those that do not show statistically significant impacts. In addition, researchers are especially likely to publish medical findings for which they have a strong financial interest or when the results are particularly exciting even if the absolute magnitude of the effects may be small.[6]

While the impact of the vested interests associated with research funding is unlikely to play as prominent a role in the VSL research as it is for companies' drug trials, the categories of potential publication selection effects are similar in terms of there being an influence on which estimates are submitted for publication and which estimates are published. Estimates that are inconsistent with economic theory, such as negative estimates of the VSL, are less likely to be published. Workers should receive more pay, not less pay, for working on dangerous jobs. Negative VSL estimates may be viewed with skepticism, as they may reflect a failure by the statistical analysis to control adequately for the attributes of the worker and the worker's job. There is an overall positive income elasticity of demand for safety, which may make it difficult to isolate a premium for job risks. The best, highest-paid jobs in the economy are not the most dangerous jobs but are relatively safe jobs. The workers in these jobs face different labor market opportunities than do workers in the very high-risk professions, often because of their superior educational backgrounds. Workers in dangerous jobs should receive a positive wage premium compared with the remuneration for the safer jobs that are available to them, but that premium may not be enough to give them more pay than workers with superior productivity.

Publication biases of other kinds may arise as well, as researchers may choose to report the VSL estimates similar to those already in the literature as being more plausible. Consequently, existing empirical evidence establishes an anchoring effect on the plausible range of values for the VSL. There are, of course, major dangers that can arise if estimates are screened out because they are believed to be unreasonable. My early estimates of VSL levels in the millions were criticized as being too large because they exceeded the present value of workers' lifetime earnings. How could the economic value of people's lives be worth more than what they earned over their lives? This apparent contradiction only arises because of an incorrect framing of what the VSL is measuring, in terms of certain lives versus statistical lives. Even setting aside the misguided emphasis on the lost-earnings approach, there could be other anchoring effects as prominent VSL studies serve as the reference point for appropriate values.

Fortunately, there are statistical methodologies that make it possible to determine the presence of publication selection effects that distort the estimated VSL, the extent of such biases, and the appropriate levels of VSL after adjusting for these effects.[7] The initial effort to adjust for these biases produced potentially devastating results for the VSL literature.[8] Focusing on a sample of what the authors regarded as the best VSL estimates in each particular study, Doucouliagos, Stanley, and Giles concluded that the estimated VSL levels in the labor market literature are overstated by 70–80 percent. After adjusting for the impact of publication selection biases, their assessment of the correct bias-adjusted VSL estimate is between $1 million and $2 million. If their conclusions are correct, then application of VSL levels that account for such biases will undercut current benefit assessments, making many risk regulation efforts that currently appear to be worthwhile no longer attractive. While these results did not generate immediate governmental concerns, beginning in 2017, regulatory policy commentators cited the publication bias findings as evidence that the governmental VSL was too high and that, as a consequence, regulatory policies were too stringent.[9]

Addressing this fundamental challenge to the integrity of VSL estimates requires that we explore the underpinnings of the methodology and assess whether there should be such a drastic reduction in the estimated VSL. If the estimates of VSL are unbiased, they should be symmetrically distributed around the average value for the sample. Figure 8.1 shows the distribution of all VSL estimates reported in studies using the preferred CFOI fatality rate data. The horizontal axis is the value of the VSL estimate, and the vertical axis is the precision of the estimate as measured by the inverse of the standard error of the VSL estimate. The VSL estimates that rank high on the vertical axis are estimated most precisely in that they have the smallest standard error for the estimate. Such diagrams are termed "funnel plots" since they should resemble an inverted funnel if there are no publication selection effects. The median VSL for this sample is $11.5 million, and the mean value is $14.3 million (in 2015 dollars). The distribution of the estimates is not perfectly symmetrical, so that large outliers make the mean value greater than the center of the distribution. However, the VSL estimates are reasonably symmetrically distributed around the median sample value.

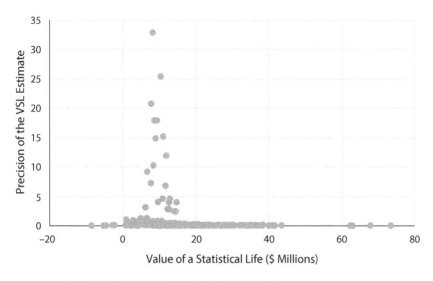

FIGURE 8.1. Funnel Plot of VSL Estimates for the CFOI Sample

The studies in the CFOI article sample even report some negative values as well as some very large positive estimates. There appears to be greater reluctance to report large negative VSL estimates than large positive VSL estimates, but overall the distribution has a fairly reasonable shape.

In contrast, the potential influence of publication selection effects is quite evident in the distribution of the authors' best estimates of the VSL from a broader set of VSL studies, not just those using the CFOI fatality rate data, as shown in figure 8.2. There is no study for which the author selected a negative VSL as the best estimate from the study. And there is no symmetry at all in the distribution of the VSL estimates. The sample mean is $12.4 million, and the median is $9.7 million (in 2015 dollars). But there is no symmetric clustering of the distribution around the median or mean value. Instead, the distribution is highly skewed, with substantial clustering of estimates at very low but positive VSL levels.

Econometric adjustments for the influence of publication selection effects leads to values that reflect these evident degrees of bias.[10] For the CFOI data, the publication-bias-corrected estimates range from $8 million to $11 million, depending on the statistical approach.

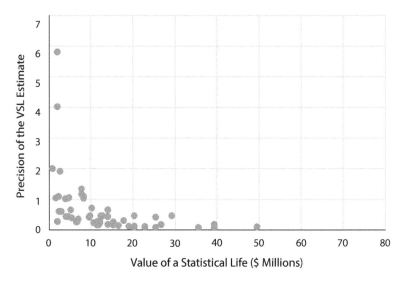

FIGURE 8.2. Funnel Plot of Best VSL Estimates from the Literature

In some samples of CFOI VSL estimates, there is no evidence of statistically significant publication selection effects, while some studies show evidence of small statistically significant publication selection effects, but the bias-corrected estimates using CFOI data are very much in line with the VSL estimates used for policy. The reliance on the superior CFOI data not only leads to less measurement error in the fatality risk data, but also has generated estimates that remain in the policy-relevant range after adjusting for the influence of possible publication selection effects.[11]

Publication selection biases are particularly prominent for international estimates of the VSL.[12] The US labor market estimates of the VSL were the first such estimates in the literature. Hence, they established an anchor for international studies that followed. The result is that the average estimated VSL for non-US studies is somewhat greater than the VSL based on CFOI data despite US income levels being higher. However, after adjusting for publication selection biases, the average international non-US VSL is considerably lower than the US estimates. Given the rampant publication biases in international studies, in chapter 6 I proposed the use of the US CFOI estimates as the baseline value, which can then be adjusted to account for income differences across countries. While other considerations may also be influential, such as international differences in life expectancy, the income differences are most pronounced and amenable to implementation as part of the effort to impute the VSL values throughout the world.

Publication selection effects are a real phenomenon. The extent of these biases is especially great for studies based on less reliable fatality rate measures, such as those using data outside the United States and those based on nongovernmental sources. However, in terms of operational implications, the approach I advocated earlier remains valid, even taking publication selection effects. Reliance on estimates based on the CFOI fatality rate data remains a sound policy evaluation approach.

Benefit Transfer Issues: Does One Size Fit All?

A fundamental practice that affects almost all benefit assessments pertains to what is known as "benefit transfer." To what extent is it appropriate to take benefit estimates from one context, such as a VSL for job risks, and apply them in other situations? The guidelines for policy analysis in both the United States and the United Kingdom recognize the benefit transfer issue with respect to benefits generally, not just the valuation of mortality risks, and they provide pertinent guidance.[13] The nature of the issues raised by benefit transfer differ in these two countries. In the United States, the reliance is on labor market estimates of the revealed-preference values of VSL, which are then applied to value mortality risks in diverse policy contexts, many of which may have little to do with occupational hazards. In the United Kingdom, the reliance is on stated-preference studies of transportation safety, which are then applied outside of the transportation context. In each instance, the benefit assessment practice assumes that the benefit levels can be transferred to these other benefit contexts. The UK policy directives do not utilize the VSL terminology but instead focus on the "value of a prevented fatality or prevented injury."

The OMB's exploration of these issues is quite detailed. When selecting an economic parameter for policy analyses, the OMB indicates a preference for revealed-preference estimates, such as those derived from labor market studies. The guidance recognizes that the same benefit value may not be appropriate in all contexts and suggests that tailoring the values to the specific situation is preferable if such a study is possible. In practice, there has been little or no tailoring of this type except with respect to agency efforts to explore possible differential values for cases of cancer.

Why might there ever be a rationale for using a different VSL in different policy contexts? All deaths lead to the loss of future welfare. Should the value assigned to the risk of such losses ever vary for different causes of death or different affected populations? For the most part, the discussions regarding problems of benefit transfer do not pertain to whether the preferences of workers differ from the preferences of motor vehicle operators or the preference of people exposed to air pollution. The focal issue usually pertains to the characteristics of the risk. Is it worse for any particular individual to be exposed to a traumatic fatality risk or to an illness with painful associated morbidity effects? The VSL consists of the sum of the value of the fatality risk and the value of the morbidity risk. For any given person exposed to risk, the fatality risk component should be the same irrespective of the context in which the person dies. The morbidity risk component may be quite different, particularly in terms of the attendant pain and suffering loss that may vary across different causes of death.

There may, of course, be differences in the morbidity component according to the nature of the fatality. The risks of death from fire or drowning are likely to be more highly valued than the risks of dying while asleep. However, most risks that are targets of regulatory interventions and product safety decisions are not painless and entail a considerable morbidity component. Some of the most feared risks, such as the risk of dying in a plane crash, may be highly valued because people overestimate the likelihood that such events will occur rather than because the nature of the deaths entails especially great morbidity effects.

Labor market estimates of VSL serve as the reference point for valuation of broad classes of fatality risks in the United States in much the same way as stated-preference valuations of transportation risks serve as the reference point in the United Kingdom. In each instance, the underlying assumption is that the benefit transfer approach is legitimate. In the United States, where labor market estimates of VSL comprise the principal reference point, the assumption is that labor market valuations also reflect the willingness to pay to reduce other kinds of mortality risks that do not involve occupational fatalities, such as deaths from air pollution, traffic accidents, adverse reactions to pharmaceuticals, and firearms. In the United Kingdom, the counterpart assumption is that the valuation of transportation-related fatalities generalizes to other risks of death.

Although transferring the benefit values to different risk situations may entail seemingly strong assumptions, the reasonable stability of the VSL estimates across different products, housing prices, and occupational domains provides some support for applying VSL estimates from the labor market to other types of risks. In recent joint research with Elissa Philip Gentry,[14] we have explored whether two types of additional labor market evidence could provide additional motivation for the benefit transfer approach. First, is there stability in the VSL for the major classes of traumatic occupational injuries? Second, what is the dominant factor that contributes to the VSL? Is it the risk of losing one's life, which is common to other risks of death, or is it the risk of incurring the morbidity effects associated with that particular cause of death?

Transportation Risks versus Job Risks

Assessing whether labor market estimates of the VSL are pertinent to transportation risks is the most important benefit transfer issue for traumatic injuries. The most extensive and costly governmental risk regulation efforts pertain to acute risks of death stemming from transportation-related hazards, not job risks. US DOT regulations consistently rank just below environmental regulations in terms of total regulatory policy costs. However, the best US revealed-preference data are not with respect to price impacts of differences in motor vehicle risks but instead pertain to the wage effects of hazards in labor market situations. To what extent is it appropriate to transfer the VSL estimates from the labor market and apply them in analyses of transportation safety?

There are sound reasons to expect strong parallels. Both job risks and transportation risks usually involve acute traumatic injuries. But the similarities are even greater given the substantial role of transportation in job-related fatalities. The Bureau of Labor Statistics categorizes fatalities in terms of both the event that gave rise to the fatality, such as transportation, and the source of the fatality, such as a motor vehicle. These categorizations have similar implications, as 85 percent of all transportation fatalities that occur on the job are related to motor vehicles.[15] The remainder of the accidents in these two categories are vehicle-only fatalities (9 percent) or transportation fatalities that are not related to vehicles (6 percent).

In our first benefit transfer study, we examined the VSL levels for job-related deaths that are transport-related and those that are not transport-related.[16] Overall, 41 percent of all worker deaths are transportation-related and 42 percent are related to deaths involving vehicles, so that the overall categorizations are quite similar. The implications of the VSL analysis also are similar whether the distinctions are based on the fatality being related to the transportation event or to the vehicle source.

Whether one categorizes fatalities as transportation-related or vehicle-related has little bearing on their overall contribution to worker fatalities or the estimated VSL. Just under half of all workplace deaths are either transportation- or vehicle-related so that the average VSL for job safety will be strongly influenced by the valuation of these transport deaths. This large transport share of occupational fatalities alone will tend to make labor market estimates of the VSL pertinent to analyses of transportation regulations.

However, it is possible to make a more refined assessment of whether it is appropriate to apply the VSL for job risks to transportation policies. Elissa Philip Gentry and I estimated the labor market VSL for transportation and non-transportation job fatalities, as well as for vehicle and non-vehicle job fatalities. In each instance, there was no statistically significant difference in the valuations. The VSL for transportation risks is not significantly different from that for non-transportation risks. There is a similar equivalence in the VSL for fatality risks associated with motor vehicles, as compared with all other kinds of fatality risks. The average VSL from the labor market, which is largely for acute risks, is applicable to both transportation and non-transportation fatalities.

This strong parallel has implications for the benefit transfer practices in both the United States and the United Kingdom. In the United States, the benefit transfer issue involves the application of revealed-preference VSL levels for occupational fatalities to transport fatalities, whereas in the United Kingdom, the emphasis is on applying stated-preference estimates from the transportation context to other kinds of risks.[17] The strong similarity of the VSL levels across occupational fatalities and transportation accidents provides support for transferring these results to other risk situations. Moreover, the stability of VSL levels across different types of occupational fatalities makes it likely that other traumatic accidental deaths will have similar values. If the principal component of the VSL is the value of the fatality risk associated with the loss of one's life, one would expect such an equivalence to hold more generally.

The Fatality and Morbidity Risk Components of the VSL

Our subsequent study disentangled the underlying components of VSL and has broad ramifications for benefit transfer practices involving other types of deaths.[18] The VSL is not simply the value of the risk of losing years of one's life. Deaths from accidents and illnesses are not generally immediate, painless events. There is also an associated morbidity aspect of fatalities, such as the pain and suffering of being killed in a fire or explosion, which may inflict a significant welfare loss. In our study, we were able to isolate the component of the labor market VSL attributable to the loss of one's life, which we termed the "value of the fatality risk," and the portion of the VSL attributable to the morbidity risk associated with the fatality, which we termed the "value of the morbidity risk." Although some job fatalities result from injuries that lead to death on the same day as the adverse event, in other instances, the deaths occur after a period of time. We captured the influence of morbidity effects using information provided in the CFOI regarding the number of days that transpired between the date of the accident and the date of the worker's death. Victims of deaths from job exertions live on average for 88 days after the fatal injury incident. Fatal victims of job-related falls and fires each live an average of 9 days after the incident. To what extent is the VSL driven by the value of the fatality risk or by the value of the morbidity risk? What we found is that empirically, it is the loss of one's life that looms greatest rather than the associated morbidity effects. The value of the fatality risk constituted over three-fourths of the VSL for traumatic job accidents. Consequently, labor market estimates of the VSL should generalize to many other contexts because the welfare loss associated with the risk of losing one's life is the dominant component of the VSL, not the pain of dying.

Regulatory agencies focusing on mortality effects from illnesses often hypothesize that the VSL for the illness-related deaths prevented by their agency's policies should be higher because of the associated morbidity effects. Since morbidity effects constitute just under one-fourth of the VSL for traumatic occupational fatalities, these deaths also are clearly not painless. Given the nontrivial VSL share for morbidity effects for traumatic fatalities, the information we need to modify these valuations for fatal illnesses is not whether particular illnesses have morbidity effects but to what degree these morbidity effects exceed those associated with occupational fatalities. The incremental differences should guide whether these other causes of death merit a higher VSL. Recent attention in particular has focused on valuing risks of cancer, where the implicit erroneous assumption often is that job-related deaths pose few morbidity effects, whereas cancer does. Almost all types of deaths regulated by government agencies entail morbidity effects. Because the risk of losing the rest of one's life dominates other considerations generating the VSL, labor market estimates of the VSL provide a useful starting point for valuing risks of other kinds of deaths. Analysts can then adjust these values based on whether there is a differential value of morbidity risk to take into account.

Cancer Risks versus Transportation Risks

Cancer and its associated treatments may cause substantial morbidity effects. Perhaps because of these effects and the prevalence of cancer, people typically place cancer in a prominent position among the most dreaded causes of death.[19] The distinctive cancer risk valuation issue is whether the associated morbidity effects are sufficiently great to warrant a cancer premium. The reference point for such an assessment of whether there should be a cancer premium is whether the value of the morbidity risks of cancer exceeds the morbidity component of the VSL for job hazards. Job-related fatalities seldom involve instantaneous, painless deaths. The morbidity component of occupational fatalities, which arise from vehicle accidents, fires, falls, exertion risks, and other hazards, accounts for 6 to 25 percent of the total estimated VSL, or a midpoint value just above $1 million. Whether there is a cancer premium that should be assigned to cancer risks depends on whether the value of the morbidity loss associated with cancer exceeds this amount.

Agencies whose regulations address cancer risks generally support such a premium, which will boost the value of their policies' estimated benefits. The cancer valuation procedure adopted in the United Kingdom is to value cancer risks twice as highly as accidental risks.[20] The UK policy guidance manual provides no empirical support for this doubling of the VSL, as it is apparently based on policymakers' subjective judgments. However, a subsequent report elaborating on the UK approach indicates that multiplying the transportation VSL by a factor of two is intended to reflect the greater public dread with respect to cancer.[21] Even with such a cancer premium, the VSL applied in the United Kingdom to the risk of cancer-related deaths is below the appropriate value based on the US VSL estimates and the income differences in the two countries. The US Environmental Protection Agency has also addressed the cancer valuation issue, hypothesizing that a 50 percent cancer premium might be a reasonable placeholder value until additional research resolves the premium issue.[22]

Revealed-preference evidence is not very instructive in obtaining a VSL for cancer risks. Occupational risk data are very comprehensive in capturing acute accidental deaths but are not well suited to tallying cancer-related deaths, which occur with a substantial latency period. Causality is often difficult to ascertain except in the unusual case of signature diseases, such as mesothelioma, which is a cancer of the lining of the lungs caused by asbestos exposures. Housing market evidence for the cancer risks from hazardous waste sites is suggestive, as the price reduction associated with cancer risk exposures implies a valuation of these cancer risks similar to labor market estimates of the VSL.[23] Given the difficulty that residents have in becoming knowledgeable about their chemical exposures and the dose-response relationships associated with these exposures, it is unlikely that such housing price evidence will make it possible to pinpoint the magnitude of any cancer premium.

Stated-preference evidence for the valuation of cancer risks from hazardous waste sites is also not definitive. The potentially alarmist responses to hazardous waste sites and people's inability to properly assess these risks lead to stated-preference responses to the valuation of these risks that are often driven by irrational fears, generating inordinately high implied VSL levels.[24]

The dominant approach to estimation of the VSL associated with cancer risks has involved the use of stated-preference surveys in which people are given information about the actual risk levels. The use of such surveys became particularly prominent with respect to the valuation of the environmental damage associated with the *Exxon Valdez* oil spill.[25] The principles that emerged from that episode included the importance of the survey providing precise specification of the commodity that people are valuing. Otherwise respondents may have different conceptualizations of what good they are buying in the hypothetical survey transaction. Asking people point blank to value the risk of cancer is unlikely to be meaningful. Different respondents will imagine different symptoms, different durations of morbidity effects, different levels of pain and suffering, and different types of cancer. Simply naming the type of cancer (e.g., lung cancer) is also unlikely to be sufficient because the consequences that different respondents associate with the particular cancer may be quite different.

In addition to specifying the nature of the disease, the survey design also requires an explicit mechanism for eliciting tradeoffs. The approach my colleagues and I introduced to the valuation literature was to use risk-risk tradeoffs rather than money-risk tradeoffs.[26] Thus, for example, the survey might ascertain whether the respondent prefers reducing a risk of ten automobile deaths to the population or a reduction of the risk of seven deaths from cancer. After being presented with a pairwise comparison of two different risks, respondents can conceptualize the tradeoffs in terms that only involve different health-related consequences rather than bringing to bear a financial metric. Using acute automobile death risks as the reference point, the survey asked respondents to equate different levels of cancer risks to different risks of automobile deaths. In the case of terminal lymph cancer, the result in an exploratory study for a North Carolina convenience sample was that the risk of a cancer death was equivalent to the risk of 1.5 automobile deaths. One can then use estimates of the VSL for acute accidents to monetize this cancer value by simply multiplying the VSL by 1.5.

A cancer valuation issue that played a prominent role in the debate over the EPA regulation of arsenic levels in drinking water pertains to the bladder cancer risks from these arsenic exposures. In a detailed exploration of the value of bladder cancer risks using a large, nationally representative sample, we found that relative to acute transportation-related fatalities, there was a cancer premium of 21 percent. In terms of absolute magnitudes of VSL, the VSL for cancer is about $2 million more than the VSL for transportation-related fatalities.[27] If the VSL for acute accident risks already includes a value of morbidity risk of $1 million, then the total morbidity risk value associated with bladder cancer is $3 million. Whether this cancer premium is sufficient to enable EPA arsenic regulations to pass a benefit-cost test depends on the assumed latency period for cancer as well as other components of the benefit and cost assessments.[28]

Other studies of cancer risk have varied the latency period and the type of cancer, with some estimates failing to show a cancer premium and others suggesting that there is a premium.[29] Thus far, there have been no studies that have found that the value of the risk of a fatal case of cancer is lower than the value of the risk of an acute accident. There is usually a modest premium for cancer risks so that the overall valuation is not that dissimilar from the labor market estimates of the VSL, which also entail a morbidity component. Moreover, if there is a latency period before the cancer is manifested, then after the cancer benefit value is discounted, the present value of reducing an expected future case of cancer may be lower than the VSL for contemporaneous acute accidents.

Terrorism Risks and Natural Disasters versus Transportation Risks

A class of risks that fortunately did not figure prominently in US policies until fairly recently is the risk of death from a terrorist attack. Terrorism risks are accompanied by an additional dimension in terms of the attack being the result of an external threat from a foreign terrorist. The nature of the deaths is very similar to that of job accidents, except in terms of the scale and context of the deaths. In the case of the 9/11 attack, the deaths from the burning and collapse of the World Trade Center and from the crashed airplanes were the results of traumatic injuries that were not that dissimilar from many workplace deaths, such as those that result from a refinery explosion or collapsed scaffolding at a construction site. However, there is a distinctive aspect to these attacks in that they may also be bundled with a perceived loss of our general sense of security and international standing resulting from a foreign attack. The attacks also kill a large number of people at a particular time, and there may be a different willingness to pay to prevent risks associated with such clusters of deaths. Survey valuations eliciting the desirability of reducing the risks of terrorism consequently include the private valuation of the lower mortality risk, as embodied in the VSL, general altruistic concerns with respect to those injured or killed, recognition of the scale of the fatality event, and broader political concerns.

The public's risk tradeoffs involving terrorism nevertheless are similar to those for VSL generally.[30] In particular, based on the trade-offs that respondents in a national survey are willing to make between terrorism deaths and traffic-related deaths, people viewed these deaths as having equivalent overall values. The nature of the differences in these values across the population follows some interesting patterns. Terrorism risk valuations are larger for those who believe that they face above-average terrorism risks, and lower for those who believe their risks are below average. Living in the West similarly makes one less concerned with these risks, as proximity to the cities attacked on 9/11 is often influential in bolstering concerns with respect to future terrorist attacks.[31] Nevertheless, even with such heterogeneity, the value placed on terrorism-related fatalities is not starkly different than the VSL generally and is well below estimates of the implicit cost per expected life associated with very restrictive anti-terrorism efforts, such as President Trump's executive order to ban immigrants from Muslim countries.[32]

The degree to which concern over one's own well-being influences broader policy valuations is evidenced in how people value risks of natural disasters. As is the case with terrorist attacks, natural disasters may lead to a cluster of deaths in which a large number of people are killed at the same time. Unlike the risks of a terrorist attack, which might conceivably arise anywhere, natural disasters tend to be more narrowly confined geographically. Hurricanes don't threaten Minnesota residents, and Florida rarely has any earthquakes. Perhaps because of the concentration of the risk, respondents in a national survey value both the risks of terrorism and traffic deaths twice as highly as deaths from natural disasters. Risks that are not perceived as local threats but are viewed as phenomena specific to other regions will command lower survey valuations. There consequently may be less political support for these natural disaster policies than one would assess if policies were based on valuing the expected deaths according to the expected number of lives saved multiplied by the VSL. It would still be appropriate to value the expected deaths using the VSL rather than a lower value that is expressed in stated-preference surveys because people perceive that they face below-average risk levels.[33]

Identified Lives versus Statistical Lives

Estimates of the VSL pertain to small risks to statistical lives rather than risks to identified lives. What we mean by an "identified life" can be distinguished several ways. The distinctions involve the level of the baseline risk, the degree to which the risk can be altered through some action or policy, and the relationship between the timing of the risk change and the risk-reducing action. How should we think about such risks? Does the VSL have any role to play as a floor or a ceiling in such valuations?

RISKS TO IDENTIFIED LIVES

In the extreme case, there may be an identified individual who faces certain death, but the probability of death attributable to this specific hazard can be reduced to zero through some intervention. Saving a person who is drowning fits this scenario. How much would our drowning victim value being saved? The person's private willingness to pay for the risk reduction is enhanced by the fact that financial resources will have less value after death. However, the amount the person can spend to save her life will be constrained by the available budget. Considering such stark cases of risk changes highlights the potential limits on lifesaving efforts and the greater ability that society may have to fund the costs of protective policies when small risks of death are involved.

A less extreme variation on identified lives is that in which the person faces certain death but a partially effective policy could reduce this probability of death to some value below 1 but not to zero. Kidney transplants for patients facing fatal renal failure often fit this scenario, as these interventions are not always successful.

A final variation on identified lives is that in which an identified person faces some nonzero probability of death that is below 1 that can be reduced either a modest amount or possibly even to zero through some intervention. Potentially effective drugs for gravely ill patients fit this profile.

THE CHALLENGES OF SAVING IDENTIFIED LIVES

The quandaries facing decision makers who must make choices involving identified lives are quite different and much greater than when small probabilities of death are involved. Suppose a municipality is confronted with a situation in which a child is trapped in a well. Rescuing her is feasible but expensive, as the cost of a rescue effort is $20 million. This amount exceeds the VSL, which the mayor's advisors have pegged at no more than $10 million. Should the municipality leave the girl in the well because the rescue cost exceeds the VSL? That would certainly not be the correct economic prescription. As with all such decisions, the task is to go back to first principles and inquire what society's willingness to pay would be for reducing that risk. We are no longer in the VSL realm of incremental money-risk tradeoffs but instead are faced with a major shift in the likelihood of death, which drops from 1 to 0 if the rescue effort is undertaken. Such visible, tragic incidents also generate an outpouring of public empathy, and society's willingness to pay to save her life would bolster the usual valuation amount. These additional altruistic components may stem in part from the infrequency of such events. There might be less public concern with any particular individual's plight if such dire situations arose on a daily basis. Fortunately, we encounter such decisions rarely.

The ramifications of the hypothetical example of the girl in the well also may extend to other situations. The photograph of one drowned Syrian refugee child may have evoked more public concern than images of a larger number of deaths.[34] The powerful imagery of the single identified death no doubt was influential. But an additional factor is that with a small number of deaths, the potential for an effective policy response appears to be more feasible. In contrast, a large number of deaths, as in the case of the 2015 sinking of a ship with hundreds of migrants off the coast of Libya, may make the policy challenge appear to be overwhelming, particularly when it is not a domestic situation for which there are effective policy mechanisms in place.

DRUG POLICIES, IDENTIFIED LIVES, AND DECISION TIMING

Although the broad reach of policies typically transforms risk reduction situations into statistical life scenarios, the distinctions between identified lives and statistical lives sometimes can become blurred. Whether a life at risk is an identified life or a statistical life may hinge on the timing of the decision. Suppose that the government is considering whether to approve funding for a costly new drug that will cure a highly fatal disease at a cost of $5 million per patient receiving the drug. At the time of the approval, suppose that the government does not know which patients will develop the disease or whose lives will be saved by the drug. The lives saved are statistical lives at that point. However, after the policy is adopted, some people will become ill with that disease. Once the illnesses have occurred, these people become identified lives. Since the governmental policy is nondiscriminatory and is targeted at the population generally, at the time of its adoption, the decision is with respect to the anonymous statistical lives that will be saved. In this instance, society's willingness to pay for the drug is guided by the VSL. After the illness is manifested, the patients become identified lives and are better able to elicit public support for the government to provide life-saving coverage, much like the scenario of the girl in the well.

The responsiveness of policies to identified lives is reflected in targeted efforts to expedite governmental approval policy of new drugs. The pressures are particularly great when the disease victims face a high probability of death so that concerns about potential drug safety are less prominent. The sluggish approval process for AIDS drugs led to the protest event called Seize Control of the FDA, which took place on October 11, 1988.[35] After the identified AIDS victims organized their efforts, they successfully lobbied to make the AIDS drugs available earlier than they would have been if the usual premarket testing for safety and efficacy was required. Within two weeks after the protest event, the FDA announced that it would be expediting the drug approval process for HIV drugs. Accelerating FDA approval of such treatments certainly was a sound and responsible policy that seeks to strike a balance between the risks of the disease and the risks of treatment rather than an exclusive focus on drug safety irrespective of the competing illness risks that are present. However, if we take societal altruism out of the calculation, then there is no compelling rationale in the identified-life situation to place a greater value on the expected lives that will be saved than is implied by the money-risk tradeoffs that the people exposed to the risk believe are appropriate. Indeed, from an economic standpoint, people usually are willing to pay less, not more, per unit of risk to reduce very large risks of death because budgetary constraints come into play. Spending funds on the order of the VSL levels to eliminate the risk of certain death is beyond almost everyone's means. People's willingness to pay for risk reductions decreases as the extent of the risk changes and the demands on their financial resources increase. Framing the policy choice in terms of the prospective small risks of death that could be reduced rather than the identified lives that could be saved leads to higher benefit assessment amounts, provided that there are no pronounced societal altruistic concerns.

Nevertheless, the possibility of substantial divergence between the VSL and the valuations of the identified lives should not be summarily dismissed. Such gaps may suggest that broader societal concerns enter and should be taken into account in the valuation process. Moreover, it may also be the case that the use of a uniform VSL is simply a bad measure of the willingness to pay for risk reduction of the particular population being protected. The VSL is not a universal constant but will vary across individuals and the characteristics of the risk.

The Potential Relevance of the Direction of Risk Change

Based on standard economic theory, the VSL that is applied should be the same whether small increases or small decreases in risk are being valued, as long as the changes are small, as job risks generally are.[36] In the case of a risk decrease, which is the more common situation for government policies and prospective private safety measures, the willingness to pay (WTP) for the risk reduction is the pertinent value. For risk increases, such as the imposition of hazardous waste risks or unexpected product defects, the relevant measure of the risk tradeoff is the willingness to accept (WTA) value.[37] The practical policy issue is whether the VSL implied by the WTP and WTA measures differ.

The impetus for the lack of equivalence between WTP and WTA can be traced to the presence of reference-point effects. In their prospect theory model, Kahneman and Tversky hypothesized that people use their current income level as a reference point and that they are especially reluctant to incur decreases from that reference point.[38] The role of reference points also extends to risk levels, as we found in an early study of consumer valuations of household chemical products that people are extremely averse to risk increases.[39] The WTA value for risk increases dwarfed the WTP value for risk decreases. Indeed, the aversion to risk increases was so great that about one-third of the consumers in our survey sample were unwilling to purchase the product for any price discount if it was reformulated and made more hazardous. Based primarily on survey evidence and hypothetical experiments, a large literature has documented widespread WTA-WTP discrepancies for environmental risks and other hazards. Reviews of this literature suggest that the WTA/WTP ratio for comparable changes in the environment or risk ranges from 3.3 to 7.2.[40] Experiments using real products, such as mugs or candy bars, have also generated apparent disparities in WTA and WTP values. The magnitude of the WTA/WTP ratio varies depending on the nature of the risk and individual characteristics.

As was also the case for publication selection bias effects, these results might lead to substantial reductions of the VSL. If one views the VSL from labor market decisions as reflecting a WTA amount for an increase in risk, and if the WTA overstates the pertinent WTP for policy by a factor from 3 to 7, then it would be appropriate to scale back the VSL by dividing the estimate by this factor. There is, however, no sound benefit transfer rationale for making such an adjustment. How consumers making hypothetical decisions feel about increases or decreases in the risk of burning their hands from using household chemical products may be quite different from how workers value actual occupational mortality risk changes in either direction.

Rather than adjusting the VSL based on experimental evidence for hypothetical transactions or for products such as candy bars, it is more instructive to explore whether the VSL in the labor market for increases in risk differs from the VSL for decreases in risk. Examining that issue is feasible using longitudinal labor market data for job changers. Workers who move to jobs with higher risk are in the WTA realm, as they should be paid more for facing greater risk, while workers who move to lower-risk jobs are in the WTP realm, as they are sacrificing a wage premium to move to a safer position. In a detailed examination of thousands of such job changers, we found that there was no statistically significant difference in the valuations. Whether the job change involved an increase in occupational fatality risk or a decrease in that risk does not affect the estimated VSL, each of which is in the usual range.[41]

Why Valuation of Product Defects May Be Different than the Value of Safety Features

Certainly a productive starting point for corporate risk analyses is to utilize government estimates of the VSL to value the expected lives saved from additional safety measures. However, relying on a single number may not capture the degree of variation in the tradeoff between costs and mortality risks, depending on the direction of change in the risk level and the particular segments of the population who are affected. The potential importance of such refinements is perhaps most pertinent in situations involving unanticipated product defects.

Proper valuation of product safety may require distinguishing between the value of risk reductions from safety improvements and the value of risk increases from product defects. Consumers' valuation of product defects, such as a faulty ignition switch that was expected to operate properly, could be quite different from the valuation of additional vehicle safety features that the consumer chose to forgo. Each situation involves a tradeoff between vehicle cost and risk, and the risk decrease from the safety feature may be the same as the risk increase from the product defect. However, product defects in which the vehicle fails to perform in a manner that is consistent with industry norms and the consumer's expectations regarding vehicle safety may be valued much more highly than safety-enhancing improvements. The rationales for different treatment include influences that can be traced to both behavioral economics factors and more conventional economic concerns.

Consider an assessment of the valuation of product defects using the VSL as the starting point for benefit valuation. Suppose the consumer is considering buying a new car and faces a choice between two models. One model has added safety features that reduce the fatality risk by 1/100,000 but costs $150 more. Because the consumer has a VSL of $10 million, the safer car is worth only $100 more, making the less-safe car the preferred alternative because it is $100 cheaper. Suppose instead that the consumer's current car has a product defect that increases the fatality risk over the life of the car by 1/100,000. Based on an average VSL of $10 million, that consumer will suffer an expected loss of $100. Since the risk changes of 1/100,000 are identical for the product defect on the current car and for the forgone safety equipment on the prospective new car, shouldn't the consumer have the same valuation in each case? If the cost to the company of recalling and repairing the defect exceeds $100, based on how much the consumer values his own well-being, is the company on solid ground in deciding to fix the cars? Would paying $100 to each owner of a defective vehicle make them just as well off as they would have been without such a defect?

Despite the risk and cost parallels of product defects and forgone safety improvements, the situations involving product defects and safety equipment for new cars may be different. For starters, the consumer is worse off after learning about the defect unless the auto manufacturer pays the consumer $100. If the consumer is not compensated for the product defect in any way, there will be a loss relative to the situation the consumer would have been in had the vehicle not developed a defect.

In the case of the product defect, something has been taken away from the consumer. The consumer has suffered a loss from the expected level of safety. There is often a profound behavioral asymmetry in how people react to such a loss rather than a comparable gain, even though this asymmetry is inconsistent with standard economic models.[42] This asymmetry is present in a wide variety of contexts, including those in which aspects of risk are involved. Consider the following experimental evidence with respect to how people have different values for positive and negative changes in health risks posed by widely used consumer products. In the first set of studies to be discussed, which we undertook for the EPA, hundreds of consumers considered a series of household chemical products.[43] The survey administrators told the consumers that the products had been reformulated. Some products posed greater risks than before, and some posed lower risks. In the case of household insecticide, consumers were willing to pay an extra $1.04 per bottle for an insecticide that reduced the inhalation risks and skin poisoning risks by 5/10,000. How did consumers react to an alternative version of the insecticide that posed an increase in risk of an identical magnitude? When the survey asked an initial sample of shoppers how much of a discount that they would require to purchase a bottle of insecticide that posed an added injury risk of 5/10,000, almost all the consumers balked at this opportunity. The consumers were not even willing to be paid to use the riskier product. The reactions were so strong that we feared that people would stop participating in the survey after being asked that question. We then revised the study so that the risk increase was only 1/10,000, or one-fifth the size of the risk decrease that they had previously considered. Even with this reduction, 77 percent of the respondents refused to buy the product, and those who did wanted a price reduction of $2.86, or almost triple what they required for a risk decrease that was five times as great. We found similar results for other types of insecticide risks and for toilet bowl cleaner risks.

These results are mirrored in our subsequent studies of how households value the safety of drinking water. Increases in the morbidity risk associated with drinking water are valued several times as highly as comparable risk decreases.[44] The starting point anchors consumers' cost and risk-level reference points, and changes from the accustomed reference point are not viewed equivalently. The potential influence of such reference-point effects is quite broad.

An underlying psychological phenomenon driving these disparities can be traced to the work of Kahneman and Tversky.[45] Their analysis did not focus on probabilities or health risks but instead dealt with changes from accustomed income levels. This loss-aversion phenomenon and related behaviors have been characterized as "status quo bias" by Zeckhauser and Samuelson.[46] Economists have documented a wide range of situations in which there are discrepancies between WTP values and WTA values.[47] For environmental goods, the average ratio of the WTA value to the WTP value is greater than 7.[48]

How one should treat disparities in the valuation of risk increases and risk decreases that arise from behavioral factors depends on the weight one places on behavioral factors. Does the difference embody a form of irrationality in which people overreact to increases in risk because they exaggerate the risk levels? In that case, a premium for product-defect risks does not appear warranted. But what if the difference in the valuations reflects a more fundamental concern that people do in fact suffer a real additional loss when something that they had has been taken away, as compared with the situation in which their baseline has never shifted but was always lower? Unless the disparity between reactions to risk increases and risk decreases can be shown to be a rational phenomenon as opposed to an overreaction of misperception of risk changes, basing compensation on the VSL remains the appropriate yardstick.

Traditional economic reasons without any behavioral underpinnings also come into play. A $10 million VSL estimate is simply an average across the worker population. One reason why involuntarily imposed risks may impose large welfare losses is that there may be wide variations in individual preferences. In a market situation in which people are voluntarily exposed to the risk and receive compensation, people can sort into the risky jobs and products consistent with their preferences. People with a lower VSL will be more willing to undertake risky pursuits and purchase less-safe cars. When the risks are imposed involuntarily, there is no such matching process. Some people with very high valuations of risk will suffer a loss if they are only compensated based on the average VSL. Life and health are also distinctive in that they are irreplaceable, thwarting efforts to suitably compensate people after the fact for risks that these people did not choose.[49]

Even people who are reluctant to bear risks always have some cutoff on expenditures, after which purchases of additional safety are not worthwhile. Explorations of the heterogeneity of the VSL in the labor market yield some estimates as high as $20 million or more.[50] Such a doubling of the VSL to reflect some people's valuation of involuntary risks that are imposed on people who are particularly averse to health risks boosts the level of benefits when undertaking a benefit assessment but does not undermine the procedure. If the average VSL across the population is $10 million, then using a value of $20 million may be correct for some people but will overvalue the risks of safety improvements to the great majority of individuals. Unlike in market contexts where known risks can be matched to consumers based on their willingness to bear risk, no such matching is possible for emerging hidden risks associated with product defects. However, if the consumer population for the product has risk preferences similar to the average worker, use of the average VSL remains appropriate.

Another possible economic rationale for treating product defects differently is that the presence of unanticipated defects may affect the consumer's overall assessment of the safety of the product. If the airbag is defective, what other things might go wrong? The existence of a product defect may serve to undermine consumers' overall sense of the safety of the product and could potentially lead them to fear other hazards. The resistance of the consumers in the household chemical survey to purchasing reformulated but riskier new products might have arisen because they wondered what kinds of additional threats might be posed by a product that has been reformulated and is now riskier than before. If one aspect of the product is now more hazardous, should we be more concerned about other potential hazards that have not yet been disclosed? And if the defect is not disclosed, consumers are unaware of what precautionary actions they should take to mitigate the risk, potentially resulting in a preventable loss in health or unnecessary precautions.

Although the underlying economic mechanisms driving consumers' aversion to losses from product defects have not all been isolated, there is ample evidence that this aversion is strong. Several articles have documented the adverse effect of product recalls on the wealth of sellers, where this measure captures both consumer demand effects as well as liability costs.[51] Moreover, the impact of product recalls on consumer demand is demonstrable. Recalls of the Ford Pinto and other models depressed sales of the defective models and boosted sales of substitutes.[52] Subsequent studies have found that consumers use the recall information as an input to their purchase decisions.[53] The effect of a recall on the perceived risk of the product may have been a general undermining of consumer confidence in the product. The substantial amount that consumers must be compensated to be indifferent to an identified product defect is not just a question of a discrepancy between WTP and WTA values. The prospect of buying a defective car may be influenced by how the defect affects one's product risk assessment more generally.

Regardless of whether one wants to incorporate the differences between WTP values and WTA values in benefit assessment, it is likely that consumers will continue to view emerging safety defects that are an unwelcome surprise as being much more problematic than having the option to purchase less expensive cars that have been equipped with fewer safety-related features. Nevertheless, the VSL usually provides appropriate guidance for valuing mortality risks and is not subject to distortions generated by alarmist responses to risk.

The Stability of the VSL

Our exploration of several prominent concerns and refinements suggests that in many situations, use of an average VSL such as $10 million is a reasonable starting point for valuation. The average VSL is quite resilient to influences that one might expect to have a dramatic impact on the VSL level. Corrections for publication selection bias have a devastating impact on VSL estimates generally but do not greatly alter the values based on the highly reliable CFOI fatality rate data. The bias-corrected values are in line with current policy-relevant levels.

Application of the VSL in different policy contexts incorporates potentially strong benefit transfer assumptions, such as whether the VSL for the risk of occupational fatalities is similar to the VSL for transportation risks and risks from terrorist attacks. There are strong parallels in the valuations across each of these contexts. Consideration of whether the well-known discrepancy between WTA and WTP values requires an adjustment in the estimated VSL found that there were no statistically significant disparities in the case of the labor market evidence that serves as the basis for US VSL estimates.

The robustness of the VSL with respect to these quite fundamental concerns suggests that application of an average VSL to different exposed populations in other risk contexts is likely to provide an excellent starting point for valuation of the risk. While it may be possible and desirable to tailor the VSL estimate more specifically to the situation, in most instances the optimal risk decisions do not hinge on such adjustments. Perhaps the main exception is for causes of death involving substantial morbidity effects. However, even in the case of cancer risks, the dominant component of the VSL is the value of the fatality risk, not the value of the morbidity risk. The prospect of losing the rest of one's future life looms much larger than the associated morbidity effects, which creates a substantial degree of stability in the VSL even if there is a justification for a modest cancer premium. Once the VSL is in a reasonable range and policymakers are no longer devaluing lives, as with the lost earnings/cost-of-death approach, the very effective risk interventions will pass muster, and the highly ineffective interventions will not be justified unless there is a truly dramatic increase in the applicable VSL.

9

How the Courts Value Lives

The Court's Task

On June 14, 2016, an alligator snatched and killed a two-year-old toddler, Lane Thomas Graves, while he was standing in shallow water along the Seven Seas Lagoon beach at Disney World's Grand Floridian Resort. After the horrific death, the press began to speculate on Disney World's prospective liability. There were no warning signs near the beach or any prominent warnings that alerted visitors to the risk of alligator attacks. Had the family chosen to file a lawsuit against Disney World and if Disney World was found to be liable for the death, how would the courts have assessed the appropriate amount of compensation that the parents should receive?[1] There is no standardized amount of compensation in wrongful death cases, but there is a standardized approach.

It is instructive to explore how the courts might treat the death of a child compared with the death of an adult. Shortly before the Disney World tragedy, Joshua Brown was killed on May 7, 2016, when the Tesla Model S that he was driving collided with a semi-trailer that was crossing the highway. At the time of the accident, the car's Autopilot feature was in control of the vehicle's operations, but it did not recognize the upcoming hazard. Suppose that Tesla is found liable for this accident because the Autopilot mechanism did not work in a manner consistent with reasonable consumer expectations and lulled drivers into a false sense of security, perhaps because of inadequate warnings.[2] On September 12, 2017, the National Transportation Safety Board concluded that overreliance on automation, lack of safeguards in the Autopilot system, and driver errors led to the crash.[3] If liability for the wrongful death is established, how would the courts assess damages in this situation, which involves a 40-year-old veteran and a technology company entrepreneur rather than a child? Whereas my proposed application of a VSL would lead to similar values for the benefit of decreasing the risks to both Lane Graves and Joshua Brown, the manner in which courts treat these wrongful death situations would be quite different in these two instances.

Tort damages have a different function than regulatory efforts and other policies that reduce fatality risks. Risk regulation situations deal with reductions in the prospective probability of death for a large population, typically involving many expected deaths. In contrast, juries in wrongful death cases are operating in hindsight. The single identified death cannot be prevented, as it has already occurred. No amount of compensation can bring the victim back to life. Rectifying the situation through monetary payments is feasible for financial losses such as property damage in an automobile accident, but financial compensation cannot replace any victim's life.

How do the courts approach compensation issues in wrongful death cases? Is there any current role for VSL estimates in this process? Application of the VSL could play a potentially instrumental role in establishing desired safety levels in the product safety situations discussed in chapters 3 and 4. Might there also be a sensible role for the VSL more generally, and if so, what should it be? As this chapter will indicate, there is no all-purpose value that should be attached to lives. That the VSL is the appropriate measure for monetizing small changes in risk does not imply that it should be the routine guide for court awards. Posing the question of what value should be attached to lives cannot be divorced from the context being considered. The value to be used depends on the objective that is being served by the pricing of lives as well as the institutional context in which the question is being posed.

When assessing the proper role of the VSL in the courts, there is a tendency to take a tort-centric perspective. Even though the focus of this chapter is on the judicial system, it is important not to lose sight of the institutional context in which the courts operate and, in particular, the role of other public and private institutions. If the liability system is the only mechanism that society has to provide either compensation or deterrence, then the responsibility is much greater than if no other government institutions are available. However, the task for the courts is diminished if market forces, regulatory policies, and government compensation programs are also available to assist in establishing incentives for safety and providing compensation for the harms that have occurred.

Although the VSL does not serve as the standard value for court awards in wrongful death cases, it has two critical functions to serve in retrospective assessments of fatalities. Legal situations in which deterrence is a critical concern, principally those involving punitive damages, can use the VSL as a penalty guideline. Similarly, government agencies can set regulatory sanctions for infractions leading to fatalities based on the VSL. Doing so would greatly boost the level of regulatory sanctions and the incentives for safety.

The Fundamentals of Damages Calculations in the Courts

Court awards in wrongful death cases encompass compensatory damages awards for the monetary and nonmonetary harm suffered by the individual and, in rare cases involving reckless or malicious behavior, an additional punitive damages award to punish the injurer. The usual compensatory damages approach in wrongful death cases follows practices based principally on addressing the loss to the survivors as well as providing a possible allowance for the pain and suffering of the deceased. The main objective is not to determine the value of the person's life to society or the value of the life to the deceased, but rather to provide appropriate compensation to the deceased's survivors. The two principal components of the loss are economic damages, or what regulatory agencies formerly called the cost-of-death approach, and noneconomic damages.[4] The framework for calculating the economic damages involves an estimate of the financial loss suffered by the survivors. The main building block of this calculation is the present value of the decedent's lifetime earnings plus fringe benefits. Medical expenses and other financial costs also may enter. The implicit principle guiding the economic damages portion of compensation is to serve as an insurance role for the financial loss incurred by the survivors. As a result, the only component of the earnings loss that gets counted is the share that would have gone to the survivors. In the case of the death of a child, speculating on future earnings is often challenging, but irrespective of the earnings loss calculation, the economic damages amount is usually very small, as most children in the current era do not ultimately become major sources of financial support for their parents. If the deceased is an adult supporting a family, the financial loss can be more significant. But even these loss amounts are somewhat diminished, as there is a deduction for the share of consumption that would have gone to the deceased rather than support of the other family members.

The noneconomic damages component addresses the pain and suffering of the deceased as well as the grief and welfare loss of the family. If the role of compensation is to serve an insurance function, then these damages payments are more problematic than the economic damages component. As I will document below, people would not generally purchase insurance to transfer income to themselves either at the time of death or to compensate for grief after the death. Doing so shifts resources away from the time when people are alive and able to derive value from these funds. However, as a practical matter, the additional pain and suffering compensation often enables the claimants to have a buffer in the award so that the payment net of the contingency fee charged by the attorney remains sufficient to address the economic loss.

The consequence of the standard calculation of the economic loss and the court's more subjective assessment of the noneconomic loss is that the family receives compensation that is generally much smaller than the VSL, where the compensation amount may be quite low in the case of the death of a child, a retiree, or other people outside the labor force. These wrongful death awards correspond to the figures used historically by auto companies to value safety improvements, as these were the amounts that the company traditionally paid in court cases. However, the wrongful death awards undervalue the reduction in the risks to life and provide inadequate guidance for firms to set the level of safety. To remedy this shortfall, should the VSL be adopted more generally as the framework to be used to set compensation in wrongful death cases? The answer to this question hinges on the principal purpose of the damages award and, in particular, on whether the intent is to provide compensation or to establish incentives for safety.

Compensation Funds

WORKERS' COMPENSATION

Before turning to the role of the courts in establishing safety incentives, consider first whether other societal compensation structures have an approach similar to that in tort cases and whether they also do not utilize the VSL as part of their structure. A prominent source of compensation for personal injuries is that provided by administrative compensation systems. It is instructive to obtain an overview of that program's practices to see if they adhere to criteria similar to those used by the courts. As is also the case for wrongful death awards, administrative compensation funds focus principally on meeting the income needs arising from injuries and deaths, rather than providing adequate incentives to reduce these risks. The longest-standing compensation systems of this type are the state-run workers' compensation programs. Covered workers are not permitted to file tort liability claims to sue their employer for injuries, but instead must rely on this administrative compensation mechanism. Although these programs consequently force workers to sacrifice a potential source of compensation, injured workers are able to receive compensation for their injuries without having to demonstrate any fault on the part of the employer. Consequently, workers are provided with compensation that addresses a broader class of injuries than if they had to file a tort liability claim and were required to show negligence on the part of the employer.

The workers' compensation system is very efficient in that most of the program costs consist of transfers to workers rather than administrative expenses. My past estimates suggest that these expenses comprise about 20 percent of total insurance premiums so that roughly 80 cents of every dollar of premiums is received by workers in terms of benefits.[5] Other insurance and litigation remedies are much less efficient. The total attorney and legal expenses for personal injury claims average 75 cents per dollar paid to injured parties, with a level of 83 cents per dollar for cases in which the claimant hired an attorney and filed a tort claim.[6] Thus, these legal expenses comprise 43–45 percent of the total amount paid to the injured party. The assurance of prompt and efficient payment through the workers' compensation system is not, however, without some compromise. Workers' compensation payments do not include an allowance for pain and suffering, as do court awards, but they do address the income loss resulting from the injury.[7]

Benefits are governed by formulas tied to the worker's earnings. The common state formula in thirty-six states is to provide compensation of two-thirds of the worker's gross earnings, which is tax free, boosting the actual economic value of the compensation to the injured worker.[8] State formulas impose caps on the amount of compensation, such as the state average weekly wage, or sometimes up to two times the state average weekly wage. There also may be a minimum benefit amount. Workers' compensation functions quite effectively in meeting the basic income loss associated with job injuries. However, the program does not attempt to address the unusually large losses in earnings that might, for example, be experienced by an injured upper-management employee.

An added dividend of the program is that the safety record of the firm affects the insurance costs, particularly for large firms. In 2014, total workers' compensation premiums written were $43.5 billion.[9] The experience rating of premiums fosters incentives for safety, as workplace fatalities would be about 30 percent greater in the absence of workers' compensation incentives.[10]

THE SEPTEMBER 11TH VICTIM COMPENSATION FUND

The recognized success of workers' compensation in providing prompt payment to injured workers and avoiding many of the costs associated with tort liability claims has generated support for the adoption of a compensation fund approach in other situations that also do not use the VSL in setting the payment amounts. The September 11th Victim Compensation Fund for the families of the 9/11 attack victims bears similarities to the workers' compensation program in that it is an administrative compensation scheme with caps on payment amounts, but with an additional allowance for pain and suffering.[11] The level of compensation was considerably more generous than that of workers' compensation. Unlike the workers' compensation situation, the victims of the attack could pursue a potential tort liability claim against the airlines, so that a fundamental purpose of the settlement program was to induce the families of those killed in the attack to not pursue the litigation option. If the family accepted the administrative compensation payment, they sacrificed the ability to file a tort liability claim. The amount of compensation included some allowance for pain and suffering as well as payment for the income loss. However, as in the case of workers' compensation, the income loss component was capped, though at a much more generous level than that of workers' compensation.

A distinctive, more controversial feature of the September 11th Victim Compensation Fund structure was that there was a deduction for collateral source payments. If the family already had extensive life insurance coverage, that amount would be subtracted from the payment amount. In general, there is no comparable deduction of collateral payments for court awards or workers' compensation. A possible rationale for such an offset is that if the objective of the fund was to insure that the family did not suffer a major financial loss, then less compensation was needed when other insurance was in place.

The presence of the damages caps and collateral source offsets had especially significant impacts for the families of the highly paid executives killed in the 9/11 attack, as their income replacement from the September 11th Victim Compensation Fund would be reduced by these provisions. Nevertheless, despite these limits, the average payout was $1.8 million, which is a reflection of the substantial income levels of those killed in the attack rather than an attempt to provide compensation comparable to that based on a VSL. The compensation fund largely succeeded in preempting any litigation, as 97 percent of the families killed in the attack accepted the settlement amounts, which had a total value of $7 billion.

GM COMPENSATION FUND FOR THE IGNITION SWITCH DEFECT

GM established a compensation fund to address the injuries and deaths associated with the ignition switch defect. Attorney Kenneth Feinberg, who also administered the September 11th Victim Compensation Fund, directed the GM fund and adopted an approach that bore some similarities to the September 11th Victim Compensation Fund. The GM fund also provided compensation for economic loss and pain and suffering but, unlike the September 11th Victim Compensation Fund, there was no cap on total payment amounts.[12] For example, under this compensation plan, a 17-year-old student who is killed and had no wages and no dependents would receive a payment of $2.2 million.[13] In recognition of the increased economic loss incurred by the families when the deceased earned a substantial income, a 40-year-old earning $75,000 per year with no children would receive a payment of $5.1 million.[14] Over 90 percent of those who were offered compensation accepted the payment amount, with a total compensation amount of $595 million being paid to the families of the deceased and nonfatal accident victims.[15] As with the September 11th Victim Compensation Fund, the administrative compensation fund succeeded in avoiding litigation of the claims in the great majority of instances and transferring income to the injured parties.

For all of these administrative compensation systems, there is no linkage to the VSL. Such a linkage might be pertinent if the compensation system was designed to provide incentives for safety. However, the emphasis is on providing compensation for basic economic losses and, in the case of the 9/11 and GM settlement funds, also to provide some additional payment for pain and suffering. Pain and suffering compensation is not a principal objective of workers' compensation, as there is no need to induce claimants to forgo litigation because they are not permitted to file tort claims against the employer. For the September 11th and GM settlement funds, claimants faced the choice of either accepting the compensation or pursuing a litigation option. An allowance for pain and suffering makes the damages components and the financial stakes more comparable in this pairwise comparison.

The Two Principal Objectives of Court Awards

To obtain a better sense of how the VSL might be used correctly in personal injury contexts, it is helpful to specify the objectives of the damages payment and indicate how the VSL might relate to these objectives. In most damages contexts, there are two concerns that are present.[16] First, if there is harm that imposes damages on a party, providing an optimal amount of insurance for the damage is desirable. Second, it is desirable to establish efficient incentives to prevent harm so that the parties take appropriate care.[17] In the case of financial losses, matters are quite simple. The damage is a financial loss so that making the party pay for the damage not only provides insurance against the loss but also generates appropriate incentives to take care.

Matters are not as straightforward for fatal accidents, as there is no single economic formula that can achieve the objectives of optimal insurance and optimal deterrence. Court awards based on economic loss may provide optimal insurance but will not generate adequate incentives for deterrence. Use of the VSL as the compensation amount will generate efficient incentives for safety, but will provide excess insurance. People generally wouldn't purchase life insurance policies to provide a compensation amount to their heirs equal to the VSL. Would, for example, people want the wrongful death payments after product accidents to be set equal to the VSL? This approach will have undesirable economic ramifications. Firms will raise the price of the products to incorporate the expected liability payments so that, in effect, the consumer will be paying for insurance coverage that is above the level that they would choose if they had control over the amount of insurance. Limiting compensation amounts to the usual measures of economic and noneconomic damages may provide efficient levels of insurance but will not provide adequate incentives for safety. Even in the absence of additional legal sanctions, there may be other policy mechanisms that come into play, such as government regulation, which can generate safety incentives in many instances.

The accepted practice for wrongful death cases in US courts is to set compensation levels for damages to primarily provide compensation for the losses experienced by the family. Whereas the focus of financial damages is on making the victim "whole" by setting the damages payment equal to the loss, such a "make whole" approach is infeasible for fatal injuries. Monetary payments, even at the level provided by the VSL, will not restore the person's welfare. The deceased obtains no benefit from such transfers after death. Anticipation of such an award before death is also unlikely to meet the "make whole" target because bequests are typically not so highly valued that a payment equal to the VSL would make a person indifferent to death.

A Constructive Role for the VSL in the Courts

While blanket adoption of the VSL as the compensatory damages measure in wrongful death cases is not warranted, there are two potential constructive roles of the VSL, each of which relates to fostering appropriate safety incentives. The first role is with respect to determination of liability. What is the appropriate level of safety for a product? Based on a conventional negligence rule, firms should balance the costs of the safety improvements against the benefits to consumers. Reliance on the value of economic and noneconomic damages in wrongful death cases is not the appropriate yardstick for measuring the importance of reducing mortality risks. The VSL is the correct price to establish efficient incentives for safety when valuing the expected deaths that will be prevented through the additional safety measure. Ideally, firms should be using the VSL in their corporate risk decisions, as proposed in chapters 3 and 4. However, even if firms do not employ these VSL statistics, the negligence tests applied by the courts should use the VSL in their determination of how much safety is sufficient.

Adoption of the VSL in determinations of liability not only will establish the correct price for the lives saved but will also frame the risk decisions in the pertinent prospective terms. What matters from the standpoint of safety decisions is whether at the time the product is put on the market, the expected lives that would be saved through greater safety were valued appropriately. This prospective framework contrasts with the hindsight bias approach that dominates retrospective jury contexts, where the tendency is to make a comparison of the identified life to the cost of improving the safety features for a single unit of the product. Note that this use of the VSL does not involve any incorporation of the VSL in the determination of damages, only in the assessment of liability.

Using the VSL to assess liability ensures that damages will be awarded when the firm does not provide adequate levels of safety. However, if the firm's safety level is inadequate and a sanction is imposed, the level of traditional economic and noneconomic damages alone will not suffice to provide adequate incentives to take care. For situations in which firms' safety decisions are remiss, government regulation and regulatory penalties to augment the influence of court awards may be influential, particularly in the case of mass-marketed consumer products.

But there may be an additional role for the courts to promote safety in the case of gross deviations from the appropriate level of safety. In these punitive damages situations, Joni Hersch and I propose that the courts use the VSL to establish a level of punitive damages that will create adequate incentives for safety.[18] In current jury instructions for punitive damages, the severity of the harm is not the critical determinant of whether punitive damages should be awarded. Jury instructions differ by state, but usually the trigger for awarding punitive damages includes requirements that the injurer was aware of the risk and was either malicious or displayed reckless and callous disregard for the well-being of those who might be injured. A pertinent framing of such concerns is whether the incentives for deterrence need to be bolstered to lead the injurer to take an efficient level of precautions. Many wrongful death cases involve horrific injuries to victims for whom compensation is clearly warranted, but demonstrating that the payment should include a punitive damages award is a more demanding test.

In punitive damages contexts, the VSL can serve as the measure of the total award amount needed to provide appropriate incentives for safety. If, for example, the appropriate VSL is $10 million, and the value of the compensatory damages award is $2 million, then $8 million is the additional punitive damages award that is appropriate for the award to create adequate incentives for safety. There may also be situations in which there are very large associated medical expenses, which would boost the appropriate compensatory damages award and total damages award. Setting the damages amount equal to the VSL creates safety incentives for the injurer. The VSL has an appropriate damages role to play in punitive damages situations because safety considerations are paramount. The use of the VSL to set compensation does provide an excessive amount of insurance irrespective of whether punitive damages are warranted. However, the compromise I am suggesting is to rely on the VSL to promote the deterrence objective in punitive damages contexts and to continue to rely on standard economic and noneconomic damages awards when safety incentives are not a salient concern.

Basing the total damages award on the VSL may, in some instances, lead to punitive damages awards that are close to the permissible upper bounds for such payments. In addition to punitive damages caps in some states, the US Supreme Court has provided more general guidance that serve as limits on the awards. The first such specification of the reasonable upper limit on punitive damages awards was in the 2003 decision in *State Farm Mutual Automobile Insurance Co. v. Campbell.* In that decision, the court suggested that a single-digit ratio of punitive damages to compensatory damages should be the upper limit: "Our jurisprudence and the principles it has now established demonstrate, however, that, in practice, few awards exceeding a single-digit ratio between punitive and compensatory damages, to a significant degree, will satisfy due process."[19] In most instances in which there are significant economic and noneconomic damages, this ratio guidance should not be constraining. However, if the compensatory damages amount is small, as in the case of the death of a child, a single-digit ratio might be an impediment to setting punitive damages utilizing the VSL. For situations of small damages amounts, the court noted that a large ratio might be warranted: "Nonetheless, because there are no rigid benchmarks that a punitive damages award may not surpass, ratios greater than those we have previously upheld may comport with due process where 'a particularly egregious act has resulted in only a small amount of economic damages.'"[20] While there are other legal guidelines that may be pertinent,[21] there seems to be no immutable barrier to using the VSL to set total damages in punitive damages contexts.

The use of the VSL in punitive damages contexts also can be generalized to incorporate the probability of detection utilizing the standard law and economic theories of deterrence.[22] Suppose that the injurer engages in stealthy behavior so that there is a 0.5 probability that the injurer will be caught and found liable for the harm. To establish appropriate incentives, a total damages level of VSL / 0.5, or 2 × VSL, will make the expected costs borne by the injurer align with the value of the harm.

Reliance on a single policy instrument—damages payments—cannot simultaneously achieve both the insurance and deterrence objectives of tort compensation. Basing damages awards on the VSL for punitive damages cases promotes the deterrence objective but provides excessive insurance. Restricting damages to the conventional economic and noneconomic damages components addresses the insurance objective but provides inadequate deterrence. In each instance, however, the fundamental damages measure is tailored to the objective that is paramount in that instance. Thus, the approach I am recommending entails compromise, but it is a targeted compromise in which the VSL is brought to bear only when deterrence is a paramount concern. When punitive damages are not awarded, there may be additional societal efforts that are operative. Often it is feasible to augment the safety incentives through regulatory standards and penalties. Regulatory interventions are particularly well suited to dealing with hazards posed by mass-marketed consumer products, as agencies can make broader market-wide assessments based on the expected benefits and costs of greater safety rather than attempting to generalize retrospectively based on the facts in a particular case. Utilizing additional policy instruments rather than relying exclusively on the courts can assist in addressing gaps in incentives that might otherwise exist.

While setting punitive damages equal to the VSL may seem to lead to very substantial payments to the injured party, application of the methodology provides much needed structure to the determination of punitive damages. Indeed, in many instances the VSL may be a damages amount that promotes restraint. The examples in chapter 3 of punitive damages awards of $100 million or more are unusual, but they are also symptomatic of the more fundamental problems facing jurors. Evidence suggests that juries are very good at assessing wrongful conduct and the seriousness of the transgression, but they face daunting challenges when asked to map these concerns into dollar punitive damages amounts.[23] Jury instructions are vague and open-ended, leading plaintiffs' attorneys to suggest irrelevant anchors to try to generate a large verdict. Application of the VSL in punitive damages contexts will assist in providing a sound approach to setting punitive damages payments.

My reliance on the VSL for setting punitive damages awards but not compensatory damages differs from the economic treatment of punitive damages by Polinsky and Shavell.[24] Their focus is on linking punitive damages awards to the probability that the injurer will be caught and found liable for the harm, which is a feature that can be incorporated in my proposed use of VSL as well. They do not advocate any punitive damages award if there is a 100 percent chance that the injurer will not escape detection. Thus, in their model, the standard punitive damages criteria pertaining to whether the injurer acted recklessly and with callous disregard of the victim are not pertinent. Rather than set punitive damages based on the VSL in the standard punitive damages situations in which deterrence is viewed as critical, they advocate raising the value of compensatory damages awards for all wrongful death cases irrespective of whether the usual punitive damages criteria are met, since "the level of compensatory damages awards in personal injury cases may be too low in practice to accomplish proper deterrence."[25] The award level needed to provide proper deterrence is the VSL. Payment of this amount in all wrongful death cases will lead to adequate deterrence but will also generate excessive insurance amounts so that their approach also entails a compromise, as will all possible solutions. My strategic application of the VSL to set damages awards is restricted to the punitive damages cases for which deterrence is warranted. Targeting the role of the VSL in this manner seeks to prevent the general problems arising from over-insurance but, at the same time, to generate safety incentives in situations where they are most needed.

The VSL Invades the Courts: Hedonic Damages

The multimillion-dollar price tag associated with VSL estimates has not escaped the attention of plaintiff attorneys. Getting a large damages number in front of the jury provides a potential anchor that jurors can use in deriving the damages payment amount. Anchors of various kinds may be particularly influential when people have no firm sense of how to set an appropriate damages amount. I am frequently contacted by attorneys who wish to introduce the VSL in court cases as a routine component of compensation. Using the VSL as a damages measure has come to be known as "hedonic damages," since the underlying economic models are usually based on hedonic (or quality-adjusted) wage equations. There is often little by way of conceptual justification for the practice, as the standard hedonic damages approach is to draw on some average VSL from the literature and apply it in the damages analysis. There is seldom an effort to tailor the estimate to the specific case so that, unlike the usual damages calculation, there is no consideration of the age, education, health status, or marital status of the deceased. This one-size-fits-all approach has led many courts to reject the use of the VSL, since it may have a tenuous connection to the value of the loss experienced in the particular case. Very few courts have permitted testimony advocating the use of hedonic damages, and numerous courts have rejected this approach.[26]

The advocacy of using the VSL in court cases is typically accompanied by reference to the government's use of the statistics in regulatory policy analyses. Presumably, according to the experts testifying about hedonic damages, the government's imprimatur on the VSL establishes it as the correct approach to monetizing lives. However, these government policy applications of the VSL are all prospective in nature, as they involve policy initiatives that will generate small reductions in mortality risks. Compensation systems such as workers' compensation and the September 11th Victim Compensation Fund do not utilize the VSL as part of the compensation formula. In wrongful death cases in which the federal government is a defendant, it would have the opportunity to introduce a VSL damages amount, but it has not. I encountered one such instance as a consulting expert to the US Department of Justice, which was handling an airplane crash claim against the Federal Aviation Administration in which the government was the defendant. Although the plaintiff's expert in this case advocated use of the VSL as the damages amount, the government attorneys consistently opposed the approach and never raised the possibility of relying on the VSL. It is incorrect to assert that application of the VSL to set damages simply reflects government practices. There is no such parallel because the purpose for which the VSL is being used is quite different and is unrelated to setting compensatory damages amounts in liability contexts.

States' provision for compensation for the "loss of enjoyment of life" often generates intractable problems for jurors. Even especially detailed instructions such as those in the state of South Carolina are unhelpful:

> Loss of the capacity to enjoy life, resulting from a personal injury, is a proper element of damages. If you find evidence of "loss of

enjoyment of life," you may award damages for this loss. Damages for "loss of enjoyment of life" compensate for the limitations, resulting from the defendant's negligence, on the injured person's ability to participate in and derive pleasure from the normal activities of daily life, or for the individual's inability to pursue his talents, recreational interests, hobbies, or avocations. "Loss of enjoyment of life" damages compensate the plaintiff not only for the subjective knowledge that one can no longer enjoy all of life's pursuits, but also for the objective loss of the ability to engage in these activities.[27]

Such instructions simply restate the valuation task but do not provide guidance for juries to set a specific damages amount.

Some states limit loss of enjoyment of life to the period when the injured party was alive, whereas other states have a broader perspective including the loss in value of life after the person's death. For example, a court decision in the state of Louisiana permitted the award of hedonic damages in addition to other categories of losses such as pain and suffering, but the hedonic damages for decedents are limited to the period when the decedent was alive.[28]

To give jurors a potential exit from this daunting task, economic experts sometimes advocated that they use hedonic damages, or the VSL, which would give jurors a methodological crutch to assist in determining the "value of the life's pleasures." Mississippi formerly was a prime venue for hedonic damages testimony until the legislature passed a statute that prohibited this approach after January 1, 2003. In Nevada and New Mexico, some courts have permitted VSL estimates to be introduced in hedonic damages cases. However, what the expert can provide to jurors may be limited to suggesting the VSL concept rather than providing a specific opinion on the value of the loss of life for the decedent.

The Problem of Duplicative Payments

In addition to testifying economics experts who sometimes recommend the use of the VSL, or hedonic damages, to set compensatory damages in wrongful death cases, prominent legal scholars have advocated an application of the VSL to boost damages to even greater levels than those associated with the hedonic damages approach.[29] Eric Posner and Cass Sunstein do not recommend employing the VSL in determining liability or in setting punitive damages, but instead advocate the general use of the VSL to augment compensatory damages. Their proposal is to base compensation on the sum of the value of the loss to the victim and the value of the loss to the survivors. Whereas compensation of the survivors is the principal objective served by current damages practices, concern for the loss to the deceased would be the dominant component of their proposal.

The loss to the victim, or what they refer to as "the hedonic loss to the victim," is the counterpart of the VSL in hedonic damages calculations.[30] While they suggest three ways of calculating the hedonic loss to the victim, the first two methods they suggest rely on measures that seek to construct the VSL based on government practices or revealed preferences of the deceased. The third approach that they suggest is more open-ended, as it asks the jury to set a "value of the life's pleasures lost by the victim." Asking jurors to make assessments such as this is similar to some current jury instructions, such as those in New Mexico and South Carolina, but is not likely to lead to meaningful answers. What is the thought experiment that jurors should envision so as to conceptualize what such a question means? Is the "value of the life's pleasures" the amount of money that the person would have to receive to be indifferent to being killed? Or rather than this willingness-to-accept amount, might it be the amount that the person would have been willing to pay to avoid certain death? Either frame of reference involving compensation or payments in the face of certain death is quite different from the VSL, which elicits the amount of compensation per unit of small risks of death.

In effect, the Posner-Sunstein proposal establishes the VSL or a comparable hedonic value of life as the basis for damages to the victim in all wrongful death cases. Reliance on the VSL as a component of damages is similar to what I suggest in punitive damages contexts, which is when deterrence considerations are prominent.

Their proposal would make the hedonic loss payment generally applicable, including claims based on negligence or other criteria, as would the Polinsky and Shavell proposal.

However, Posner and Sunstein's damages proposal goes further in that it includes an additional layer of damages beyond the VSL. They advocate augmenting the hedonic loss compensation with a variant of the usual economic and noneconomic loss components, or the standard compensatory damages value. More specifically, there would be payments for the usual nonmonetary loss components, such as "grief, mental distress, loss of companionship, and the like." In addition, there would be compensation for the economic loss, or "the amount of money that would make the survivor just as well off (financially) as he would have been if the death had not occurred." There is no problem of inadequate insurance or inadequate deterrence under their proposal. Rather, there is a problem of over-insurance coupled with excessive deterrence. Thus, the nature of the compromise is different than under my proposal and under the status quo.

In my view, basing damages on the sum of the VSL and the standard compensatory damages approach is duplicative. The VSL incorporates the deceased's prospective value of all such losses that will occur after death. The underlying conceptual rationale for the VSL is that it reflects the money-risk tradeoff accounting for all consequences of the death. Posner and Sunstein's proposed double counting will lead to excessive levels of deterrence even in situations where punitive damages are usually warranted. In situations where only compensatory damages are warranted, it will lead to excessive insurance, with the amount of over-insurance equal to the VSL. Their assessment that the proposal would "have a significant impact on tort awards, especially for the elderly in non-hedonic-loss states" dramatically understates the transformation of the tort liability landscape that would result from the adoption of this approach. Boosting wrongful death awards by perhaps an order of magnitude will have profound ramifications.

If the underlying principle of basing damages on the VSL plus the compensatory damages amount is the correct deterrence approach, then to have a consistent risk reduction approach, it should replace the VSL in all decisions regarding the determination of safety levels, including the figures government agencies use to value mortality risks. However, there is no compelling economic rationale for augmenting the VSL by the cost-of-death values when setting the appropriate levels of safety. The VSL by definition reflects how much people value changes in risk. As a result, I advocate a more limited, targeted use of the VSL in judicial contexts.

Misuses of the VSL when There Are No Deaths

The multimillion-dollar litigation stakes created by introduction of the VSL has generated interest in attempts to apply the VSL using happiness scores and disability scales even in situations in which there has been no fatality. The first and more far-fetched application of VSL is in conjunction with happiness scores. I first encountered this attempt to apply the VSL in the context of the *Exxon Valdez* oil spill.[31] This catastrophic oil spill had a variety of diverse adverse impacts on the fishing and recreation industries in Alaska. However, there were also attempts to recoup the nonmonetary losses incurred by Alaskan residents based on reported happiness scales. The following stylized example illustrates the nature of the approach. Suppose that on a 10-point scale, surveys found that people reported a happiness level of 9 before the oil spill occurred and that after the spill, the happiness level is 6. For purposes of this calculation, let the VSL be $10 million. Following the logic of the happiness scale approach, Alaskan residents have lost one-third of their happiness so that the value of their loss is (1/3) × $10 million, or $3.3 million per resident.

Combining the VSL with happiness scales in this manner has no conceptual foundation whatsoever and involves two pivotal assumptions. The utilization of the VSL assumes that the objective of the payment is prevention of the risk, not compensation for the loss. Moreover, even if the objective is deterrence, there must be a basis for chaining the VSL with happiness scales, which are concepts that have no meaningful economic relationship. Would decreasing the public's happiness score by one-third really be comparable to a risk that killed one-third of all Alaskan residents? That is the implicit assumption involved in this chaining of the happiness scores with the VSL. Whereas death is forever, happiness scores may be ephemeral. After Exxon paid compensation for the economic losses and the fishing industry rebounded, the reported happiness no doubt increased, making the downward happiness event only a temporary phenomenon. The fundamental problem is that the happiness scales used by psychologists are entirely unrelated to the theory underlying the VSL.

A more frequent misuse of the VSL in the courtroom is in conjunction with impairment ratings or disability scales. As in the case of happiness scales, these ratings likewise have no conceptual link to the VSL. These ratings are intended to provide a sense of the degree of impairment following a disabling injury and are often linked to impairment with respect to specific functions. Unlike happiness scales, they seem to be more concrete in terms of being related to the physical consequences associated with the injury. Suppose that for a particular disability scale, a moderate disability has a score of 20 percent disability. If the pertinent VSL is $10 million, is it appropriate to assign a value to this temporary disability of $0.20 \times \$10$ million, or $2 million? Making a calculation such as this assumes that a moderate disability is equivalent to a one-fifth chance of death. As with happiness scales, these hybrid calculations mix and match the VSL with conceptually unrelated approaches. These misuses of the VSL also make the implicit assumption that the VSL is not a deterrence number but is a compensatory damages amount that can be adjusted proportionally using some arbitrary scale.

Principles for Addressing Pain and Suffering

Pain and suffering constitute one important component of mortality risks. The breakdown of VSL into the value of the fatality risk and the value of the morbidity risk indicates that the pain and suffering component exceeds $1 million for acute accidents and may be somewhat higher in the case of fatalities accompanied by prolonged morbidity effects, as with cancer. Pain and suffering does matter and is an important component of the VSL. Should such values be used in the context of setting pain and suffering awards in wrongful death cases? As is the case with VSL generally, these values are pertinent for deterrence and are not values for purposes of compensation. And in the punitive damages contexts in which the application of the VSL is appropriate, setting damages based on the entire VSL, not just the fatality risk valuation component, already incorporates the value of the associated pain and suffering.

Pain and suffering awards also arise in the context of nonfatal injuries, raising similar conceptual issues. Understanding the economic theory pertaining to the optimal levels of insurance compensation is instructive and has similar implications for fatalities as well as for very severe injuries. Some of the best-known court awards involved substantial compensation for pain and suffering. A well-known example involving pain and suffering as well as medical expenses is the award to the woman who spilled a hot cup of McDonald's coffee on her lap, leading to a $2.9 million award that was subsequently reduced to $640,000. There clearly is a deterrence rationale for preventing the infliction of such pain and suffering, but is this a harm for which compensatory damages for the pain and suffering component are desirable?

There are several types of pain and suffering losses that might be candidates for compensation. In addition to the physical pain suffered at the time of the injury and during treatment for the injury, there also may be anguish and terror associated with an impending injury, such as during an airplane crash. The accident victim also may have suffered a loss of enjoyment of life either through death or permanent disability. Finally, the family of the deceased may experience a loss of love and companionship after a fatality. These are all legitimate loss components. But how should we think about these impacts from the standpoint of appropriate levels of compensation, setting aside issues of deterrence?

A useful thought experiment is to inquire whether people would choose to purchase insurance for such injuries if such insurance was available on an actuarially fair basis. The standard economic prescription is that optimal insurance levels will equate the incremental effect on welfare (i.e., the marginal utility of income) in the injured and healthy conditions.[32] In the case of fatalities, empirical evidence indicates that people place a lower value on bequests than they do on having money while they are alive. However, even in the case of non-fatal injuries, the marginal utility of money may be diminished after major injuries. Serious physical injuries may limit the ability to derive additional well-being through consumption expenditures. There may, of course, be tremendous value that can be derived through rehabilitation expenditures, handicap-accessible ramps, and assisted care for severe injuries. These types of expenses are included as part of the medical and rehabilitation components of economic damages and are not pertinent to the quite different matter of whether pain and suffering per se should be insured.

As a practical matter, people do not generally purchase insurance for the pain and suffering associated with accidents. One problem is that there is the potential for misrepresentation of the ailment. Monitoring the severity of the pain may be difficult, especially if it is based on self-reports. However, there are more fundamental forces at work. My empirical studies with William N. Evans on the structure of individual utility functions implies that serious job injuries reduce the marginal utility of income so that full income replacement after an injury is not desirable.[33] As a result, based on these impacts, the optimal level of earnings replacement that workers would choose is 0.85, or less than full replacement of their earnings loss after on-the-job injuries. In contrast, minor consumer product injuries, such as temporary hand burns from toilet bowl cleaner, do not lower the marginal utility of income.[34] These inflictions of pain and suffering are tantamount to monetary losses, and full insurance of these losses would be appropriate.

At first glance, our results for the implications of pain and suffering may seem to be contradictory.[35] Either injuries reduce the marginal utility of income or they don't. However, the effect of the injury depends on the severity and whether it impairs a person's ability to derive utility from additional expenditures. Serious injuries lead to such impairments, but minor injuries do not. In the example of the temporary hand burn, the injured consumer will have fully returned to normal health by the time any compensation for the injury is paid so that there would be no diminishment of the welfare benefit that can be derived from the compensation.

These results suggest that the economic case for pain and suffering compensation for serious injuries and deaths is often problematic. Pain and suffering clearly matter in cases where deterrence concerns are paramount or for minor harms that don't impede people's ability to enjoy consumption expenditures. This lack of a broad economic justification for pain and suffering compensation has led legal scholars such as Jeffrey O'Connell to advocate tort liability reform that is not unlike the structure of workers' compensation in that there would be expedited compensation of victims but without pain and suffering awards.[36] A practical rationale for keeping a pain and suffering component of damages is that these payments provide the leeway to cover claimants' legal fees. In order for the compensation to serve an insurance function and cover the economic losses that were incurred, claimants must receive a payment that enables them to cover their legal expenses and still have enough funds to address the economic losses that were incurred. For these reasons, even tort reform proposals that advocate eliminating pain and suffering generally include a provision for reasonable legal expenses associated with the claim.

Judicial Restraints on Arbitrary Valuations of Mortality Risks

A final judicial role with respect to the VSL can be in providing quality control with respect to irresponsible selection of the VSL levels by government agencies. Might there be a judicial check on agency practices that set wildly inappropriate values on mortality risks? While agencies may undertake such policies that are not subject to benefit-cost tests, major new regulatory proposals are subject to administrative requirements to analyze benefits and costs. To not be in violation of the Administrative Procedure Act, agencies must not act arbitrarily. One might raise the broader issue of whether agencies have acted arbitrarily if they do not utilize benefit-cost analysis in making policy decisions.[37] However, here I focus on the narrower issue of whether agencies have acted arbitrarily by failing to use reasonable estimates of the VSL to value mortality risk reductions in their benefit-cost analyses. A potential check on such abuses is judicial review of the agency's analysis. To date there have been more than several dozen judicial reviews of benefit-cost analyses, leading to some regulations being overturned because of shortcomings in the analysis, such as the failure to analyze pertinent benefit and cost components.[38]

One might envision agencies advocating departures in either direction from reasonable levels of the VSL. Consider two possible extremes. An administration committed to deregulation might suggest reverting to the cost-of-death approach for valuing mortality risks, reducing the value placed on these risks by an order of magnitude to about $1 million. As a result of this reduction in lifesaving benefits, the agency in turn can justify the repeal of existing regulations and adoption of less stringent new regulations. At the other extreme are advocates who oppose the monetization of mortality risks, arguing that the welfare effects are too sacred to be valued in monetary terms. Thus, under this approach, the expected lives saved would receive no specific monetary value in the benefits calculation because such risks are "priceless."[39]

The practical ramifications of these seemingly opposite positions may be quite similar. In each instance, the risk reduction benefits will receive either a greatly diminished monetary value or no explicit monetary value. Moreover, it is likely that agencies will claim that they of course will take these mortality risk effects into account in their qualitative discussion of benefits. However, the consequence is likely to be the undervaluation of lives in each instance, as was the case before agencies adopted the VSL approach.

Whether the courts could overturn benefit-cost analyses adopting these practices may vary with the nature of the departure from the VSL. The cost-of-death approach is outside of the mainstream economics procedures for valuing mortality risks. Since there is no technical barrier to performing the analysis correctly, it is likely that challenges to such analyses would be successful. Overturning the complete failure to monetize the expected lifesaving benefits because of the sacred nature of life may be more difficult. But in practice, no agency ever places an infinite value on risks to life. It is usually possible to calculate the cost per expected life saved by the regulation, which serves as a measure of how much the agency has implicitly valued such risks even without attaching an explicit figure to the risk. Because judicial reviews of such agency actions are not routine and legal challenges are not always successful, the ideal solution is for government agencies to value risks to life properly rather than be compelled to do so by the courts.

Implications for the VSL in the Courts

There are three related junctures at which the VSL could play a pivotal role in the courts' treatment of personal injury cases: the amount of compensation, the determination of liability, and the establishment of efficient incentives for risk reduction. Regrettably, there is no single economic formula that can address all of these matters. The compromise I have suggested is reliance on standard approaches in setting compensatory damages, use of the VSL in determining liability, and application of the VSL in setting the total damages amount when there is a substantial shortfall in safety so that punitive damages are warranted. This selective application of the VSL is an effort to strike a balance between providing meaningful economic incentives and avoiding the problem of excess insurance amounts.

Consider first the compensation objective. Examination of the damages practices in the courts and in various administrative compensation schemes highlights the wide disparities between the VSL and conventional damages approaches for wrongful death. The courts do not get the answer wrong by failing to adopt the VSL as the default compensatory damages measure in wrongful death cases. There have been some limited attempts to introduce hedonic damages in the courtroom as well as proposals in the literature to adopt the VSL as a routine basis for damages compensation, but there has not been widespread adoption of the VSL for these purposes. Doing so would escalate tort damages and generate inordinately excessive insurance amounts.

The courts also have yet to adopt the use of the VSL for the second function, which is with respect to ascertaining the adequate level of investment in safety. There are two situations in which such tradeoffs can arise. The first is in the courts. Determining whether the firm is negligent requires an assessment of the value of safety improvements, for which the VSL can provide assistance by both establishing the value of safety and framing the risk reduction decision as a prospective choice involving risks rather than a comparison of an identified victim with the cost of the safety improvement—a hindsight comparison that even responsible firms will generally lose. The related use of the VSL is by firms in setting the level of product safety. As I proposed in chapter 3, provision of a safe harbor for use of the VSL in risk analyses could facilitate efforts by companies to undertake meaningful, responsible risk analyses.

A third, and as of yet never utilized, role of the VSL is in setting punitive damages to provide adequate incentives for safety when there are extreme departures from the requisite level of safety. For such cases of reckless disregard for safety, basing damages on the VSL will generate adequate incentives for deterrence. This targeted use of the VSL will foster safety incentives when they are most needed without creating the widespread problem of excessive insurance that would arise if compensatory damages were always based on the VSL.

The only shortfall of this proposal is that when compensatory damages do not include the VSL, companies may lack the incentive to invest in the requisite amount of safety. They will, however, face a determination of liability based on the VSL, and if their safety decisions reflect a sufficient disregard for safety, they will be subject to punitive damages based on the VSL. The underlying difficulty is that a single mechanism—the damages award in a wrongful death case—cannot simultaneously ensure an efficient level of insurance and an efficient level of safety incentives. To the extent that there are remaining gaps from a risk reduction standpoint, it is important to recall that the entire burden of promoting safety does not rest with the courts. Government regulations in which the stringency of regulations are tied to the VSL can establish an efficient overall level of safety, particularly for mass-marketed consumer products. Market forces and administrative compensation schemes also may come into play.

The approach I advocate represents a tremendous expansion in how the courts and firms would utilize the VSL in determining liability and setting punitive damages. The focus on how this liability structure would affect the overall performance of tort liability should not lead us to lose sight of the additional dividend of reliance on the VSL in terms of how different people will be treated under my proposed remedy. Current approaches to damages incorporate large components of inequality. Children and those with low earnings fare particularly poorly, and those with more substantial financial resources receive preferential treatment based on the structure of the damages formulas. Application of the VSL in determining liability and setting punitive damages would serve as an equalizer in terms of ensuring adequate levels of safety and setting effective, comparable levels of punitive damages.

10

Setting Safety Guideposts for Private and Public Institutions

The Morality of the VSL Approach

The value of a statistical life serves as a mechanism for incorporating the public's preferences for safety into a wide range of institutional policies. While its use has been greatest in governmental assessments of perspective regulations, it can also assist in transforming corporate risk decisions, judicial practices, and regulatory sanctions. In each of these domains, the increased reliance on the VSL as a safety guidepost will enhance safety and lead to greater health risk protections. Given this record of enhancing safety, it is perhaps puzzling that most of the criticism of the VSL has been from advocates of more vigorous regulatory policies.

One possible explanation for this opposition to the VSL is a lack of understanding of the VSL concept and its implications. The "economic value of life" conjures up images of an accountant tallying up a person's income or taxes that they pay as a measure of their worth to society. It may also be the case that few people outside of the government are aware of the more protective policies that have emerged because government agencies have adopted the VSL approach.

However, in many of my discussions with environmental and union activists, I have found that the resistance to the VSL is not about the VSL but is really more general uneasiness about basing policies on benefit-cost tests. Because of the central role of the VSL in governmental regulatory analyses, advocates of regulatory approaches that dispense with any grounding on a comparison of costs and benefits blame the VSL for the necessity of balancing the two. The nature of their complaint typically goes beyond any specific VSL number. Rather, their plea is to have policy practices that are unfettered by any attempt to ensure that the benefits are commensurate with the costs. The VSL serves as the target for their attack, but it is the entire policy analysis apparatus that they would like to jettison. However, benefit-cost tests exist independently of the use of the VSL.

The alternative of not placing a dollar value on mortality risk reductions might serve to diminish controversy, but will lead to less protective policies. There is no feasible option of valuing expected lives by an infinite amount, which is an approach frequently suggested by the math-challenged critics of the VSL. So long as societal resources are constrained, we will have to set finite financial limits on safety-related efforts. Application of the VSL has pushed these limits outward and has boosted the desired level of stringency of risk regulations.

Although we cannot place an infinite value on fatality risks, perhaps we could sidestep the controversy by not setting any price on safety, thus avoiding the purported commodification of human life. Failure to monetize the mortality risk benefits will make them less consequential than the seemingly more real cost numbers. The genesis of governmental evaluation of regulations began with an exclusive focus on costs and inflationary impacts. Impacts such as fatality risk reductions and environmental impacts merited qualitative discussion but were not the key drivers of the assessment. The adoption of the VSL is consistent with government agencies' efforts over several decades to demonstrate that policy outcomes that are not readily priced in markets also merit substantial dollar values and are just as real in terms of economic impact as are the costs of providing greater levels of safety.

Societal valuation of lives is not a new phenomenon. The courts have been doing this for decades using amounts that substantially undervalue the importance of preventing deaths. These procedures are so ingrained that there is very little public criticism of the methods used by the courts. This immunity to criticism is especially remarkable given the tying of the compensation amounts to the income levels of those whose losses are being assessed and the current societal concern with income inequality. Regulatory agencies searching for an economic framework to value reduced risks of death originally adopted the courts' methodology for setting damages in wrongful death cases, which they termed the cost-of-death approach. This framework is better suited for compensating the families after a fatality than for ascertaining how much it is worth to reduce the risk of death. Surprisingly, the cost-of-death approach's bottom basement valuation of life generated little controversy.

In contrast, some observers view it as immoral to use the procedure that is now most commonly referred to as the value of a statistical life, even though it boosted the value of mortality risk reductions by an order of magnitude greater than the cost-of-death approach and led to the justification of more protective regulations. Apparently, not identifying what was being valued by couching it in the terminology of the "cost of death" kept the nature of the valuations that were being made under wraps. Shifting to the VSL approach and identifying the risk-cost tradeoffs makes the sensitive nature of governmental risk regulation decisions more open to public scrutiny. Government agencies periodically search for a more opaque term than the VSL to disguise the sensitive valuations being made. But regardless of whether agencies succeed in adopting an obfuscatory terminology for money-risk tradeoff benefit values, the fundamental nature of government valuation practices will continue to involve sensitive balancing of costs and risks either explicitly or implicitly.

The current shortfall is the failure to fully exploit more generally the insights provided by the VSL. There are three broad classes of social institutions involved in making safety decisions, providing incentives for safety, and determining compensation for injuries—the market, the courts, and government regulation. Each of these institutions could expand the role of VSL and, in doing so, serve as a more constructive force for promoting safety. In each instance, the proposed change does not involve some subtle modification of the level of the VSL. The general range of the VSL estimates is well established. Rather, there is an opportunity to greatly broaden the menu of the uses of the VSL, which to date has largely been confined to benefit assessments in the analysis of proposed major regulations.

The Safety Challenges for Corporations

The deficiencies of firms' product safety decisions loom especially large. Companies formerly used the cost-of-death approach in their attempts at risk analyses of product safety but have never embraced the use of the VSL. In many instances, as epitomized by the GM experience, there has been complete abandonment of systematic risk analyses. As a result, exploiting the guidance provided by the VSL in conjunction with systematic risk assessments could transform the character of corporate risk policies. The chronology of corporate practices bears remarkable similarities to that of government agencies. Particularly in the automobile industry, companies made early attempts at meaningful risk analyses, relying on a cost-of-death measure of the value of lives rather than the VSL, as did government agencies. However, companies never made the shift to the VSL as they were pummeled in legal proceedings for product risk-cost analyses using the cost-of-death approach. The enormous liability costs that were inflicted as a result of these ill-conceived efforts undoubtedly contributed to the complete abandonment of a comprehensive effort to assess the costs and risks associated with different product decisions rather than searching for a sounder risk analysis approach. Companies' failure to attempt meaningful risk analyses is not in consumers' interests or that of the companies.

Rather than shunting risk valuation issues to the side and, in some cases, suppressing all meaningful attempts to consider risk-related matters, companies should be encouraged to use the VSL in setting product safety levels. From a conceptual standpoint, the VSL has a natural role to play in such analyses. The revealed-preference estimates of VSL could enable companies to incorporate firm empirical evidence on consumer preferences when choosing the product characteristics to provide. These VSL estimates reflect the value that consumers would place on safety if they were cognizant of the product risk attributes. Thus, use of the VSL in effect replicates what a well-functioning market should achieve.

Companies' failure to adopt risk analysis practices that mimic those of regulatory agencies is not due to ignorance. Corporate officials and their trade associations frequently intervene to influence the economic content of governmental regulatory impact analyses. However, companies have not ventured forth into similar analytical terrain because undertaking meaningful risk analyses poses potential liability hazards to the firm. As past experience with corporate risk analyses has demonstrated, systematic risk analyses may expose companies to public misunderstandings of the product design process, leading to the imposition of punitive damages. Undertaking such a risk assessment demonstrates that the company was aware of the risk, which is a frequent criterion in jury instructions for the award of punitive damages. My experimental evidence with jury-eligible citizens suggests that even responsible corporate risk analyses may encounter enormous resistance. Regulatory agencies do not risk being sanctioned for undertaking comprehensive risk-cost tradeoffs, and indeed, executive orders require them to do so. However, the threat of punitive damages looms particularly large for corporations that market a potentially dangerous product for which they have undertaken a risk analysis. Simply educating companies on the wisdom of risk analyses based on the VSL will not suffice unless companies also have additional legal protections. The objective of such protections is not to exempt companies from liability for making unsafe products. Such liability would be unaffected. However, companies should not be faulted for undertaking a systematic risk analysis to better inform their product safety decisions. Statutory provision of a safe harbor for companies that undertake such analyses would be ideal. Plaintiffs should not be permitted to introduce evidence regarding risk analyses that indicate that the company sought to strike an efficient balance between cost and risk. Companies would, however, have the leeway to introduce such evidence regarding risk analyses to demonstrate their corporate responsibility. In much the same way that medical malpractice apology laws shield physicians from having the apology used against them in court, plaintiffs likewise would not be able to use the act of undertaking a risk analysis as evidence of reckless company behavior.

In the absence of statutory safe harbor laws, regulatory agencies could issue guidance for companies to structure safety-related matters in that agency's domain. In most instances, this guidance need not be more complicated than the US Office of Management and Budget's guidelines for regulatory analysis coupled with agency guidance on the valuation of mortality risks. The existence of such guidance would give companies a reference point for justifying the critical importance of thinking systematically about risk before putting products on the market. The level of protection afforded by such guidelines would be comparable to that of a regulatory compliance defense in that it would be potentially helpful but not exculpatory.

Expanding the Role of the VSL in the Courts

Unlike the situation for corporate risk analyses, the courts have occasionally used the VSL estimates, though the cost-of-death measure remains the dominant approach. Unfortunately, the adoption of the VSL in judicial contexts has often involved a misuse of the VSL as a substitute for the cost-of-death measure in routine wrongful death cases, thus providing an excessive level of insurance to the decedent's survivors. The enthusiasm for establishing a high VSL anchor for damages awards has been the dominant approach rather than exploiting the substantive import of the VSL, which is that this risk-cost tradeoff measure serves as the guidepost for appropriate safety and deterrence efforts.

There is consequently the opportunity to extend the traditional role of the courts to incorporate the VSL in two contexts. First, the determination of whether products have struck an appropriate balance between risk and cost should be based on a benefit-cost test in which the VSL serves as the price for the expected lives that will be saved through additional safety measures. In addition to setting the correct price to induce efficient levels of safety, this approach also casts the assessment of whether firms were negligent in terms of the prospective benefits that would be generated by additional safety measures and the associated costs. Companies are making decisions with respect to costs across a product line and risk probabilities, not costs to avert an identified death where the victim is known in advance. In contrast, standard jury assessments are distorted by the impact of hindsight bias and the comparison of identified lives lost with unit safety costs per product. Thus, the use of the VSL has a twofold benefit. Not only does it establish an efficient price for safety, but it also transforms the jury's task to that of determining whether the prospective expected lives saved warranted the extra costs rather than comparing an identified victim's life with the modest unit cost of safety improvements.

The second role of the VSL in the judicial system is with respect to setting total damages amounts in wrongful death cases in which punitive damages are warranted. Jurors have little meaningful guidance for setting punitive damages awards, as jury instructions provide no concrete assistance in mapping jurors' concerns into a punitive damages amount. There have been more than one hundred blockbuster punitive damages awards in excess of $100 million, many of which were for situations involving corporate risk analyses. This utilization of the VSL will provide much needed structure and discipline to setting punitive awards and will also establish the penalty level needed to create incentives for safety. Whereas there currently is some sporadic, limited role of the VSL in setting hedonic damages, the adoption of the VSL approach to punitive damages and to determining liability is distinct from any existing uses of the VSL by the courts.

Expanding the Government's Use of the VSL

Fostering incorporation of the VSL in companies' product risk decisions and giving the VSL a greater role in the courtroom will have a constructive impact, but these changes alone may not be sufficient to ensure adequate levels of safety. Government regulatory practices and other policy efforts constitute a third institutional avenue in which there are opportunities for an expanded role of the VSL with respect to both the evaluation and the implementation of policies.

One might assume that there are few additional opportunities for the VSL to influence government practices. Government agencies already use the VSL to a greater extent than private companies or the judicial system. Government agencies have been at the forefront in integrating the VSL in regulatory analyses and in establishing standards for health, safety, and environmental quality. While there are various ways in which these agency practices concerning regulatory analyses might be improved, for the most part, regulatory agencies have adopted VSL analyses that are in the general range of reasonable estimates.

However, the government does more with respect to risk than simply promulgate major new regulations. Even for existing regulations, there are many policy-related decisions and implementation efforts that entail critical judgments regarding risk. Efforts that do not involve new regulations, ranging from flood control measures to food safety inspection practices, likewise involve considerations of cost and risk. The potential dividends from adopting the VSL to guide these agency practices were illustrated by the hazardous waste cleanup example in chapter 7. Without having to promulgate any new major regulations that would require a regulatory impact assessment, the US Environmental Protection Agency routinely makes decisions regarding which hazardous waste sites most merit cleanup and which do not. Targeting these remediation efforts based on the expected risk reduction values based on the VSL would be more protective of the populations exposed to risk than the current policy regime. Widespread utilization of the VSL in the targeting of risk policies would lead to sounder priorities than the current reliance on influences such as the political clout of the region's legislators and local voting histories.

Perhaps the most promising governmental opportunity for expanding the use of the VSL is with respect to regulatory sanctions. Even though the VSL establishes the appropriate deterrence price to

induce regulated firms to set efficient levels of safety, current practices for setting regulatory sanctions do not incorporate the VSL.
Indeed, statutory provisions often cap regulatory sanctions at surprisingly trivial levels that assign to lost lives the level of importance
that one might accord to infractions such as incorrectly completed
paperwork. The result is that there is a tremendous inadequacy in
the financial incentives for safety that are generated.

The GM ignition switch experience documented in chapter 4
illustrated the shortfall in regulatory sanctions for this highly publicized defect-induced carnage. Although some might fault the
National Highway Traffic Safety Administration for not being sufficiently aggressive in its sanctions of GM, the critical deficiency was
not NHTSA's response to the defects but the statutory restriction
on fines, which were limited to $7,000 per violation and $35 million for a series of violations. Although the maximum permissible
penalty amounts for NHTSA and other agencies have since been
updated for inflation, they remain inadequate. Removing these caps
and establishing a formal link between regulatory sanctions involving fatalities and the VSL used in agency regulatory analyses would
greatly bolster the incentives that regulatory sanctions could provide
to promote transportation safety.

The rationale for more stringent penalties coupled with statutory
amendments to permit setting penalties at a level commensurate
with the VSL is not limited to transportation-related hazards. This
approach should become the norm for all health, safety, and environmental regulations. Consider the sanctions imposed by the
Occupational Safety and Health Administration after workplace fatalities. The median penalty for safety violations related to the death
of a worker was $7,000 for federal OSHA enforcement actions and
$3,500 for state-run OSHA plans in fiscal year 2015.[1] In each case,
the level of sanctions is about three orders of magnitude less than is
warranted based on the VSL. There is some administrative leeway
to impose greater sanctions, which agency officials should exploit.
Even after the inflation-adjusted increase in penalty levels in 2016,
OSHA penalties remain modest. The maximum penalty amounts
are $12,471 for serious violations, $12,471 per day for failure to abate

hazards beyond the abatement date, and $124,709 for willful or repeated violations.[2] Although there is the possibility of criminal sanctions for violations causing deaths, since the advent of OSHA in 1970, there have been only eighty-nine criminal prosecutions.[3] If convicted, the maximum monetary sanction is limited to $500,000 for companies.[4] In comparison, the financial incentives for safety provided by wage premiums for fatal and nonfatal risks combine with workers' compensation costs to total over $100 billion annually. Government sanctions for risk-related violations must be considerably greater than they are now to augment these market incentives in a meaningful way.

The NHTSA and OSHA are not the only agencies with caps on permissible penalty amounts. The Food and Drug Administration can levy fines up to $26,723 per medical device violation, with a limit of $1,781,560 in a single proceeding.[5] Similarly, food safety fines are capped at $75,123 per violation for individuals, $375,613 for companies, with a maximum fine of $751,225 in a single proceeding. Likewise, the EPA has a series of quite modest maximum penalty amounts for various statutory violations relating to water pollution, air pollution, hazardous waste disposal, and other environmental programs.[6]

As in the case of the US Department of Transportation, the agenda for bolstering regulatory sanctions for risk-related agencies is twofold. First, in situations involving deaths, the sanctions for regulatory violations should be linked as closely as possible to the VSL. To the extent that agencies have administrative leeway to raise current penalty levels, they should exploit it. Second, Congress should greatly increase the statutory limits with respect to sanctions that can be imposed for regulatory violations, particularly for hazards involving risks of serious injury and death. Given that the core features of these statutes have remained largely unchanged for almost half a century, other than for updates for inflation, and were drafted before there were any estimates of what is now the VSL, it is not too soon to begin rethinking how these agencies can better accomplish their missions.

Similar constraints on penalty levels have prevailed in other countries as well. Under the UK Health and Safety at Work Act of 1974, the monetary penalties for health and safety offenses in magistrates' courts were previously capped at £20,000.[7] While this maximum was removed for all offenses committed after March 12, 2015, the enforcement guidance documents do not make any reference to the use of the VSL or indications that the penalty levels might be a couple orders of magnitude greater than the previous penalty maximum.[8]

Evidence on labor market performance provided by the VSL studies may assist government agencies in identifying contexts where there are evident failures both in market operations and current regulatory remedies. A prominent example is that of Mexican immigrant workers, who face above-average job risks but do not receive appropriate remuneration for these substantial additional risks. The deficiencies are especially acute for immigrant workers who are not fluent in English, as they receive no evident wage premium at all for the hazards they incur. Such gaps highlight the situations where there is both a market failure and a regulatory failure in which inordinate exposures to risk remain.

Application of the VSL also can provide a reference point for establishing a sensible approach to what we mean by risk equity, which has been a recurring governmental concern that has lacked strong guidance for what is meant by equitable. Establishing equitable risk tradeoffs in terms of the amount expended per expected life saved is a more meaningful risk equity concept than attempting to equalize risk levels or incremental risk levels across the population. Evidence with respect to hazardous waste cleanup efforts demonstrates that policies based on such risk tradeoffs would be more effective in saving lives and protecting minority groups than the current policies undertaken under the banner of environmental equity. In this and in many other situations, equity and efficiency may be complementary objectives with respect to government efforts to promote safety.

Fine-Tuning This Unified Approach

The VSL provides a single guidepost that establishes a consistent price for safety across the principal societal institutions. Corporations can use the VSL in making corporate risk decisions to establish levels of product safety. The courts can use the VSL in judging the adequacy of these decisions and in setting punitive damages. And government agencies can use the VSL in policy analyses and in setting regulatory sanctions. The VSL has the remarkable ability to set a consistent and efficient price for safety across each of these domains.

My proposed overhaul of risk-related practices by firms, the courts, and government agencies relies on the insights provided by a general application of VSL guidance, but if refinements are needed, they would be feasible. Much of the stability of the VSL across different contexts stems from the dominant component of the VSL being the value of the fatality risk component of the VSL. It is the risk of the loss of life rather than the associated morbidity effects that is the principal concern. As a result, the VSL estimates based on labor market studies are likely to have broad applicability with respect to other risks of death. Those studies relying on the more recent CFOI fatality data are the most credible and also the least subject to publication selection biases. Using these estimates as the baseline, one can then augment these values for risks of death such as cancer that may command a modest premium.

It is also possible to refine VSL estimates based on characteristics such as income and age. The dependence of the VSL on income follows the expected patterns and suggests that the VSL estimates in the United States should exceed those in other countries with lower income levels. However, the extent of the current gap between the US VSL and those in other countries is often too great. There appears to be an international tendency to undervalue lives just as US agencies once did. Examination of age variations in the VSL demonstrates that there is greater stability in the VSL with respect to age than one might expect based on differences in remaining life expectancy. In most situations, whether they involve broadly based government policies or mass-marketed consumer products, fine-tuning of the VSL to reflect such heterogeneity is not a key issue.

We already know a great deal about the VSL. A lack of knowledge is not the barrier to exploiting its potential in promoting safety. The present economic approach to health, safety, and environmental risks embodies enormous inconsistencies across different institutions and across countries. While the VSL is now entrenched in government regulatory analyses, the VSL has not fulfilled its logical role in the operations of firms, the courts, and government agencies throughout the world. Utilization of the VSL establishes an efficient monetary guidepost for safety in a variety of contexts, not just in regulatory analyses. Moreover, just as the shift from the cost-of-death approach to the VSL led to more stringent regulatory policies, greater utilization of the VSL in these other domains will generate greater protections from risk. Broader adoption of the VSL will rectify the systematic underpricing of lives, providing the guideposts for a safer society.

Chapter One: How Pricing Lives Saves Lives

1. My 1976 dissertation was published as W. Kip Viscusi, *Employment Hazards: An Investigation of Market Performance* (Cambridge, MA: Harvard University Press, 1979).

2. See Thomas C. Schelling, "The Life You Save May Be Your Own," in *Problems in Public Expenditure Analysis*, ed. Samuel B. Chase, Jr. (Washington, DC: Brookings Institution, 1968).

3. My role in this regulatory debate is discussed in Pete Earley, "What's a Life Worth? How the Reagan Administration Decides for You," *Washington Post Magazine*, June 9, 1985, p. 36.

4. National Safety Council, *Injury Facts: 2016 Edition* (Itasca, IL: National Safety Council, 2016), p. 2.

5. There were also deficiencies in the fatality rate used in those studies, including all mortality risks of people in different occupations rather than their job-specific risks, overstating the level of the risk variable and leading to a downward bias in the estimated value of a statistical life. Such low estimates appear in Richard Thaler and Sherwin Rosen, "The Value of Saving a Life: Evidence from the Labor Market," in *Household Production and Consumption*, ed. Nestor E. Terleckyj (New York: National Bureau of Economic Research, 1976).

6. See US Office of Management and Budget, Office of Information and Regulatory Affairs, *2015 Report to Congress on the Benefits and Costs of Federal Regulations and Agency Compliance with the Unfunded Mandates Reform Act* (2015), p. 13, https://obamawhitehouse.archives.gov/sites/default/files/omb/inforeg/2015_cb/2015-cost-benefit-report.pdf [https://perma.cc/ERR4-VQ3L]. This report concludes, "The largest benefits are associated with regulations that reduce the risks to life." Regulations by the Environmental Protection Agency and the US Department of Transportation are most influential, as documented in table 1–1, pp. 9–10.

7. Even critics of the VSL approach make a similar observation that "the value of life is easily the single most important number in the economics of health and environmental protection, frequently accounting for the great majority of the benefits in cost-benefit studies." See Frank Ackerman and Lisa Heinzerling, *Priceless: On Knowing the Price of Everything and the Value of Nothing* (New York: New Press, 2004), pp. 61–62.

8. For discussion of the commodification of lives resulting from use of the VSL, see Mark Kelman, *A Guide to Critical Legal Studies* (Cambridge, MA: Harvard University Press, 1987); and Lisa Heinzerling and Mark V. Tushnet, *The Regulatory and Administrative State: Materials, Cases, Comments* (New York: Oxford University Press, 2006).

9. Richard Berkman and W. Kip Viscusi, *Damming the West* (New York: Grossman, 1973).

10. The role of risk beliefs has been a continuing empirical concern, beginning with my doctoral dissertation, Viscusi, *Employment Hazards*, and W. Kip Viscusi, *Risk by Choice: Regulating Health and Safety in the Workplace* (Cambridge, MA: Harvard University Press, 1983). Note too that from the standpoint of economic theory, not all workers need to perceive the risk, only the marginal worker whose preferences affect the required wage at the firm.

11. W. Kip Viscusi and Charles J. O'Connor, "Adaptive Responses to Chemical Labeling: Are Workers Bayesian Decision Makers?" *American Economic Review* 74, no. 5 (1984): 942–956.

12. Many of the results of these studies appeared in the following two books: W. Kip Viscusi and Wesley A. Magat, *Learning about Risk: Consumer and Worker Responses to Hazard Information* (Cambridge, MA: Harvard University Press, 1987); and Wesley A. Magat and W. Kip Viscusi, *Informational Approaches to Regulation* (Cambridge, MA: MIT Press, 1992).

13. The objective of warnings is to provide information that will foster an understanding of the risks and responsible behavior. Our studies yielded several principles for the design of effective warnings policies. First, effective warnings are those that provide new information in a convincing manner. Reminder warnings that do not provide new information or that seek to browbeat consumers into changing their behavior are ineffective. Second, parsimonious readable warnings are preferable. In practice, warnings often suffer from label clutter whereby consumers are unable to ferret out the key message of the warning, such as pertinent precautions. Readability does not require that warnings shout out a message, only that the warning format and text be easily accessible. Finally, we documented the effect of information overload whereby providing too much information tends to obscure the most important warnings message. Over time, this concern becomes particularly pertinent for consumer products as companies and government agencies add warnings concerning additional, less prominent hazards without taking into account the effect of information overload on the overall efficacy of the warning.

Chapter Two: How the Government Values Risks to Life

1. Adam Smith, *The Wealth of Nations* (1776), Modern Library Edition (New York: Random House, 1994).

2. See Michael J. Moore and W. Kip Viscusi, "Doubling the Estimated Value of Life: Results Using New Occupational Fatality Data," *Journal of Policy Analysis and Management* 7, no. 3 (1988): 476–490.

3. For a review of the capabilities of the CFOI data and economists' use of these data to estimate VSL, see W. Kip Viscusi, "Using Data from the Census of Fatal Occupational Injuries to Estimate the 'Value of a Statistical Life,'" *Monthly Labor Review* (October 2013): 1–17.

4. As discussed in chapter 8, if one also adjusts for publication selection effects, the mean VSL is $9.8 million, and if one also adjusts for study-specific differences, the value rises to $10.7 million. See W. Kip Viscusi, "The Role of Publication Selection Bias in Estimates of the Value of a Statistical Life," *American Journal of Health Economics* 1, no. 1 (2015): 27–52, p. 34.

5. W. Kip Viscusi and Joseph E. Aldy, "The Value of a Statistical Life: A Critical Review of Market Estimates throughout the World," *Journal of Risk and Uncertainty* 27, no. 1 (2003): 5–76, p. 18. The $7 million estimate in that article has been converted to 2015 dollars. The best practices guidance in Australia also cites these estimates. See Australian Government, Department of the Prime Minister and Cabinet, Office of Best Practice Regulation, "Best Practice Regulation Guidance Note: Value of Statistical Life," December 2014, https://www.pmc.gov.au /sites/default/files/publications/Value_of_Statistical_Life_guidance_note.pdf [https://perma.cc/77C5-22LL].

6. US Department of Transportation, "Guidance on Treatment of the Economic Value of a Statistical Life (VSL) in US Department of Transportation Analyses—2015 Adjustment," June 17, 2015, https://www.transportation.gov/sites /dot.gov/files/docs/VSL2015_0.pdf [https://perma.cc/Y8DU-XV9Q].

7. Glenn Blomquist, "Value of Life Saving: Implications of Consumption Activity," *Journal of Political Economy* 87, no. 3 (1979): 540–558.

8. Jahn K. Hakes and W. Kip Viscusi, "Automobile Seatbelt Usage and the Value of Statistical Life," *Southern Economic Journal* 73, no. 3 (2007): 659–676.

9. Glenn C. Blomquist, Ted R. Miller, and David T. Levy, "Values of Risk Reduction Implied by Motorist Use of Protective Equipment: New Evidence from Different Populations," *Journal of Transport Economics and Policy* 30, no. 1 (1996): 55–66.

10. For example, see Christopher Garbacz, "More Evidence on Smoke Detector Effectiveness and the Value of Saving a Life," *Population Research and Policy Review* 10, no. 3 (1991): 273–287; and Robin R. Jenkins, Nicole Owens, and Lanelle Bembenek Wiggins, "Valuing Reduced Risks to Children: The Case of Bicycle Safety Helmets," *Contemporary Economic Policy* 19, no. 4 (2001): 397–408.

11. Mark K. Dreyfus and W. Kip Viscusi, "Rates of Time Preference and Consumer Valuations of Automobile Safety and Fuel Efficiency," *Journal of Law and Economics* 38, no. 1 (1995): 79–105.

12. Ted Gayer, James T. Hamilton, and W. Kip Viscusi, "Private Values of Risk Tradeoffs at Superfund Sites: Housing Market Evidence on Learning about Risk," *Review of Economics and Statistics* 82, no. 3 (2000): 439–451, p. 449.

13. Chris Rohlfs, Ryan Sullivan, and Thomas Kniesner, "New Estimates of the Value of a Statistical Life Using Air Bag Regulations as a Quasi-Experiment," *American Economic Journal: Economic Policy* 7, no. 1 (2015): 331–359.

14. Glenn C. Blomquist, "Motorist Use of Safety Equipment: Expected Benefits or Risk Incompetence?" *Journal of Risk and Uncertainty* 4, no. 2 (1991): 135–152.

15. Kenneth Arrow, Robert Solow, Paul R. Portney, Edward E. Leamer, Roy Radner, and Howard Schuman, "Report of the NOAA Panel on Contingent Valuation," *Federal Register* 58, no. 10 (January 11, 1993): 4601–4614.

16. Mariam Coaster, Baxter P. Rogers, Owen D. Jones, W. Kip Viscusi, Kristen L. Merkle, David H. Zald, and John C. Gore, "Variables Influencing the Neural Correlates of Perceived Risk of Physical Harm," *Cognitive, Affective, & Behavioral Neuroscience* 11, no. 4 (2011): 494–507. The experimental subjects also rated health risks presented in the frequency format relative to a specified population as being greater than those presented using a probability format.

17. M. W. Jones-Lee, M. Hammerton, and P. R. Philips, "The Value of Safety: Results of a National Sample Survey," *Economic Journal* 95, no. 377 (1985): 49–72.

18. For a meta-analysis of these and other estimates, see Viscusi and Aldy, "Value of a Statistical Life."

19. These statistics are updated to 2015 dollars using information from table 7.2 of W. Kip Viscusi, "The Value of Individual and Societal Risks to Life and Health," in *Handbook of the Economics of Risk and Uncertainty*, ed. Mark J. Machina and W. Kip Viscusi (Amsterdam: Elsevier, 2015), pp. 436–441.

20. My report provided the basis for my subsequent article, W. Kip Viscusi, "The Value of Risks to Life and Health," *Journal of Economic Literature* 31, no. 4 (1993): 1912–1946.

21. US Department of Health and Human Services, Food and Drug Administration, "Labeling for Bronchodilators to Treat Asthma; Cold, Cough, Allergy, Bronchodilator, and Antiasthmatic Drug Products for Over-the-Counter Human Use," *Federal Register* 76, no. 143 (July 26, 2011): 44475–44489.

22. US Office of Management and Budget, Circular A-4, "Regulatory Analysis," September 17, 2003, https://georgewbush-whitehouse.archives.gov/omb/circulars/a004/a-4.html [https://perma.cc/DCG4-DXNH].

23. US Department of Transportation, "Guidance" (2015).

24. US Environmental Protection Agency, "Valuing Mortality Risk Reductions for Policy: A Meta-Analytic Approach" (February 2016), p. 34, https://yosemite.epa.gov/sab/sabproduct.nsf/0/0CA9E925C9A702F285257F380050C842/$File/VSL%20white%20paper_final_020516.pdf [https://perma.cc/4LWD-NS2Z].

25. US Department of Health and Human Services, Office of the Assistant Secretary for Planning and Evaluation, *Guidelines for Regulatory Impact Analysis* (2016).

26. Chris Rohlfs, "The Economic Cost of Conscription and an Upper Bound on the Value of a Statistical Life: Hedonic Estimates from Two Margins of Response to the Vietnam Draft," *Journal of Benefit-Cost Analysis* 3, no. 3 (2012): 1–37. His VSL estimates are in the $1.6–$5.2 million range based on college enrollments to avoid the draft, and in the $7.4–$12.1 million range based on military enlistment decisions.

27. Thomas J. Kniesner, John D. Leeth, and Ryan S. Sullivan, "A New Approach to Evaluate Safety and Force Protection Investments: The Value of a Statistical Life," in *Military Cost-Benefit Analysis: Theory and Practice*, ed. Francois Melese, Anke Richter, and Binyam Solomon (New York: Routledge, 2015).

28. The international data are drawn from table 3.1 of Urvashi Narain and Chris Sall, *Methodology for Valuing the Health Impacts of Air Pollution: Discussion of Challenges and Proposed Solutions* (Washington, DC: World Bank Group, 2016), p. 25. These data are updated to 2015 dollars.

29. Australian Government, "Best Practice Regulation Guidance Note." The Australian figure is $4.2 million Australian dollars.

30. OECD, *Mortality Risk Valuation in Environment, Health and Transport Policies* (Paris: OECD Publishing, 2012).

31. UK Department for Transport, Highway Economics Note No. 1, "2005 Valuation of the Benefits of Prevention of Road Accidents and Casualties," January 2007. Converted to 2015 US dollars, the total value was $2,108,280.

32. For example, the survey by Jones-Lee, Hammerton, and Philips asked respondents how much they would be willing to pay to reduce different risks of death and how much they would be willing to pay for various safety features, leading to VSL estimates that included all components of potential loss. See Jones-Lee, Hammerton, and Philips, "Value of Safety."

33. US Bureau of Labor Statistics, "Revisions to the 2014 Census of Fatal Occupational Injuries (CFOI)," April 21, 2016, http://www.bls.gov/iif/cfoi_revised14 .htm [https://perma.cc/LYY7-2JUT].

34. This value is likely to be low, as many estimates are in the range of $70,000. For a review of these values, see Viscusi and Aldy, "Value of a Statistical Life."

35. US Bureau of Labor Statistics, "Nonfatal Occupational Injuries and Illnesses Requiring Days Away from Work, 2014," press release, November 10, 2016, http://www.bls.gov/news.release/pdf/osh2.pdf [https://perma.cc/ML9L -X6CL]. The total number of such injuries was 1,153,490.

36. Insurance Information Institute, *The Insurance Fact Book* (New York: Insurance Information Institute, 2016), p. 117.

37. Michael J. Moore and W. Kip Viscusi, *Compensation Mechanisms for Job Risks: Wages, Workers' Compensation and Product Liability* (Princeton, NJ: Princeton University Press, 1990).

38. This can be done in two principal ways. In my analysis of the proposed OSHA hazard communication regulation, I converted the reduced injuries into death risk equivalents based on the implicit value of job injuries. Alternatively, one could calculate regulatory costs net of benefits other than mortality risk reductions and analyze the value of these net costs per expected life saved. These shorthand summaries are helpful in tracking overall policy performance but are no substitute for a complete analysis of policy benefits and costs, as it is the net difference between benefits and costs that is the main matter of interest.

39. John F. Morrall III, "Saving Lives: A Review of the Record," *Journal of Risk and Uncertainty* 27, no. 3 (2003): 221–237. These values are in 2015 dollars.

40. See US Office of Management and Budget, Office of Information and Regulatory Affairs, *2015 Report to Congress on the Benefits and Costs of Federal Regulations and Agency Compliance with the Unfunded Mandates Reform Act* (2015), p. 13, https://obamawhitehouse.archives.gov/sites/default/files/omb/inforeg /2015_cb/2015-cost-benefit-report.pdf [https://perma.cc/ERR4-VQ3L]. Although some of the benefit estimates remain controversial, there has been a greater emphasis on regulatory proposals that have calculated benefits sufficient to justify the regulatory costs.

41. This and the subsequent Superfund estimates are from James T. Hamilton and W. Kip Viscusi, *Calculating Risks? The Spatial and Political Dimensions of Hazardous Waste Policy* (Cambridge, MA: MIT Press, 1999), p. 125. Cost estimates have been converted to 2015 dollars.

42. Ibid., chapters 4 and 5 examine the conservatism biases in EPA risk analyses for hazardous waste sites.

43. W. Kip Viscusi and James T. Hamilton, "Cleaning up Superfund," *Public Interest* 124 (Summer 1996): 52–60.

Chapter Three: The Hazards of Corporate Valuations of Product Risks

1. 174 Cal. Rptr. 348, 358 (Ct. App. 1981).

2. See Gary T. Schwartz, "The Myth of the Ford Pinto Case," *Rutgers Law Review* 43, no. 4 (1991): 1013–1068.

3. Ibid., 1020–1026.

4. Mark Dowie, "Pinto Madness," *Mother Jones*, September/October 1977, http://www.motherjones.com/politics/1977/09/pinto-madness [http://perma .cc/GDE7-36FD].

5. *Carroll v. Otis Elevator Co.*, 896 F.2d 210, 215–216 (7th Cir. 1990).

6. *Ford Motor Co. v. Stubblefield*, 319 S.E.2d 470, 475 (Ga. Ct. App. 1984).

7. Ibid., 481.

8. *Ford Motor Co. v. Miles*, 141 S.W.3d 309, 319 (Tex. App. 2004).

9. *Miles v. Ford Motor Co.*, 922 S.W.2d 572, 579 (Tex. App. 1996), remanded for procedural errors, *Ford Motor Co. v. Miles*, 967 S.W.2d 377 (Tex. 1998).

10. Ibid., 588–589.

11. See *Jimenez v. Daimler Chrysler Corp.*, 269 F.3d 439, 443 (4th Cir. 2001); *Jimenez v. Chrysler Corp.*, No. 2: 96–1269–11, 1997 WL 743644, at 1 (LRP Jury) (SC Oct. 8, 1997).

12. Donald C. Dilworth, "Jurors Punish Chrysler for Hiding Deadly Defect," *Trial*, February 1, 1998, available at http://www.thefreelibrary.com/Jurors +punish+Chrysler+for+hiding+deadly+defect.-a020379898 [http://perma.cc /3XXS-XD3Z].

13. 447 S.E.2d 302, 310 (Ga. Ct. App. 1994).

14. See Edward C. Ivey, "Value Analysis of Auto Fuel Fed Fire Related Fatalities," memorandum, June 29, 1973, transcript available at http://www.cnn.com

/US/9909/10/ivey.memo [https://perma.cc/X7KM-CBH8]; Terence Moran, "GM Burns Itself," *American Lawyer*, April 1993, pp. 68, 73.

15. For a description of strategies, proceedings, and deliberations in the *GM Corp. v. Moseley* trial, see Moran, "GM Burns Itself," 69.

16. Ivey, "Value Analysis," 2.

17. *GM Corp. v. Moseley*, 447 S.E.2d 302, 305 (Ga. Ct. App. 1994).

18. Walter Olson, "The Most Dangerous Vehicle on the Road," *Wall Street Journal*, February 9, 1993.

19. Moran, "GM Burns Itself," 82.

20. See Andrew Pollack, "$4.9 Billion Jury Verdict in G.M. Fuel Tank Case," *New York Times*, July 10, 1999, http://www.nytimes.com/1999/07/10/us/4.9 -billion-jury-verdict-in-gm-fuel-tank-case.html [http://perma.cc/TM3S-U6LN]; "GM Hit by $4.9 Billion Verdict," *CNN Money*, July 9, 1999, http://money.cnn .com/1999/07/09/home_auto/gm_verdict/ [http://perma.cc/2XEE-R6AS].

21. See Ann W. O'Neill, Henry Weinstein, and Eric Malnic, "GM Ordered to Pay $4.9 Billion in Crash Verdict," *Los Angeles Times*, July 10, 1999, http://articles .latimes.com/1999/jul/10/news/mn-54658 [https://perma.cc/A76F-VF57]; and Frank Swoboda and Caroline E. Mayer, "Jury Hits GM with Historic Crash Verdict," *Washington Post*, July 10, 1999, http://www.washingtonpost.com/wp-srv /national/longterm/supcourt/stories/jury071099.htm [http://perma.cc/3GWC -U6QZ].

22. Michael White, "$4.9 Billion Awarded in Gas Tank Accident," *Topeka Capital-Journal*, July 10, 1999, http://cjonline.com/stories/071099/bus_gmaward .shtml#.V3WKDbgrKUk [http://perma.cc/NYS4-8C2P].

23. Swoboda and Mayer, "Jury Hits GM."

24. Editorial, "Casino Justice," *Washington Post*, July 13, 1999, at A18.

25. Ibid., quoting Brian J. Panish, lawyer for the accident victims.

26. Ibid.

27. The value of fifty-five fatalities at $7 million per fatality is $385 million. With five million automobiles produced each year, the safety benefit per automobile is ($385 million/5 million automobiles), or $77.00 benefit per vehicle, which is almost an order of magnitude greater than the $8.59 per vehicle cost.

28. Jeffrey Ball and Milo Geyelin, "General Motors Is Ordered by a Jury to Pay $4.9 Billion in Fuel-Fire Case," *Wall Street Journal*, July 12, 1999, http://www.wsj .com/articles/SB931552704721866921 [https://perma.cc/2QW5-TB92].

29. See J. Stratton Shartel, "Defense Timeline Plays Key Role in Trial against GM," *Inside Litigation*, July 1996, pp. 1, 3.

30. Further details of the first of these studies are reported in W. Kip Viscusi, "Corporate Risk Analysis: A Reckless Act?" *Stanford Law Review* 52, no. 3 (2000): 547–597; and W. Kip Viscusi, "Punitive Damages: How Jurors Fail to Promote Efficiency," *Harvard Journal on Legislation* 39, no. 1 (2002): 139–167. The sample in this first study was 489, and 206 jury-eligible citizens participated in a sequel.

31. Viscusi, "Corporate Risk Analysis," 554.

32. Ibid., 556, 594. Another scenario involving a cost per life saved of $1 million yielded similar results, with 92 percent of the mock jurors favoring punitive damages, with a median award of $1 million. All scenarios discussed in the text below involve a cost per life saved of $4 million.

33. Viscusi, "Punitive Damages."

34. Ibid., 155.

35. Ibid.

36. Ibid., 166. However, the geometric mean award dropped to $2.1 million as compared with $3.0 million for the no analysis scenario.

37. For example, the paramount importance of promising safety is incorporated in the title of the Safe Drinking Water Act, which governs environmental criteria for drinking-water safety. Similarly, companies must show the safety and efficacy of pharmaceutical products. Federal Food, Drug & Cosmetic Act § 505, 21 USC § 355(b) (2012).

38. James F. Blumstein, "Medical Malpractice Standard-Setting: Developing Malpractice 'Safe Harbors' as a New Role for QIOs?" *Vanderbilt Law Review* 59, no. 4 (2006): 1017–1049. This insightful article provides general guidance with respect to the design and implementation of safe harbor protections.

39. See Benjamin Ho and Elaine Liu, "Does Sorry Work? The Impact of Apology Laws on Medical Malpractice," *Journal of Risk and Uncertainty* 43, no. 2 (2011): 141–167.

40. A representative apology law, such as that in Virginia, provides that "the portion of statements, writings, affirmations, benevolent conduct, or benevolent gestures expressing sympathy, commiseration, condolence, compassion, or a general sense of benevolence, together with apologies that are made by a health care provider . . . to the patient . . . shall be inadmissible as evidence of an admission of liability" (Va. Code Ann. § 8.01–581.20:1).

41. Caroline Cecot and W. Kip Viscusi, "Judicial Review of Agency Benefit-Cost Analysis," *George Mason Law Review* 22, no. 3 (2015): 575–617.

42. Company profits, sales, and advertising budgets are examples of company characteristics that are less pertinent than the VSL. Even anchors with no stated rationale are influential. See Reid Hastie, David A. Schkade, and John W. Payne, "Do Plaintiffs' Requests and Plaintiffs' Identities Matter?" in *Punitive Damages: How Juries Decide* (Chicago: University of Chicago Press, 2002), p. 73.

Chapter Four: Corporate Risk Analyses and Regulatory Sanctions: Lessons from the GM Ignition Switch Recall

1. US Department of Transportation, National Highway Traffic Safety Administration, "TQ14–001 Consent Order," May 16, 2014, www.nhtsa.gov/staticfiles /communications/pdf/May-16-2014-TQ14-001-Consent-Order.pdf [https:// perma.cc/A95H-LALY]. See also Jeff Plungis and Tim Higgins, "GM to Pay Record $35M Fine over Ignition-Switch Recall," *Product Safety and Liability Reporter*, May 19, 2014, p. 534.

2. The nature of the defect is described in detail in US Department of Justice, Southern District of New York, Letter to Anton R. Valukas, Esq., et al, "Re: General Motors Company—Deferred Prosecution Agreement," September 16, 2015, https://www.justice.gov/usao-sdny/file/772311/download [https://perma.cc/PVJ3-2P5D]. See, in particular, exhibits A and B, pp. 16–46.

3. The engineer is quoted in *Elliott v. General Motors LLC* (*In re Motors Liquidation Co.*), 15–2844 (2d Cir. July 13, 2016).

4. The GM documentation of "more than a dozen" fatalities is discussed in Anton R. Valukas, *Report to Board of Directors of General Motors Company Regarding Ignition Switch Recalls* (May 29, 2014), p. 11, http://www.beasleyallen.com/webfiles/valukas-report-on-gm-redacted.pdf [https://perma.cc/8FW5-RH5G].

5. See Kirsten Korosec, "Ten Times More Deaths Linked to Faulty Switch than GM First Reported," *Fortune*, August 24, 2015, http://fortune.com/2015/08/24/feinberg-gm-faulty-ignition-switch/ [https://perma.cc/N5CB-WVF4]. There were also 275 injuries.

6. Jeff Bennett, "GM to Recall 8.45 Million More Vehicles in North America," *Wall Street Journal*, June 30, 2014, http://www.wsj.com/articles/gm-to-recall-7-6-million-more-vehicles-in-u-s-1404153705 [http://perma.cc/F6Z2-L3TS].

7. See Department of Transportation, "TQ14–001 Consent Order," 9; and Valukas, *Report to Board of Directors*.

8. One of the words GM officials were told to avoid was "defect." See exhibit B in Department of Transportation, "TQ14–001 Consent Order," 41.

9. Stephen Breyer, *Breaking the Vicious Circle: Toward Effective Risk Regulation* (Cambridge, MA: Harvard University Press, 1993), 13–14.

10. The other auto safety problem of comparable scale is the unintended acceleration of Toyota vehicles. The extent to which this phenomenon is due to driver error or a defect in the cars' computer system was widely debated. In 2014, Toyota reached a $1.2 billion settlement with the US Department of Justice. See Charles Levinson, Jeff Bennett, and Devlin Barrett, "Toyota to Pay $1.2 Billion to Settle U.S. Probe," *Wall Street Journal*, March 19, 2014, http://www.wsj.com/articles/SB10001424052702304256404579449070848399280 [https://perma.cc/G7TU-K74V].

11. Valukas, *Report to Board of Directors*, 1–5, 17, 22. The affected vehicles were part of GM's small-car product line designed to meet federal emission requirements and to be inexpensive, "cost conscious" vehicles.

12. Ibid., 21.

13. Ibid., 1. There also have been more than one hundred claims for fatalities linked to the ignition switch. "GM Fund Receives 107 Death Claims Blaming Faulty Switches," *Wall Street Journal*, August 26, 2014, http://www.wsj.com/articles/gm-fund-receives-107-death-claims-blaiming-faulty-ignition-switches-1409105410 [https://perma.cc/2DQ9-7LJL].

14. GM CEO Mary Barra reported this estimate in testimony before the US Congress on April 1, 2014. See Tom Krisher and Marcy Gordon, "New CEO Barra

Faces Tough Task in Shedding Old GM," *Yahoo! News*, April 2, 2014, http://news.yahoo.com/ceo-barra-faces-tough-task-shedding-old-gm-040907777.html [http://perma.cc/BX7M-BFJN]. The recall cost in 2014 has turned out to be much greater. See Chris Isidore, "GM Total Recall Cost: $4.1 Billion," *CNN.com*, February 4, 2015, http://money.cnn.com/2015/02/04/news/companies/gm-earnings -recall-costs/ [http://perma.cc/6WRH-DZXQ].

15. Paul Lienert and Marilyn Thompson, "GM Avoided Defective Switch Redesign in 2005 to Save a Dollar Each," *Reuters*, April 2, 2014, http://www.reuters .com/article/us-gm-recall-delphi-idUSBREA3105R20140402 [https://perma.cc /Z4M3-EXKS]. See also US Department of Justice, US Attorney's Office, Southern District of New York, "Manhattan U.S. Attorney Announces Criminal Charges against General Motors and Deferred Prosecution Agreement with $900 Million Forfeiture," press release, September 17, 2015, https://www.justice.gov/usao -sdny/pr/manhattan-us-attorney-announces-criminal-charges-against-general -motors-and-deferred [https://perma.cc/VM4H-85AW]; and Jeff Bennett, "GM Report to Address Missteps," *Wall Street Journal*, June 2, 2014, at B1, B7.

16. See exhibit C in US Department of Justice, Letter to Valukas, "Deferred Prosecution Agreement," 27.

17. Ibid.

18. Committee on Energy and Commerce, US House of Representatives, *Staff Report on the GM Ignition Switch Recall: Review of NHTSA*, September 16, 2014.

19. NHTSA Acting Administrator David Friedman used language similar to that in the risk analysis court cases: "GM engineers knew about the defect. GM investigators knew about the defect. GM lawyers knew about the defect. But GM did not act to protect Americans from that defect." See Michael A. Fletcher, "GM Releases Results of Ignition-Switch Probe," *Washington Post*, June 5, 2014, https://www.washingtonpost.com/business/economy/gm-to-release-results -of-ignition-switch-probe/2014/06/05/31c09d90-ec3b-11e3-9f5c-9075d5508f0a _story.html [https://perma.cc/K4H5-GPKQ]; and Bennett, "GM Report to Address Missteps," B7.

20. For documentation of this and all subsequent statements regarding GM's contacts with NHTSA, see Department of Transportation, "TQ14–001 Consent Order."

21. Ibid., 41, exhibit B.

22. Ibid.

23. Ibid.

24. Ibid., 39.

25. Ibid.

26. Valukas, *Report to Board of Directors*, 70.

27. Ibid., 256.

28. Ibid., 2.

29. Ibid., 68–69.

30. Ibid., 255.

31. Ibid., 140.

32. See "GM Ignition Compensation Claims Resolution Facility Announces an Extension of the Claims Filing Deadline," *GM Ignition Compensation Claims Resolution Facility*, November 17, 2014, original press release archived at http://perma.cc/EG6L-FFCU.

33. Ashby Jones, "GM Says It Has a Shield from Some Liability," *Wall Street Journal*, June 15, 2014, http://www.wsj.com/articles/gm-says-it-has-a-shield-from-some-liability-1402874861 [https://perma.cc/Z9JW-8FFF].

34. *Elliott v. General Motors LLC* (*In re Motors Liquidation Co.*), 15–2844 (2d Cir. July 13, 2016). In April 2017, the US Supreme Court turned away GM's appeal of that decision.

35. Hiroko Tabuchi, "The Quest to Save a Few Dollars per Airbag Led to a Deadly Crisis," *New York Times*, August 27, 2016.

36. The number of valid death claims ultimately found to be related to the ignition switch defect continued to increase, eventually reaching 124 deaths. As of January 26, 2015, the administrator of the GM settlements, Kenneth Feinberg, had certified fifty valid claims. See Linda Sandler, "GM's Confirmed Ignition Deaths Hit 50 as Claims Deadline Nears," *Bloomberg News*, January 26, 2015, http://www.bloomberg.com/news/2015-01-26/gm-s-confirmed-ignition-deaths-hit-50-as-claims-deadline-nears.html [http://perma.cc/V78D-FX3U].

37. This deterrence value assumes that NHTSA can identify all lives lost by a company's failure to report the defect. If there is a probability above zero that the company will be able to conceal its behavior, the appropriate penalty will be greater, as discussed below in the context of punitive damages.

38. Department of Transportation, "TQ14–001 Consent Order," 2.

39. US Department of Transportation, "Notice of Increase in Civil Penalty for Violations of National Traffic and Motor Vehicle Safety Act," *Federal Register* 81, no. 55 (March 22, 2016): 15413.

40. Mike Spector, "GM Ignition-Switch Offers $595 Million to Victims," *Wall Street Journal*, December 10, 2015, http://www.wsj.com/articles/gm-ignition-switch-fund-offers-595-million-to-victims-1449755042 [https://perma.cc/KE74-YVLM].

41. US Department of Justice, Letter to Valukas, "Deferred Prosecution Agreement."

42. Ibid., 7.

43. 49 USC § 30165(a)(1) (2012); 49 CFR § 578.6(a) (2014); and Department of Transportation, "Notice of Increase in Civil Penalty."

44. A. Mitchell Polinsky and Steven Shavell, "Punitive Damages: An Economic Analysis," *Harvard Law Review* 111, no. 4 (1998): 869–972. Earlier scholars that they cite on this issue include Jeremy Bentham. The specific proposal here follows that of Joni Hersch and W. Kip Viscusi, "Saving Lives through Punitive Damages," *Southern California Law Review* 83, no. 2 (2010): 229–262.

45. GM reported the defect in 2014. See Department of Transportation, "TQ14–001 Consent Order," 2. In 2005, GM considered proposed fixes of the ignition switch problem, and in 2007, a Wisconsin trooper issued a report on an

ignition-switch-related fatality and sent it to GM, though there is no evidence that the report was read. See Valukas, *Report to Board of Directors*, 115.

46. US Department of Justice, Letter to Valukas, "Deferred Prosecution Agreement," exhibit B, 2, 5.

47. Paul M. Barrett, "The GM Fiasco and Overuse of Secret Settlements: Four Blunt Points," *Bloomberg Businessweek*, June 25, 2014, http://www.businessweek .com/articles/2014-06-25/the-gm-fiasco-and-the-overuse-of-secret-settlements -four-blunt-points [http://perma.cc/GSB6-JZGA].

48. Joni Hersch, "Breast Implants: Regulation, Litigation, and Science," in *Regulation through Litigation*, ed. W. Kip Viscusi (Washington, DC: Brookings Institution, 2002). Note that these product defects included subsequently well-established morbidity risk problems with breast implants that were targeted by government regulations, such as product leakage, and extended well beyond the more widely debated risks linked to leakage such as that of autoimmune diseases.

49. For an example of a regulation that requires automobile manufacturers to disclose any known defects relating to motor vehicle safety, see 49 USC § 30118(c)(1) (2012).

Chapter Five: The Devaluation of Life: Should Age Matter?

1. Among the many press accounts of this incident is Katharine Q. Seelye and John Tierney, "E.P.A. Drops Age-Based Cost Studies," *New York Times*, May 8, 2003, http://www.nytimes.com/2003/05/08/us/epa-drops-age-based-cost -studies.html [https://perma.cc/ZRD4-UGCF]; Cindy Skrzycki, "Under Fire, EPA Drops the 'Senior Death Discount,'" *Washington Post*, May 13, 2003, https:// www.washingtonpost.com/archive/business/2003/05/13/under-fire-epa-drops -the-senior-death-discount/e14279ed-9109-40e5-998b-fd3a1620799c/ [https:// perma.cc/UN8V-EZDJ]; "What's a Granny Worth? Cost Benefits Must Be Based on Good Science and Sound Economics," *Washington Times*, July 7, 2003, http://www.washingtontimes.com/news/2003/jul/6/20030706-104810-2250r/ [https://perma.cc/X3H4-M3C4].

2. This analysis involved the use of two UK surveys with percentage discounts of −10 percent and −41 percent. See John D. Graham, "Saving Lives through Administrative Law and Economics," *University of Pennsylvania Law Review* 157, no. 2 (2008): 395–540.

3. The fatality data are from the US Environmental Protection Agency, *Technical Addendum: Methodologies for the Benefit Analysis of the Clear Skies Act of 2003* (Washington, DC: US Environmental Protection Agency, 2003), and the senior discount figure of 37 percent is from the US Environmental Protection Agency, *Technical Addendum: Methodologies for Benefit Analysis of the Clear Skies Initiative* (Washington, DC: US Environmental Protection Agency, 2002).

4. Somewhat surprisingly, the EPA apparently did not consider the US labor market estimates of the age variation in the valuation of mortality risks. The first

detailed analysis along these lines was Michael J. Moore and W. Kip Viscusi, "The Quantity-Adjusted Value of Life," *Economic Inquiry* 26, no. 3 (1988): 369–388.

5. M. W. Jones-Lee, M. Hammerton, and P. R. Philips, "The Value of Safety: Results of a National Sample Survey," *Economic Journal* 95, no. 377 (1985): 49–72.

6. M. Jones-Lee and M. Spackman, "The Development of Road and Rail Transport Safety Valuation in the United Kingdom," *Research in Transportation Economics* 43, no. 1 (2013): 23–40. The stated-preference mean estimates of $6 million to $7.5 million in 2015 dollars based on the pre-Brexit exchange rates are higher than the median values selected by the government. The US mean estimates also exceed the US median values but not to as great a degree as in the UK stated-preference studies.

7. HM Treasury, *The Green Book: Appraisal and Evaluation in Central Government* (London: TSO, 2011), p. 62. The value of preventing transport fatalities was £1.145 million, in year 2000 prices. The figure in the text adjusts for the year 2000 British pound–US dollar exchange rate and the US dollar price level adjustment from 2000 to 2015.

8. The EPA senior discount estimates were based on a response to one question, Question 18(a), in Jones-Lee, Hammerton, and Philips, "Value of Safety," 56, for which they estimated a positive and statistically significant age effect and a negative and statistically significant age squared effect. For the other key survey questions 18(b), 20(a), 20(b), and 20(c), the age variable is never statistically significant while the age squared variable is usually statistically significant and negative.

9. The Clear Skies controversy stimulated further research on the VSL-age relationship. The steady relationship is in a stated-preference study by Anna Alberini, Maureen Cropper, Alan Krupnick, and Nathalie B. Simon, "Does the Value of a Statistical Life Vary with Age and Health Status? Evidence from the US and Canada," *Journal of Environmental Economics and Management* 48, no. 1 (2004): 769–792; and the flat pattern until age 70 is in Alan Krupnick, Anna Alberini, Maureen Cropper, Nathalie Simon, Bernie O'Brien, Ron Goeree, and Martin Heintzelman, "Age, Health and the Willingness to Pay for Mortality Risk Reductions: A Contingent Valuation Survey of Ontario Residents," *Journal of Risk and Uncertainty* 24, no. 2 (2002): 161–186. Other stated-preference studies have found different patterns, including a declining pattern with age. For a review of these studies, see Alan Krupnick, "Mortality-Risk Valuation and Age: Stated Preference Evidence," *Review of Environmental Economics and Policy* 1, no. 2 (2007): 261–282.

10. Daniel Kahneman and Amos Tversky, "Prospect Theory: An Analysis of Decision under Risk," *Econometrica* 47, no. 2 (1979): 263–292.

11. Hara Associates, *Benefit/Cost Analysis of Proposed Tobacco Products Information Regulations*, prepared for Health Canada and Consulting and Audit Canada, June 5, 2000.

12. European Commission, "Recommended Interim Values for the Value of Preventing a Fatality in DG Environment Cost Benefit Analysis" (2001), http://

ec.europa.eu/environment/enveco/others/pdf/recommended_interim_values
.pdf [https://perma.cc/BSA7-L2AZ].

13. The empirical basis for these statistics and others cited in this and the following paragraph is W. Kip Viscusi and Joseph E. Aldy, "Labor Market Estimates of the Senior Discount for the Value of Statistical Life," *Journal of Environmental Economics and Management* 53, no. 3 (2007): 377–392. The patterns for age differences are steeper by 1-digit industry and flatter by 3-digit industry, since much of the difference in risk levels is in terms of age differences in the industry mix within these categories as people age. But the general result that older workers are in fact exposed to substantial job risks remains true.

14. Additional assumptions are also usually required for this result, such as the availability of actuarially fair insurance markets and perfect capital markets. See Donald S. Shepard and Richard J. Zeckhauser, "Survival versus Consumption," *Management Science* 30, no. 4 (1984): 423–439.

15. The quality aspect of a QALY value can reflect age variations in the level of well-being so that constant valuations are not necessarily required if there are changes in health status that influence the QALY value.

16. The studies discussed in this section are the following: Viscusi and Aldy, "Labor Market Estimates"; Joseph E. Aldy and W. Kip Viscusi, "Age Differences in the Value of Statistical Life: Revealed Preference Evidence," *Review of Environmental Economics and Policy* 1, no. 2 (2007): 241–260; Joseph E. Aldy and W. Kip Viscusi, "Adjusting the Value of a Statistical Life for Age and Cohort Effects," *Review of Economics and Statistics* 90, no. 3 (2008): 573–581; and W. Kip Viscusi and Joni Hersch, "The Mortality Cost to Smokers," *Journal of Health Economics* 27, no. 4 (2008): 943–958.

17. The values shown are updated to 2015 dollars and are the cohort-adjusted estimates in W. Kip Viscusi and Joseph E. Aldy, "The Value of a Statistical Life: A Critical Review of Market Estimates throughout the World," *Journal of Risk and Uncertainty* 27, no. 1 (2003): 5–76.

18. The value of these components is based on the estimates in Viscusi and Aldy, "Labor Market Estimates."

19. Per-Olov Johansson, "On the Definition and Age-Dependency of the Value of a Statistical Life," *Journal of Risk and Uncertainty* 25, no. 3 (2002): 251–263.

20. Thomas J. Kniesner, W. Kip Viscusi, and James P. Ziliak, "Life-Cycle Consumption and the Age-Adjusted Value of Life," *Contributions to Economic Analysis & Policy* 5, no. 1 (2006): article 4.

21. This result is for the long-term exposure benefit estimates. The short-term exposure estimates perform similarly. See table 2 of Aldy and Viscusi, "Labor Market Estimates," 387.

22. See table 5 of Kniesner, Viscusi, and Ziliak, "Life Cycle Consumption," 28.

23. US Environmental Protection Agency, *Regulatory Impact Analysis—Control of Air Pollution from New Motor Vehicles: Tier 2 Motor Vehicle Emissions Standards and Gasoline Sulfur Control Requirements*, Report EPA420-R-99-023 (Washington, DC: US Environmental Protection Agency, 1999).

24. The calculations of lost life expectancy also include the influence of discounting deferred benefits. The data discussed in this section are drawn from W. Kip Viscusi, Jahn K. Hakes, and Alan Carlin, "Measures of Mortality Risks," *Journal of Risk and Uncertainty* 14, no. 3 (1997): 213–233.

25. Elizabeth Arias, National Center for Health Services, "United States Life Tables, 2008," *National Vital Statistics Reports* 61, no. 3 (2012).

26. Sarah Lichtenstein, Paul Slovic, Baruch Fischhoff, Mark Layman, and Barbara Combs, "Judged Frequency of Lethal Events," *Journal of Experimental Psychology: Human Learning and Memory* 4, no. 6 (1978): 551–578.

27. For the sample with judgments anchored on motor vehicle accident rates, the adjusted R^2 for the mortality risk estimates equation jumps from 0.43, including only the total number of deaths in the analysis, to a value of 0.92, also accounting for lost life expectancy. The performance based on electrocution-anchored judgments is similar, with the R^2 rising from 0.52 to 0.93. See Viscusi, Hakes, and Carlin, "Measures of Mortality Risks." There is also evidence that people discount the future life-expectancy losses in the perception of risks. For illnesses with a ten-year lag, the implicit rate of discount that respondents applied in assessing the risks was 10.8 percent for the motor vehicle accident–anchored judgments and 8.8 percent for the electrocution-anchored perceptions. The implicit discount rate drops to 3–4 percent for illnesses with a twenty-five-year lag.

28. More specifically, these estimates track the value of a statistical life adjusted for the worker's discounted life expectancy.

29. These patterns are for the cohort-adjusted estimates in Aldy and Viscusi, "Adjusting the Value."

30. See Viscusi and Hersch, "Mortality Cost to Smokers." Estimates differ by gender because the estimates of VSL based on a log wage equation are proportional to the worker's wage rate, which is lower for women. Although the VSLY is lower for women, the length of life to which a VSLY is applied is greater for women.

31. Research in progress at the US Department of Health and Human Services is now utilizing the VSLY approach similar to that adopted in Viscusi and Hersch, "Mortality Cost to Smokers."

32. National Institute for Health and Care Excellence, "Judging Whether Public Health Interventions Offer Value for Money," September 2013, http://nice.org .uk/advice/lgb10/chapter/introduction [https://perma.cc/5ZLJ-HYRE]. Their cutoffs focus on the value of a quality-adjusted life year, which should have a value similar to a VSLY, or the VSLY may be lower if health status declines.

33. See, e.g., US Department of Health and Human Services, "Organ Procurement and Transplantation Network," *Federal Register* 63, no. 63 (April 2, 1998): 16296–16338.

34. US Department of Health and Human Services, Food and Drug Administration, "Use of Materials Derived from Cattle in Human Food and Cosmetics," *Federal Register* 81, no. 53 (March 18, 2016): 14718–14732, citing Aldy and Viscusi, "Age Differences."

35. Similar difficulties arise if one applies a constant value per discounted remaining life year, which will also generate a valuation that steadily declines with age.

36. Seth Borenstein, "An American Life Worth Less Today," *Associated Press*, July 10, 2008; David A. Fahrenthold, "Cosmic Markdown: EPA Says Life Is Worth Less," *Washington Post*, July 19, 2008, http://www.washingtonpost.com/wp-dyn /content/story/2008/07/19/ST2008071900185.html [https://perma.cc/MU4P -PSEX]; Stephen Colbert, "The Word—Priceless," *The Colbert Report*, July 14, 2008, http://www.cc.com/video-clips/e8zxmm/the-colbert-report-the-word— -priceless [https://perma.cc/73HN-EJK5].

37. I review the various procedures used by the EPA in W. Kip Viscusi, "The Devaluation of Life," *Regulation & Governance* 3, no. 2 (2009): 103–127.

38. Janusz R. Mrozek and Laura O. Taylor, "What Determines the Value of Life? A Meta-Analysis," *Journal of Policy Analysis and Management* 21, no. 2 (2002): 253–270; and Viscusi and Aldy, "Value of a Statistical Life." The EPA also relied on a third meta-analysis for corroboration since it was not yet published. See Ikuho Kochi, Bryan Hubbell, and Randall Kramer, "An Empirical Bayes Approach to Combining and Comparing Estimates of the Value of a Statistical Life for Environmental Policy Analysis," *Environmental & Resource Economics* 34, no. 3 (2006): 385–406.

Chapter Six: Should There Be Preferential Treatment of the Rich?

1. Matthew D. Adler, *Well-Being and Fair Distribution: Beyond Cost-Benefit Analysis* (New York: Oxford University Press, 2012).

2. W. Kip Viscusi and Joseph E. Aldy, "The Value of a Statistical Life: A Critical Review of Market Estimates throughout the World," *Journal of Risk and Uncertainty* 27, no. 1 (2003): 5–76. The other meta-analyses of the income elasticity of VSL used in that study include Jin-Tan Liu, James K. Hammitt, and Jin-Long Liu, "Estimating Hedonic Wage Function and Value of Life in a Developing Country," *Economics Letters* 57, no. 3 (1997): 353–358; Ted R. Miller, "Variations between Countries in Values of Statistical Life," *Journal of Transport Economics and Policy* 34, no. 2 (2000): 169–188; Bradley J. Bowland and John C. Beghin, "Robust Estimates of Value of a Statistical Life for Developing Economies," *Journal of Policy Modeling* 23, no. 4 (2001): 385–396; and Janusz R. Mrozek and Laura O. Taylor, "What Determines the Value of Life? A Meta-Analysis," *Journal of Policy Analysis and Management* 21, no. 2 (2002): 253–270. The elasticities that the authors reported were 0.53 (Liu et al. 1997), 0.89 (Miller 2000), 0.46 (Mrozek and Taylor 2002), and 1.66 (Bowland and Beghin 2001).

3. Hristos Doucouliagos, T. D. Stanley, and W. Kip Viscusi, "Publication Selection and the Income Elasticity of the Value of a Statistical Life," *Journal of Health Economics* 33 (2014): 67–85. The sample used in this analysis was based on that of François Bellavance, Georges Dionne, and Martin Lebeau, "The Value of a

Statistical Life: A Meta-Analysis with a Mixed Effects Regression Model," *Journal of Health Economics* 28, no. 2 (2009): 444–464.

4. See, e.g., Louis Kaplow, "The Value of a Statistical Life and the Coefficient of Relative Risk Aversion," *Journal of Risk and Uncertainty* 31, no. 1 (2005): 23–34; and Louis R. Eeckhoudt and James K. Hammitt, "Background Risks and the Value of a Statistical Life," *Journal of Risk and Uncertainty* 23, no. 3 (2001): 261–279.

5. The 0.62 value is based on the estimates using what is termed the "precision-effect estimate with standard error." Using a variety of other formulations, the estimates ranged from 0.25 to 0.63.

6. This estimate is based on the quantile regression models reported in Thomas J. Kniesner, W. Kip Viscusi, and James P. Ziliak, "Policy Relevant Heterogeneity in the Value of Statistical Life: New Evidence from Panel Data Quantile Regressions," *Journal of Risk and Uncertainty* 40, no. 1 (2010): 15–31.

7. See Dora L. Costa and Matthew E. Kahn, "Changes in the Value of Life, 1940–1980," *Journal of Risk and Uncertainty* 29, no. 2 (2004): 159–180.

8. W. Kip Viscusi and Clayton J. Masterman, "Income Elasticities and the Global Values of a Statistical Life," *Journal of Benefit-Cost Analysis* 8, no. 2 (2017): 226–250.

9. In addition to advocating a higher VSL for DOT generally, I also recommended that FAA be permitted to use a higher VSL than the rest of the agency. See W. Kip Viscusi, *Fatal Tradeoffs: Public and Private Responsibilities for Risk* (New York: Oxford University Press, 1992); and W. Kip Viscusi, "The Value of Risks to Life and Health," *Journal of Economic Literature* 31, no. 4 (1993): 1912–1946. Advocacy of a higher VSL when beneficiaries pay for the policy is what Cass Sunstein has termed the "easy cases." See Cass R. Sunstein, *Valuing Life: Humanizing the Regulatory State* (Chicago: University of Chicago Press, 2014).

10. These estimates are from K. R. Shanmugan, "Valuations of Life and Injury Risks," *Environmental and Resource Economics* 16, no. 4 (2000): 379–389.

11. Many of the pertinent issues are examined in James K. Hammitt and Lisa A. Robinson, "The Income Elasticity of the Value per Statistical Life: Transferring Estimates between High and Low Income Populations," *Journal of Benefit-Cost Analysis* 2, no. 1 (2011): 1–29.

12. The income differences across countries are based on the OECD tabulation of the household net adjusted disposable income levels. See OECD, "Better Life Index, Income" (2016), http://www.oecdbetterlifeindex.org/topics/income [https://perma.cc/2CCH-KDWM]. The policy relevant VSL estimates are from chapter 2.

13. The estimates below were presented at the 2017 Society for Benefit-Cost Analysis conference session, "Valuing Mortality Risk Reductions in Low- and Middle-Income Countries: Addressing Data Gaps and Inconsistencies." Here, I use the $10 million US VSL figure rather than a $9.6 million estimate adjusting for publication biases.

14. Office Memorandum from Lawrence M. Summers, Subject: GEP, the World Bank/IMFMIGA, December 12, 1991.

15. Gardiner Harris, "Bangladesh Factory Owners Charged in Fire That Killed 112," *New York Times*, December 22, 2013.

16. US Department of Transportation, "Guidance on Treatment of the Economic Value of a Statistical Life (VSL) in U.S. Department of Transportation Analyses—2015 Adjustment," June 17, 2015, https://www.transportation.gov /sites/dot.gov/files/docs/VSL2015_0.pdf [https://perma.cc/Y8DU-XV9Q]; US Environmental Protection Agency, "Valuing Mortality Risk Reductions for Environmental Policy: A White Paper," December 10, 2010. A more recent draft EPA review is "Valuing Mortality Risk Reductions for Policy: A Meta-Analytic Approach," US EPA Office of Policy, National Center for Environmental Economics for Review by the EPA's Science Advisory Board, Environmental Economics Advisory Committee, February 2016.

17. US Department of Transportation, "Guidance," 8; and US Environmental Protection Agency, "Valuing Mortality Risk Reductions," 43.

18. US Environmental Protection Agency, "Public Health and Environmental Radiation Protection Standards for Yucca Mountain, NV," *Federal Register* 70, no. 161 (August 22, 2005): 49014–49065.

19. *State of Nevada v. US Environmental Protection Agency*, DC Circuit, US Court of Appeals, July 9, 2004.

20. US Environmental Protection Agency, "Public Health," 49037.

21. Nobel laureate Thomas Schelling has made similar observations with respect to global climate change policies.

22. Robert J. Gordon, *The Rise and Fall of American Growth: The U.S. Standard of Living since the Civil War* (Princeton, NJ: Princeton University Press, 2016).

23. See the July 1991 decision in *UAW v. OSHA*, (DC Cir.), 89–1559; and Stephen F. Williams, "Second Best: The Soft Underbelly of Deterrence Theory in Tort," *Harvard Law Review* 106, no. 4 (1993): 932–944.

24. Letter from James MacRae, Acting Administrator, US Office of Management and Budget, Office of Information and Regulatory Affairs, to Nancy Risque-Rohrbach, Assistant Secretary for Policy, US Department of Labor, March 10, 1992.

25. Ralph L. Keeney, "Mortality Risks Induced by Economic Expenditures," *Risk Analysis* 10, no. 1 (1990): 147–159; Randall Lutter and John F. Morrall III, "Health-Health Analysis: A New Way to Evaluate Health and Safety Regulation," *Journal of Risk and Uncertainty* 8 no. 1 (1994): 43–66; Kenneth S. Chapman and Govind Hariharan, "Controlling for Causality in the Link from Income to Mortality," *Journal of Risk and Uncertainty* 8, no. 1 (1994): 85–93; and John D. Graham, Bei-Hung Chang, and John S. Evans, "Poorer Is Riskier," *Risk Analysis* 12, no. 3 (1992): 333–337.

26. W. Kip Viscusi, "Mortality Effects of Regulatory Costs and Policy Evaluation Criteria," *RAND Journal of Economics* 25, no. 1 (1994): 94–109.

27. Higher income levels also enable people to undertake some health-harming activities. Accounting for smoking and drinking relationships with income reduces the level of expenditures that has a counterproductive effect. See Randall Lutter, John F. Morrall III, and W. Kip Viscusi, "The Cost-Per-Life-Saved

Cutoff for Safety-Enhancing Regulations," *Economic Inquiry* 37, no. 4 (1999): 599–608.

Chapter Seven: Promoting Risk Equity through Equitable Risk Tradeoffs

1. William J. Clinton, "Federal Actions to Address Environmental Justice in Minority Populations and Low-Income Populations," *Federal Register* 59, no. 32 (February 16, 1994): 7629–7633.

2. See, e.g., Vicki Been, "What's Fairness Got to Do with It? Environmental Justice and the Siting of Locally Undesirable Land Uses," *Cornell Law Review* 78, no. 6 (1993): 1001–1085; Vicki Been, "Analyzing Evidence of Environmental Justice," *Journal of Land Use & Environmental Law* 11, no. 1 (1995): 1–36; Commission for Racial Justice, *Toxic Wastes and Race in the United States: A National Report on the Racial and Socio-economic Characteristics of Communities with Hazardous Waste Sites* (New York: United Church of Christ, 1987); James T. Hamilton, "Politics and Social Costs: Estimating the Impact of Collective Action on Hazardous Waste Facilities," *RAND Journal of Economics* 24, no. 1 (1993): 101–125; James T. Hamilton, "Testing for Environmental Racism: Prejudice, Profits, Political Power?" *Journal of Policy Analysis and Management* 14, no. 1 (1995): 107–132; Rae Zimmerman, "Issues of Clarification in Environmental Equity: How We Manage Is How We Measure," *Fordham Urban Law Journal* 21, no. 3 (1993): 633–669. James T. Hamilton and W. Kip Viscusi, *Calculating Risks? The Spatial and Political Dimensions of Hazardous Waste Policy* (Cambridge, MA: MIT Press, 1999); James T. Hamilton, "Environmental Equity and the Siting of Hazardous Waste Facilities in OECD Countries: Evidence and Policies," in *International Yearbook of Environmental and Resource Economics 2005/2006: A Survey of Current Issues*, ed. Henk Folmer and Tom Tietenberg (Northampton, MA: Edward Elgar, 2005); Vicki Been and Patrick J. Rohan, "Environmental Justice and Equity Issues" in *Zoning and Land Use Controls*, ed. Gary I. Cohen (New York: Matthew Bender, 1995).

3. W. Kip Viscusi, Jahn K. Hakes, and Alan Carlin, "Measures of Mortality Risks," *Journal of Risk and Uncertainty* 14, no. 3 (1997): 213–233. For comparison, all estimates are costs per normalized life saved, thus holding life expectancy constant. The set of regulatory policies in this article and their costs are based on previous assessments by former US Office of Management and Budget economist John F. Morrall III.

4. See, in particular, table 2 and the discussion in W. Kip Viscusi, "The Value of Risks to Life and Health," *Journal of Economic Literature* 31, no. 4 (1993): 1912–1946, which was based on my report to the FAA. The income adjustment assumed that the VSL varied proportionally with income.

5. W. Kip Viscusi, *Fatal Tradeoffs: Public and Private Responsibilities for Risk* (New York: Oxford University Press, 1992). If the higher costs reduce consumer demand for air travel, as would occur if consumers are unaware of the safety benefits of the regulation, then corporate profits will be affected as well.

6. Cass R. Sunstein, *Valuing Life: Humanizing the Regulatory State* (Chicago: University of Chicago Press, 2014).

7. Ted Gayer, James T. Hamilton, and W. Kip Viscusi, "The Market Value of Reducing Cancer Risk: Hedonic Housing Prices with Changing Information," *Southern Economic Journal* 69, no. 2 (2002): 266–289; Ted Gayer, James T. Hamilton, and W. Kip Viscusi, "Private Values of Risk Tradeoffs at Superfund Sites: Housing Market Evidence on Learning about Risk," *Review of Economics and Statistics* 32, no. 3 (2000): 439–451; Ted Gayer and W. Kip Viscusi, "Housing Price Responses to Newspaper Publicity of Hazardous Waste Sites," *Resource and Energy Economics* 24 (2002): 33–51.

8. This estimate is based on US Surgeon General reports and other government data and is presented in W. Kip Viscusi, "Risk Beliefs and Preferences for E-Cigarettes," *American Journal of Health Economics* 2, no. 2 (2016): 213–240.

9. Joni Hersch and W. Kip Viscusi, "Smoking and Other Risky Behaviors," *Journal of Drug Issues* 28, no. 3 (1998): 645–661.

10. W. Kip Viscusi and Joni Hersch, "Cigarette Smokers as Job Risk Takers," *Review of Economics and Statistics* 83, no. 2 (2001): 269–280.

11. W. Kip Viscusi and Joni Hersch, "The Mortality Cost to Smokers," *Journal of Health Economics* 27, no. 4 (2008): 943–958.

12. This discussion draws on Joni Hersch and W. Kip Viscusi, "Immigrant Status and the Value of Statistical Life," *Journal of Human Resources* 45, no. 3 (2010): 749–771.

13. Scott Richardson, John Ruser, and Peggy Suarez, "Hispanic Workers in the United States: An Analysis of Employment Distributions, Fatal Occupational Injuries, and Non-fatal Occupational Injuries and Illnesses," in *Safety Is Seguridad: A Workshop Summary* (Washington, DC: National Academies Press, 2003), 43–82.

14. The statistics in the remainder of this paragraph are drawn from National Safety Council, *Injury Facts: 2016 Edition* (Itasca, IL: National Safety Council, 2016).

15. A fuller description of his approach can be found in Paul R. Portney, "Trouble in Happyville," *Journal of Policy Analysis and Management* 11, no. 1 (1992): 131–132.

16. See Hamilton and Viscusi, *Calculating Risks?*

17. Ibid.

18. Stephen Breyer, *Breaking the Vicious Circle: Toward Effective Risk Regulation* (Cambridge, MA: Harvard University Press, 1993).

19. See, in particular, chapter 7 of Hamilton and Viscusi, *Calculating Risks?*

20. Ibid.

21. Ibid., based on data presented in chapter 9.

Chapter Eight: Fine-Tuning the Selection of the Pertinent VSL

1. US Department of Transportation, "Guidance on Treatment of the Economic Value of a Statistical Life (VSL) in U.S. Department of Transportation

Analyses—2015 Adjustment," June 17, 2015, https://www.transportation.gov
/sites/dot.gov/files/docs/VSL2015_0.pdf [https://perma.cc/Y8DU-XV9Q].

2. US Environmental Protection Agency, National Center for Environmental
Economics, *Guidelines for Preparing Economic Analyses* (Washington, DC: US
Environmental Protection Agency, 2010, updated May 2014), appendix B.

3. US Office of Management and Budget, Circular A-4, "Regulatory Analysis," September 17, 2003, https://georgewbush-whitehouse.archives.gov/omb
/circulars/a004/a-4.html [https://perma.cc/DCG4-DXNH].

4. Examples of these reviews include W. Kip Viscusi, "The Value of Risks
to Life and Health," *Journal of Economic Literature* 31, no. 4 (1993): 1912–1946;
Janusz R. Mrozek and Laura O. Taylor, "What Determines the Value of Life? A
Meta-Analysis," *Journal of Policy Analysis and Management* 21, no. 2 (2002): 253–
270; W. Kip Viscusi and Joseph E. Aldy, "The Value of a Statistical Life: A Critical
Review of Market Estimates throughout the World," *Journal of Risk and Uncer-
tainty* 27, no. 1 (2003): 5–76; Ikuho Kochi, Bryan Hubbell, and Randall Kramer,
"An Empirical Bayes Approach to Combining and Comparing Estimates of the
Value of a Statistical Life for Environmental Policy Analysis," *Environmental &
Resource Economics* 34, no. 3 (2006): 385–406; and François Bellavance, Georges
Dionne, and Martin Lebeau, "The Value of a Statistical Life: A Meta-Analysis
with a Mixed Effects Regression Model," *Journal of Health Economics* 28, no. 2
(2009): 444–464.

5. Kerry Dwan, Douglas G. Altman, Juan A. Arnaiz, Jill Bloom, An-Wen
Chan, Eugenia Cronin, Evelyne Decullier, Philippa J. Easterbrook, Erik Von Elm,
Carrol Gamble, Davina Ghersi, John P. A. Ioannidis, John Simes, and Paula R.
Williamson, "Systematic Review of the Empirical Evidence of Study Publication
Bias and Outcome Reporting Bias," *PLoS ONE* 3, no. 8 (2008): e3081; and Kerry
Dwan, Carrol Gamble, Paula R. Williamson, and Jamie J. Kirkham, "Systematic
Review of the Empirical Evidence of Study Publication Bias and Outcome Re-
porting Bias—An Updated Review," *PLoS ONE* 8, no. 7 (2013): e66844.

6. John P. A. Ioannidis, "Why Most Published Research Findings Are False,"
PLoS Medicine 2, no. 8 (2005): e124.

7. A comprehensive introduction to the methodological issues is provided by
T. D. Stanley and Hristos Doucouliagos, *Meta-Regression Analysis in Economics
and Business* (London: Routledge, 2012).

8. Ibid. See also Hristos Doucouliagos, T. D. Stanley, and Margaret Giles, "Are
Estimates of the Value of a Statistical Life Exaggerated?" *Journal of Health Economics* 31, no. 1 (2012): 197–206.

9. "The Value of a Statistical Life: Economics and Politics," *Strata* (March
2017), http://www.strata.org/VSL/ [https://perma.cc/CWZ8-EZ6R].

10. W. Kip Viscusi, "The Role of Publication Selection Bias in Estimates of the
Value of a Statistical Life," *American Journal of Health Economics* 1, no. 1 (2015):
27–52.

11. Correcting for publication selection effects for the income elasticity of
VSL leads to estimates consistent with meta-analysis results that do not account
for such selection effects. See Hristos Doucouliagos, T. D. Stanley, and W. Kip

Viscusi, "Publication Selection and the Income Elasticity of the Value of a Statistical Life," *Journal of Health Economics* 33 (2014): 67–75.

12. W. Kip Viscusi and Clayton Masterman, "Anchoring Biases in International Estimates of the Value of a Statistical Life," *Journal of Risk and Uncertainty* 54, no. 2 (2017): 103–128.

13. US Office of Management and Budget, Circular A-4, "Regulatory Analysis." In the United Kingdom, the guidance document is HM Treasury, *The Green Book: Appraisal and Evaluation in Central Government* (London: TSO, 2011).

14. W. Kip Viscusi and Elissa Philip Gentry, "The Value of a Statistical Life for Transportation Regulations: A Test of the Benefits Transfer Methodology," *Journal of Risk and Uncertainty* 51, no. 1 (2015): 53–77.

15. Ibid.

16. Ibid.

17. See HM Treasury, *The Green Book*, and stated-preference studies in the United Kingdom such as M. W. Jones-Lee, *The Economics of Safety and Physical Risk* (Oxford: Basil Blackwell, 1989); M. W. Jones-Lee, M. Hammerton, and P. R. Philips, "The Value of Safety: Results of a National Sample Survey," *Economic Journal* 95, no. 377 (1985): 49–72; and Judith Covey, Angela Robinson, Michael Jones-Lee, and Graham Loomes, "Responsibility, Scale and the Valuation of Rail Safety," *Journal of Risk and Uncertainty* 40, no. 1 (2010): 85–108.

18. Elissa Philip Gentry and W. Kip Viscusi, "The Fatality and Morbidity Components of the Value of Statistical Life," *Journal of Health Economics* 46 (2016): 90–99.

19. See Susan Chilton, Michael Jones-Lee, Francis Kiraly, Hugh Metcalf, and Wei Pang, "Dread Risks," *Journal of Risk and Uncertainty* 33, no. 3 (2006): 165–182.

20. UK Health and Safety Executive, *Reducing Risks, Protecting People: HSE's Decision-Making Process* (Norwich, UK: Crown, 2001); and HM Treasury, *The Green Book*.

21. Michael Zand, Clark Rushbrook, Ian Spencer, Kyran Donald, and Anna Barnes, *Cost to Britain of Work-Related Cancer*, UK Health and Safety Executive, Research Report RR1074 (London: Crown, 2016), 27. The report notes, "The aim of this was to reflect, in a very approximate way, the limited evidence available at the time, which indicated some public 'dread' of cancer (e.g., Jones-Lee et al. 1985)."

22. US Environmental Protection Agency, "Valuing Mortality Risk Reductions for Environmental Policy: A White Paper," December 10, 2010.

23. Ted Gayer, James T. Hamilton, and W. Kip Viscusi, "Private Values of Risk Tradeoffs at Superfund Sites: Housing Market Evidence on Learning about Risk," *Review of Economics and Statistics* 32, no. 3 (2000): 439–451.

24. Gary H. McClelland, William D. Schulze, and Brian Hurd, "The Effect of Risk Beliefs on Property Values: A Case Study of a Hazardous Waste Site," *Risk Analysis* 10, no. 4 (1990): 485–497.

25. Kenneth Arrow, Robert Solow, Paul R. Portney, Edward E. Leamer, Roy Radner, and Howard Schuman, "Report of the NOAA Panel on Contingent Valuation," *Federal Register* 58, no. 10 (January 11, 1993): 4601–4614.

26. Our earlier efforts focused on the valuation of chronic bronchitis risks using risk-risk tradeoffs, and our first cancer risk valuation was in Wesley A. Magat, W. Kip Viscusi, and Joel Huber, "A Reference Lottery Metric for Valuing Health," *Management Science* 42, no. 8 (1996): 1118–1130. This initial study did not indicate that there was any cancer latency period.

27. W. Kip Viscusi, Joel Huber, and Jason Bell, "Assessing Whether There Is a Cancer Premium for the Value of a Statistical Life," *Health Economics* 23, no. 4 (2014): 384–396.

28. A critique of the regulation that claims that the costs exceed the benefits is by Jason K. Burnett and Robert W. Hahn, "A Costly Benefit: Economic Analysis Does Not Support EPA's New Arsenic Rule," *Regulation* 24, no. 3 (2001): 44–49. Adopting their assumptions but using our estimates of the VSL leads to benefits exceeding costs if there is no latency period, but costs exceeding benefits if the latency period is a decade or more.

29. James K. Hammitt and Jin-Tan Liu, "Effects of Disease Type and Latency on the Value of Mortality Risk," *Journal of Risk and Uncertainty* 28, no. 1 (2004): 73–95; George Van Houtven, Melonie B. Sullivan, and Chris Dockins, "Cancer Premiums and Latency Effects: A Risk Tradeoff Approach for Valuing Reductions in Fatal Cancer Risks," *Journal of Risk and Uncertainty* 36, no. 2 (2008): 179–199; and James K. Hammitt and Kevin Haninger, "Valuing Fatal Risks to Children and Adults: Effects of Disease, Latency, and Risk Aversion," *Journal of Risk and Uncertainty* 40, no. 1 (2010): 57–83.

30. W. Kip Viscusi, "Valuing Risks of Death from Terrorism and Natural Disasters," *Journal of Risk and Uncertainty* 38, no. 3 (2009): 191–213.

31. Baruch Fischhoff, Roxana M. Gonzalez, Deborah A. Small, and Jennifer S. Lerner, "Judged Terror Risk and Proximity to the World Trade Center," *Journal of Risk and Uncertainty* 26, no. 2/3 (2003): 137–151.

32. The initial immigration ban was overturned by the US Court of Appeals for the Ninth Circuit. According to one estimate, if the executive order had been effective in reducing terrorist attacks in the United States by 50 percent, the cost would have been $525.5 million per expected life saved, given the very small risk of dying from refugee terrorist attacks. See Alex Nowrasteh, "Trump's Deplorable Travel Ban," *Foreign Affairs*, February 10, 2017.

33. Ideally, one can construct a VSL accounting for these beliefs by, for example, dividing their willingness to pay for the risk reduction by their perception of the risk rather than an average societal value.

34. Photojournalist Nilüfer Demir photographed 3-year-old Aylan Kurdi, who had drowned on the shore of Bodrum, Turkey. Demir reported for Dogan News Agency (DHA). See Charles Homans, "The Boy on the Beach," *New York Times*, September 3, 2015. A similar photo of a single live, but injured Syrian child, Omran Dagneesh, also received prominent worldwide coverage; see Anne Barnard, "An Injured Child, Symbol of Syrian Suffering," *New York Times*, August 19, 2016.

35. This incident and its consequences are chronicled in Jennifer Brier, *Infectious Ideas: U.S. Political Responses to the AIDS Crisis* (Chapel Hill, NC: University of North Carolina Press, 2009).

36. The underlying reasoning for equivalence of this type for small changes in risk dates back to the theory of risk and insurance generally in Kenneth J. Arrow, *Essays in the Theory of Risk Bearing* (Chicago: Markham Publishers, 1971).

37. For advocacy that the potential applicability of WTA values may be substantial, see Jack L. Knetsch, Yohanes E. Riyanto, and Jichuan Zong, "Gain and Loss Domains and the Choice of Positive and Negative Changes," *Journal of Benefit-Cost Analysis* 3, no. 4 (2012): 1–18.

38. Daniel Kahneman and Amos Tversky, "Prospect Theory: An Analysis of Decisions under Risk," *Econometrica* 47, no. 2 (1979): 263–291.

39. W. Kip Viscusi, Wesley A. Magat, and Joel Huber, "An Investigation of the Rationality of Consumer Valuations of Multiple Health Risks," *RAND Journal of Economics* 18, no. 4 (1987): 465–479.

40. For the 3.3 ratio, see Tuba Tunçel and James K. Hammitt, "A New Meta-Analysis on the WTP/WTA Disparity," *Journal of Environmental Economics and Management* 68, no. 1 (2014): 175–187. For the 7.2 ratio, see John K. Horowitz and Kenneth E. McConnell, "A Review of WTA/WTP Studies," *Journal of Environmental Economics and Management* 44, no. 3 (2002): 426–447.

41. Thomas J. Kniesner, W. Kip Viscusi, and James P. Ziliak, "Willingness to Accept Equals Willingness to Pay for Labor Market Estimates of the Value of a Statistical Life," *Journal of Risk and Uncertainty* 48, no. 3 (2014): 187–205. The estimated baseline VSL estimates were $10.3–$11.4 million.

42. See Kahneman and Tversky, "Prospect Theory." Loss aversion also may affect consumers. See also W. Kip Viscusi and Joel Huber, "Reference-Dependent Valuations of Risk: Why Willingness-to-Accept Exceeds Willingness-to-Pay," *Journal of Risk and Uncertainty* 44, no. 1 (2012): 19–44, pp. 19, 20.

43. Wesley A. Magat, W. Kip Viscusi, and Joel Huber, "Risk Valuations and the Rationality of Consumer Behavior," in Wesley A. Magat and W. Kip Viscusi, *Informational Approaches to Regulation* (Cambridge, MA: MIT Press, 1992), 53–54.

44. Viscusi and Huber, "Reference-Dependent Valuations," 27–36.

45. Kahneman and Tversky, "Prospect Theory," 277–78.

46. William Samuelson and Richard Zeckhauser, "Status Quo Bias in Decision Making," *Journal of Risk and Uncertainty* 1, no. 1 (1988): 7–59, pp. 47–48.

47. For a summary of existing studies analyzing circumstances under which individuals' willingness to pay to avoid a certain risk differs from their willingness to accept payment to subject themselves to a certain risk, see Tunçel and Hammitt, "A New Meta-Analysis."

48. Horowitz and McConnell, "Review of WTA/WTP Studies," 428.

49. Even in a standard consumer product situation, if the product that has been taken away cannot be replaced, compensating consumers based on the purchase price will not adequately compensate any consumer whose valuation exceeded the purchase price.

50. Thomas J. Kniesner, W. Kip Viscusi, and James P. Ziliak, "Policy Relevant Heterogeneity in the Value of Statistical Life: New Evidence from Panel Data Quantile Regressions," *Journal of Risk and Uncertainty* 40, no. 1 (2010): 15–31, p. 28.

51. Examples of such analyses include Gregg Jarrell and Sam Peltzman, "The Impact of Product Recalls on the Wealth of Sellers," *Journal of Political Economy* 93, no. 3 (1985): 512–536; George E. Hoffer, Stephen W. Pruitt, and Robert J. Reilly, "The Impact of Product Recalls on the Wealth of Sellers: A Reexamination," *Journal of Political Economy* 96, no. 3 (1988): 663–670; and Jayendra Gokhale, Raymond M. Brooks, and Victor J. Tremblay, "The Effect on Stockholder Wealth of Product Recalls and Government Action: The Case of Toyota's Accelerator Pedal Recall," *Quarterly Review of Economics and Finance* 54, no. 4 (2014): 521–528.

52. Steven M. Crafton, George E. Hoffer, and Robert J. Reilly, "Testing the Impact of Recalls on the Demand for Automobiles," *Economic Inquiry* 19, no. 4 (1981): 694–703.

53. Robert J. Reilly and George E. Hoffer, "Will Retarding the Information Flow on Automobile Recalls Affect Consumer Demand?" *Economic Inquiry* 21, no. 3 (1983): 444–447; George E. Hoffer, Stephen W. Pruitt, and Robert J. Reilly, "Market Responses to Publicly-Provided Information: The Case of Automotive Safety," *Applied Economics* 24, no. 7 (1992): 661–667.

Chapter Nine: How the Courts Value Lives

1. There was no lawsuit filed by the parents and no publicized settlement amount. The family established the Lane Thomas Foundation shortly after the death. Although it is not known whether Disney World contributed to the foundation, the president of Disney World indicated that "we continue to provide ongoing support for the family." See Sandra Pedicini, "Family Won't Sue Disney over Alligator Attack," *Orlando Sentinel*, July 20, 2016.

2. Following the accident, the family retained a personal injury lawyer to explore possibly litigation options. See Stephen Gandel, "Tesla Autopilot Crash Victim's Family Has Hired a Personal Injury Lawyer," *Fortune*, July 11, 2016. Note, too, that in 2017, NHTSA concluded that a defect in the Autopilot mechanism did not cause the accident. See US Department of Transportation, National Highway Traffic Safety Administration, Monthly Defect Investigation Report #PE16-007, "Automatic Vehicle Control Systems: MY2014–2016 Tesla Model S and Model X," January 19, 2017. Nevertheless, attorneys filed a class action lawsuit against Tesla, alleging that its Model S and Model X cars were "dangerously defective." See "Tesla Sued Over 'Dangerously Defective' Autopilot Software," *Bloomberg BNA Product Safety and Liability Reporter*, April 21, 2017.

3. National Transportation Safety Board Office of Public Affairs, "Driver Errors, Overreliance on Automation, Lack of Safeguards, Led to Fatal Tesla Crash," press release, September 12, 2017, https://www.ntsb.gov/news/press-releases /Pages/PR20170912.aspx [https://perma.cc/HSX3-MZEJ].

4. There are also other minor subcomponents of these broad categories depending on the situation. For deceased adults, for example, there may be damages claims for lost services to the household as well as loss of consortium.

5. W. Kip Viscusi, *Reforming Products Liability* (Cambridge, MA: Harvard University Press, 1991).

6. Joni Hersch and W. Kip Viscusi, "Tort Liability Litigation Costs for Commercial Claims," *American Law and Economics Review* 9, no. 2 (2007): 330–369.

7. The duration of the payment amount may also depend on the nature of the injury, such as whether it involved the loss of a finger or a thumb.

8. H. Allan Hunt, Social Security Administration, Office of Policy, "Benefit Adequacy in State Workers' Compensation Programs," *Social Security Bulletin* 65, no. 4, (2003/2004), available at https://www.ssa.gov/policy/docs/ssb/v65n4/v65n4p24.pdf [https://perma.cc/4MXT-BRR4]; H. Allan Hunt and Marcus Dillender, "Benefit Adequacy in State and Provincial Workers' Compensation Programs," *Employment Research* 21, no. 4 (2014): 1–4.

9. Insurance Information Institute, *The Insurance Fact Book* (New York: Insurance Information Institute, 2016), 117.

10. Michael J. Moore and W. Kip Viscusi, *Compensation Mechanisms for Job Risks: Wages, Workers' Compensation and Product Liability* (Princeton, NJ: Princeton University Press, 1990).

11. The guidelines for the 9/11 compensation fund are presented in September 11th Fund, 28 CFR § 104. See Kenneth R. Feinberg, *Final Report of the Special Master for the September 11th Victim Compensation Fund of 2001: Volume 1* (2004), 110, table 12; Air Transportation Safety and System Stabilization Act, Pub. L. 107–42, 115 Stat. 230; and Kenneth R. Feinberg, *What Is Life Worth? The Inside Story of the 9/11 Fund and Its Effort to Compensate the Victims of September 11th* (New York: PublicAffairs, 2005).

12. "Feinberg Announces GM Ignition Compensation Claims Resolution Facility," *GM Recall Lawsuits*, press release, June 30, 2014, http://www.gmlawsuitrecall.com/etc/gm_recall_lawsuit/files/website/231962224-Feinberg-Press-Release-Final.pdf [https://perma.cc/LUD9-W56P]; "GM Ignition Compensation Claims Resolution Facility Final Protocol for Compensation of Certain Death and Physical Injury Claims Pertaining to the GM Ignition Switch Recall," *GM Recall Lawsuits* (June 30, 2014), http://www.gmlawsuitrecall.com/etc/gm_recall_lawsuit/files/website/231962904-Final-Protocol-June-30-2014.pdf [https://perma.cc/XGL8-8B79].

13. "GM Announces Compensation Fund," *GM Recall Lawsuits*, http://www.gmlawsuitrecall.com/victims_compensation_fund [https://perma.cc/8R69-B5YP].

14. Ibid.

15. Mike Spector, "GM Ignition-Switch Fund Offers $595 Million to Victims," *Wall Street Journal*, December 10, 2015.

16. A review of the principles at work is provided in Steven Shavell, *Foundations of Economic Analysis of Law* (Cambridge, MA: Harvard University Press, 2004).

17. A related objective is to foster incentives to engage in the efficient level of the risky activity.

18. This use of the VSL is discussed more fully in Joni Hersch and W. Kip Viscusi, "Saving Lives through Punitive Damages," *Southern California Law Review* 83, no. 2 (2010): 229–262.

19. *State Farm Mut. Auto Ins. Co. v. Campbell*, 538 U.S. 408, 425 (2003).

20. Ibid. (quoting *Gore,* 517 U.S. at 582).

21. In *Exxon Shipping Co. v. Baker*, 128 S. Ct. at 2673, the court suggested that a 1:1 limit for punitive awards relative to compensatory damages awards was appropriate in maritime cases.

22. For a fuller articulation of the relation of my approach to the law and economics theories of punitive damages, see Hersch and Viscusi, "Saving Lives."

23. Cass R. Sunstein, Reid Hastie, John W. Payne, David A. Schkade, and W. Kip Viscusi, *Punitive Damages: How Juries Decide* (Chicago: University of Chicago Press, 2002).

24. A. Mitchell Polinsky and Steven Shavell, "Punitive Damages: An Economic Analysis," *Harvard Law Review* 111, no. 4 (1998): 869–962.

25. Ibid., 941.

26. Thomas R. Ireland, "Recent Legal Decisions Regarding Hedonic Damages: An Update," *Journal of Forensic Economics* 13, no. 2 (2000): 189–204; Thomas R. Ireland, "The Last of Hedonic Damages: Nevada, New Mexico, and Running a Bluff," *Journal of Legal Economics* 16, no. 1 (2009): 91–109; and Thomas R. Ireland, "Trends in Legal Decisions Involving Hedonic Damages from 2000 to 2012," *Journal of Legal Economics* 19, no. 1 (2012): 61–88.

27. Ralph King Anderson, *South Carolina Requests to Charge—Civil* (Columbia: South Carolina Bar, 2002), § 13–9 (2002), SC-JICIV 13–9: Damages—Elements of Actual Damages—Loss of Enjoyment of Life.

28. *McGee v. A C and S, Inc.*, 933 So. 2d 770, (La. 2006).

29. Eric A. Posner and Cass R. Sunstein, "Dollars and Death," *University of Chicago Law Review* 72, no. 2 (2005): 537–598.

30. They suggest various ways in which they would attempt to make this damages component specific to the individual, but the methods they propose are not feasible, such as inquiring what amount of money the victim would have required to accept the risk probability. There are ways in which the VSL could be tailored to the situation, such as accounting for variations by age and income.

31. I served as an expert for NOAA and the US Department of Justice in the litigation, but these groups did not present a damages calculation based on the VSL and happiness scales.

32. Kenneth J. Arrow, *Essays in the Theory of Risk Bearing* (Chicago: Markham, 1971). Arrow's result for financial risks embodies the general principle of equating the marginal utility of income for the loss and no-loss states.

33. W. Kip Viscusi and William N. Evans, "Utility Functions that Depend on Health Status: Estimates and Economic Implications," *American Economic Review* 80, no. 3 (1990): 353–374.

34. W. Kip Viscusi and William N. Evans, "Estimation of State-Dependent Utility Functions Using Survey Data," *Review of Economics and Statistics* 73, no. 1 (1991): 94–104.

35. More recent discussion of these issues is in Amy Finkelstein, Erzo F. P. Luttmer, and Matthew J. Notowidigdo, "What Good Is Wealth without Health? The Effect of Health on the Marginal Utility of Consumption," *Journal of the European Economic Association* 11, no. S1 (2013): 221–258.

36. Jeffrey O'Connell, "An Alternative to Abandoning Tort Liability: Elective No-Fault Insurance for Many Kinds of Injuries," *Minnesota Law Review* 60, no. 3 (1976): 501–565; Joni Hersch, Jeffrey O'Connell, and W. Kip Viscusi, "An Empirical Assessment of Early Offer Reform for Medical Malpractice," *Journal of Legal Studies* 36, no. 2 (2007): S231–S259.

37. This is the focus of Cass R. Sunstein, "Cost-Benefit Analysis and Arbitrariness Review," *Harvard Environmental Law Review* 41, no. 1 (2017): 1–41.

38. Caroline Cecot and W. Kip Viscusi, "Judicial Review of Agency Benefit-Cost Analysis," *George Mason Law Review* 22, no. 3 (2015): 575–617. This article reviews thirty-eight court decisions involving challenges to agency benefit-cost analysis practices.

39. Frank Ackerman and Lisa Heinzerling, *Priceless: On Knowing the Price of Everything and the Value of Nothing* (New York: New Press, 2004).

Chapter Ten: Setting Safety Guideposts for Private and Public Institutions

1. AFL-CIO, *Death on the Job: The Toll of Neglect*, 25th ed. (April 28, 2016), 2, https://aflcio.org/sites/default/files/2017-03/1647_DOTJ2016_0.pdf [https://perma.cc/TZN8-HRC6]. Although there is the possibility of criminal sanctions for violations causing deaths, since the advent of OSHA in 1970 there have only been eighty-nine criminal prosecutions.

2. US Department of Labor, "OSHA Penalty Adjustments to Take Effect after August 1, 2016," OSHA Fact Sheet 3879 (2016), https://www.osha.gov/Publications/OSHA3879.pdf [https://perma.cc/V6CW-LSM8].

3. AFL-CIO, *Death on the Job*.

4. US Department of Labor, *OSHA Inspections*, OSHA Publication 2098 (Washington, DC: US Government Printing Office, 2002).

5. Department of Health and Human Services, "Adjustment of Civil Monetary Penalties for Inflation," *Federal Register* 81, no. 172 (September 6, 2016): 61538–61582.

6. US Environmental Protection Agency, "Civil Monetary Penalty Inflation Adjustment Rule," *Federal Register* 81, no. 127 (July 1, 2016): 43091–43096.

7. Health and Safety Executive, "Maximum Penalties for Section 33 HSWA Offences," in *HSE Enforcement Guide (England and Wales)* (Norwich, UK: Crown, 2003), available at http://www.hse.gov.uk/enforce/enforcementguide/court

/sentencing-penalties.htm [https://perma.cc/T65K-V5SB]. Compensation for injuries may also be ordered. The Crown Court does not have a limit on fines.

8. Health and Safety Executive, *Enforcement Policy Statement* (October 2015–V1), available at http://www.hse.gov.uk/pubns/hse41.pdf [https://perma.cc/2GUW-VXZV].

INDEX

Italicized pages refer to figures and tables

A NOTE ON THE TYPE

This book has been composed in Adobe Text and Gotham. Adobe Text, designed by Robert Slimbach for Adobe, bridges the gap between fifteenth- and sixteenth-century calligraphic and eighteenth-century Modern styles. Gotham, inspired by New York street signs, was designed by Tobias Frere-Jones for Hoefler & Co.